EGO
Development and Psychopathology

EGO
Development and Psychopathology

David P. Ausubel

TRANSACTION PUBLISHERS
New Brunswick (U.S.A.) and London (U.K.)

Library of Congress Catalog Number: 96-6118
ISBN: 1-56000-266-2
Printed in the United States of America

Library of Congress Cataloging-in-Publication Data

Ausubel, David Paul.
  Ego development and psychopathology / David P. Ausubel.
    p. cm.
  Includes index.
  ISBN 1-56000-266-2 (alk. paper)
  1. Mental illness—Etiology.   2. Ego (Psychology).   3. Developmental psychology.   I. Title.
  RC455.4.E35A87 1996
  616.89'071—dc20   96-6118
                                                                        CIP

To Gloria

Everything else being equal, commonsensical theories are usually (but not always or necessarily) more valid or veridical than those lacking in common sense—largely because of the difference between them in congruence with commonsensical considerations. But a theory not in accord, or seriously at odds, with common sense has rarely if ever been validated.

Contents

List of Tables

Preface

In this book, I attempt to present a plausible developmental classification and psychogenic theory and explanation of the causes of the principal mental disorders that is based on my original theory of ego development, first formulated in 1948–1952. Its appearance at this time with a clinical emphasis is, I believe, particularly appropriate now that the psychologically atheoretical neurobiological approach is virtually unchallenged, and that the influence of other psychogenic approaches, such as psychoanalysis and its variants (e.g., psychoanalytic ego psychology) in the fields of psychiatry and clinical psychology is apparently waning.

It certainly has not been the case that there have been no other developmental approaches to psychopathology; the Freudian, Adlerian, and Eriksonian are only a few of the more influential ones that could be mentioned. The main difference between the approach advocated and adopted in this book and these others is that the stages of ego development have been derived empirically from longitudinal and cross-sectional developmental data rather than speculatively on a largely a-priori basis. The major source of these data on ego development has been published research from the Gesell Child Development Institute at Yale University and, to a lesser extent, from similar institutes at various other American universities.

I certainly do not wish to imply that there is no place at all for speculation in ego development or psychopathology theory. It is essential on a tentative basis where valid evidence is unobtainable or unavailable, if one is to avoid large unacceptable explanatory gaps in the theory in question. But in such cases, it is imperative not only that the law of parsimony be scrupulously observed, but also that the empirically unsupported theoretical proposition be consistent with, and inferred from, the most relevant and related evidence, logic, and theoretical principles that are available. For example, the self-concepts of the preverbal child can only be validly hypothesized from the differential treatment he receives from his parents at this age and from his known reaction capacities in related and relevant areas of development.

The central thesis of this book is that the most significant and critical factors predisposing persons to various mental disorders are critical developmental defects (complete or partial deficiencies, failures, distortions, overcompensations) that arise at critical transitional phases of ego development. This does not imply in the least that these factors are singly determinative, but rather that they interact with genic, temperamental, and coping predispositions; with the individual's degree of exposure and resistance to stress; with his adaptive resources; and with cultural influences and situational vicissitudes.

Mental disorder, therefore, like all complex behavioral and social phenomena, is obviously a product of multiple causality. However, I have chosen to classify mental disorders in terms of their developmental history largely because developmental factors, in my opinion, have greater discriminating power in delineating etiological, functional, and phenomenological similarities and differences among the various clinical syndromes, as well as exhibit greater explanatory power both for mental-health professionals, patients, and interested lay intellectuals than the factors underlying other possible classificatory schemes.

Although some effort is made, in a general way, to compare and contrast the theoretical orientation of this book to competing theories, my principal objective is not to do so systematically or definitively, but rather to present a coherent, self-consistent, and comprehensive developmental theory of psychopathology and to relate it as cogently as possible, for explanatory purposes, to the phenomenology and related clinical problems of psychiatric diagnosis. I believe that this type of noneclectic approach is much more helpful, to the general reader, students, and trainees alike, in understanding psychiatric syndromes and patients than a hodgepodge compendium of unintegrated and often contradictory theoretical positions with respect to controversial issues in psychiatry that neither acknowledges, specifies, nor attempts to reconcile these contradictions. Psychiatric treatment is also not covered in any systematic fashion but only insofar as it bears incidentally on more general problems of ego development and psychopathology.

It should be emphasized, however, that this book does not purport to be a *textbook* of, or a complete reference work on, psychiatry. It is addressed chiefly to those mental health professionals who are the *primary* diagnosticians and therapists of mentally ill individuals, that is, psychiatrists, clinical psychologists, and psychiatric social workers; it can be profitably read by them in an adjunctive sense (as a sourcebook of ego development and its relation to psychopathology), as well as by students and trainees in these disciplines, and by general and alcohol and drug counselors, special education teachers, and others who: (1) are interested in a self-consistent and noneclectic psychogenic and developmental theory of psychiatry and abnormal and clinical psychology that is related to most of the empirical and clinical psychiatric and psychological evidence relevant for a psychogenic approach to mental disorder; and (2) who desire to know how such a developmental theory can be psychodynamically related, in a general way, to the phenomenology and treatment of the *principal* mental disorders so as to be able to make more psychological sense of them.

Apart from etiological developmental issues, no attempt is additionally made definitively to consider other causative factors, for example, genetic factors or ethnic, cultural, and psychosocial stress factors, or to cover in sufficient detail all of the clinical syndromes, diagnostic techniques, and treatment modalities necessarily and customarily included in a textbook of psychiatry. Also, although all mental disorders are not discussed in this book, all of the major ones are, plus a representative sample of the more important lesser ones to which ego-development theory is most applicable.

Even though, as indicated above, this book is primarily intended for mental-health specialists and for workers in allied fields, it will also hopefully be read by the large body of intellectual, well-educated, and psychologically sophisticated lay persons (i.e., professionals who are engaged in fields other than mental health) who are also deeply interested in psychological development and mental disorder. Intellectuals in our culture have always been traditionally and differentially interested in the theoretical basis of mental as opposed to physical disorders. At one point in time, this interest was expressed in reading literature about the moral and spiritual basis of these disorders; but during the past six decades or so, it was manifested in avid reading of the different schools of psychoanalytic theory. (Parenthetically, it might be noted that among physicians, psychiatrists have tended to be the relative intellectuals.)

Since this book largely presents an original and relatively new theoretical underpinning for the classification and interpretation of the major mental disorders that is based largely on my own thinking and clinical experience with respect to ego development and the psychopathological consequences of developmental defects and deficiencies (rather than on a compilation, history, critique, or integration of prior and current theoretical views and clinical studies by authorities in the field involving large bibliographies), it would, in my opinion, be not only highly misleading but also pretentious to attempt to bolster and "document" my theoretical propositions by meticulously citing a host of only tangentially related references. Generally speaking, therefore, they are cited in only relatively few obviously necessary instances. This minor departure from traditionally academic style and format, I believe, will also prove to be more congenial and less foreboding to the more general nonmental health professional readers of this book.

It should be noted parenthetically that in order to make this book more applicable to clinical practice, the actual nomenclature of the various clinical syndromes generally follows the *Diagnostic and Statistical Manual IV of the American Psychiatric Association,* even though a new developmental model of psychiatric classification is proposed. This does not create any conceptual difficulties, however, because the standard DSM nomenclature is almost completely phenomenological in nature, making relatively few etiological distinctions. Thus, the names of the various DSM-IV syndromes can be easily placed in my developmental classification without generating conceptual confusion and contradictions reflective of conflicting causal assumptions. In those relatively few instances where I believe that the older clinical name for a given disorder helps to establish a new clinical distinction made in this book (e.g., Process and Reactive Schizophrenia), the older names are used textually and their DSM equivalents are found in parentheses.

Last, I wish to gratefully acknowledge the feedback, critique, and helpful suggestions of my wife, Gloria, for improving the content, clarity, and organization of this book and also for her invaluable assistance in helping to prepare the manuscript for publication. I am also grateful to Dr. Irving Louis Horowitz, Editorial Chairman and President Emeritus of Transaction Publishers for helping me better to define and delimit the appropriate scope and focus of this volume.

David P. Ausubel
Esopus, New York

I

Ego Development

1

The Natural History of Ego Development: Ego Omnipotence and Satellization during Infancy and Childhood

The investigation of the self-concept in early infancy is obviously fraught with serious scientific hazards. In the absence of verbal reports from the child regarding his perception of self and universe, we must have recourse to speculation and inference from the way he is treated, from the demands made upon him, from his established reactive capacities, and from a subjective estimate of the degree of cognitive sophistication that determines his perception of these things. In making such inferences, the greatest single source of error is an "adultomorphic" approach, which can never be avoided completely.

But despite this limitation and the probable impossibility of ever obtaining objectively verifiable data, speculation is still necessary and desirable in order to avoid important gaps in our theory of personality development. Later stages of ego development are naturally dependent in part upon beginning stages in the evolution of a notion of self—even if the infant cannot tell us what they are. Speculative formulations are as allowable here as in other theoretical areas, provided they are plausible, obey the law of parsimony, are logically reconcilable with related empirical data at a later stage of development, and are uttered with the humility and tentativeness befitting their status as hypotheses rather than as definitively established facts. And in this particular instance there is the additional requirement that they be consistent with the presumed cognitive maturity of infants.

Definition of Concepts

To avoid confusion later, it is necessary to distinguish at the outset among the terms *self, self-concept, ego,* and *personality,* which constitute, in the order given, an ascending hierarchy of complexity and inclusiveness. The *self* is a constellation of individual perceptions and memories that consists of the visual image of the appearance of one's body, the auditory image of the sound of one's name, images of kinesthetic sensations and visceral tension, memories of personal events, and so forth. The *self-concept,* on the other hand, is an abstraction of the essential and distinguishing characteristics of the self that differentiate an individual's "selfhood" from the environment and from other selves. In the course of personality development, various evaluative attitudes, values, aspirations, motives, and obligations become associated with the self-concept. The organized system of interrelated self-attitudes, self-motives, and self-values that results may be called the *ego.*

This constellation of ego referents, in turn, undergoes conceptualization: a least common denominator is abstracted that constitutes at any given stage of development the conceptual essence of the person's notion of himself as a functioning individual who is endowed with certain attributes related to his role and status. Insofar as this abstraction (the ego concept) or *identity* is a discriminable and self-recognizable content of awareness characterized by personal identifiability and *some* continuity (not immutability) over time, it enjoys a measure of psychological substantiveness. Thus, as long as one does not reify it (i.e., attribute corporeality, activity, motivation, etc., to it), it is justifiable to refer to the ego as a *psychological* entity or structure.

Personality is a still more inclusive term than ego. It includes all of the behavioral, emotional, attitudinal, and motivational predispositions of individuals at a given point in their life history that determine how they will interact with, and respond to, stimuli both from within and without. Thus, it embraces the peripheral, transitory, and trivial, as well as the central, aspects of their reactive potentialities and their cognitive as well as their motivational, emotional, and moral traits.

This distinction between ego and personality highlights the crucial role of the ego in the individual's personality organization. His psychological world can be ordered in terms of degree of ego involvement, with concentric zones of objects, persons, groups, values, and activities varying in degree of affective proximity to his ego. The more central zones are areas of prime concern and significance. What happens in these areas is a source of pride or shame, success or failure and gives rise to such feelings as increased or decreased self-esteem, optimism or pessimism, self-confidence or self-doubt, anxiety, elation, depression, anger, envy, and so forth. It is these central ego-implicated components of personality that lend it whatever continuity, consistency, and generality it exhibits.

Organization of the Remaining Introductory-Theoretical (Pre-clinical) Chapters

Chapters 1 and 2 shall provide a normative overview of ego development that delineates both the age-level changes in ego structure accompanying major shifts in the biosocial status of the developing individual, as well as major variants of the norm. The development of moral values and of conscience, although an integral aspect of ego development, will be considered in chapter 3. General psychopathological considerations that follow from deficiencies, defects, failure, distortions, and so forth in ego development, plus other psychogenic determinants of mental disorder, for example, genic, stress, mental mechanisms, will constitute a separate chapter (4). General aspects of anxiety, a complex emotional fear state that is closely related to ego-development outcomes and also serves as one of the major links between ego development and psychopathological entities, will be considered in a separate chapter (5).

The theoretical approach to psychopathology adopted in this book is that both normal and pathological personality functioning can be most cogently explained in terms of an individual's ego structure at a given point in his or her life cycle. Because in large measure this structure reflects how and in what manner he/she has passed through critical transitional phases of ego development, it behooves us to attempt to understand this process thoroughly—the nature of its component sequential stages, their determinants and developmental outcomes, and the implications of these outcomes (degree of success or failure in completing developmental tasks) both for current normal and pathological personality functioning and for later stages of ego development.

This does not mean, as pointed out earlier, that ego development is the *only* significant determinant of normal and aberrant personality functioning. Genic predispositions, current situational stress, sociocultural factors, temperamental and constitutional variables, and so forth, must always be taken into consideration since mental disorder is always a product of multiple causality. Nevertheless, ego development, in my opinion, may be considered the most significant and differential determining (etiological) factor and, hence, the most appropriate basis of an etiological and/or psychopathological classification of mental illness. It must also be remembered that the impact of all of these other variables is represented as a precipitate in current ego structure and functioning inasmuch as the latter, in turn, served in the past as determinants of developing ego structure.

An Interactional Approach to Ego Development

Ego development may be viewed as the result of a process of continuous interaction between current social experience and existing personality (ego) structure that is mediated by perceptual and cognitive processes. According to this interactional view, neither the direction nor the patterning of ego development is predetermined by endogenous genic factors or by the sequential unfolding of psychosexual drives. Instead, a wide range of interpersonal experience (both current and internalized within personality) constitutes the major determinant of inter- and intracultural uniformities in ego development.[1] Such experience is prerequisite to the genesis of the ego and of ego attributes, including psychosexual drives. Its salient components are not specific infant care practices that impinge on erogenous zones but, rather, significant dimensions of parental attitudes, shifts in role and status, and changes in parental and cultural demands and expectations. From exposure to influences such as these, ego drives are generated autonomously rather than being sublimated from prestructured libidinal drives.

Major Determinants of Ego Development

The more important variables that participate in ego development may be classified as social (external), endogenous (internal), and perceptual-cognitive (mediating). *Social* variables include all aspects of institutional, intergroup, intragroup, and interpersonal relationships and organization that affect the course of ego development. They not only comprise the current stimulus conditions that help determine the direction of behavior and development at any particular moment, but also, through a process of internalization, contribute significantly to the growing structure of personality.

Endogenous (or internal) variables constitute the growth matrix of ego development. They are a product of all previous relevant interactions between heredity and environment, and selectively predispose or limit the direction of change in response to current experience. Internal variables include personality and temperamental traits, level of motor and cognitive capacity, physiological factors, and, most important, the prevailing state of ego organization itself. Thus, it is clear that most significant personality development is not a simple and immediate function of social experience. Always interposed between the two are both perceptual and cognitive factors and the ego structure that the individual brings into the social situation.

Perceptual variables play a mediating role in the interactional process underlying ego development. Before social experience (e.g., parent attitudes, cultural norms), various competencies related to self, and different ego needs, motives, and attributes can be brought together in the same interactional field, they must first be related to perceptually (i.e., give rise to a clear content of awareness). The stimulus world, therefore, whether of internal or external origin, is not the proximate antecedent of behavior or development; the perceptual world is.[2] Thus, although a child's role and status in the home and his parents' behavior toward him are objective social events in the real world, they affect his ego development only to the extent and in the form in which they are perceived. This does not imply that the perceived world *is* the real world but that perceptual reality is both psychological reality and the actual (mediating) variable that influences behavior and development.

Insofar as perception itself undergoes systematic developmental changes during the life cycle, level of perceptual maturity must be considered a determining as well as a mediating factor in ego development. Perceptual immaturity insulates the young infant from awareness of environmental threat and from the attitudinal effects of parental practices. For example, it does not enable the child to appreciate fully either his executive dependence and incompetence or the meaning of parental deference to his needs during infancy. This immaturity also obviates awareness of subtle interpersonal attitudes and of the functional and reciprocal nature of social rules and obligations within the childhood peer group. On the other hand, increased perceptual maturity is one of the factors enabling the two- to three-year-old child to evaluate more realistically his actual degree of power and volitional independence in the home situation and, thus, contributes to the ego devaluation and satellization occurring during this stage of ego development.

Adultomorphic views of infants and children that fail to take their perceptual and cognitive immaturity into account have generated many fanciful notions about child development, as well as numerous fad-like child-rearing practices. It has been alleged, for example, that neonates react with catastrophic anxiety to "the psychological trauma of birth" inherent in biological separation from the mother; that they are aware of their parents' rejecting attitudes and guilt feelings; that they suffer irreversible loss in "bonding" (attachment behavior) if separated from the mother, both immediately after delivery and during the lying-in period, as well as at any time during the first six months; that their personality development is permanently affected in a serious negative way by such practices as bottle feeding; by maternal self-preoccupation, anxiety, and tenseness in administering routine child care; and by frequent exposure to strangers.

Actually, infants respond only very transiently and superficially to all of these situations—not only because of their perceptual and cognitive immaturity, but also because they have as yet no clearly defined sense of self to which these experiences could be referred and thereby constitute threat, hazard, or deprivation to same. Persuasive testimony in support of these hypotheses is furnished by the fact that neither strangers nor separation from the sole accustomed caretaker reliably induce serious effects on infants' behavior, emotional expression, or physical well-being until after six months of age. In fact, before this latter age not even such simple differentiated emotions as fear or anger are exhibited by infants; and more complex emotions such as anxiety, insecurity, and jealousy are not manifested until later in the first year of life.

How can these evidences of growth in perceptual maturity be explained? One obvious possibility is that perceptual maturity, at least in part, is a function of cognitive capacity and sophistication that tend to increase with age and experience. Here we must consider the impact on perception of increased ability to verbalize, to manipulate symbols and abstractions, to form categorical judgments, to make more subtle differentiations within the stimulus field, to avoid animistic thinking, and to disregard irrelevant instances of concomitance in reaching judgments of causality. Some aspects of perceptual maturation, however, are, in turn, probably attributable to normative modifications of ego structure itself (e.g., changed perceptions of parents and peers following upon ego devaluation).

Cognitive processes (e.g., acquiring new meanings, generalizing, abstracting, deducing, inducing, making judgments, etc.) similarly serve both as mediating factors and as determinants of ego development. The cognitive contents (cognitions) to which they give rise are either concepts, concept names, or propositions. Because of the availability of cognitive processes in human mental functioning, it is possible, for example, for the self-concept and the ego to become abstract conceptual entities (structures) and for the developing child both to make comparative judgments of self and others and to make inferences about causality. All of the more complex components of ego structure, such as self-esteem, self-judgments, ego aspirations, and so forth, must also be considered cognitions resulting from the cognitive processes involved in acquiring propositional meanings, concept meanings, and concept names, as well as in comprehending and generating propositions. In the absence of verbal representation or language they could exist in only very rudimentary form.

Unlike most other concepts and propositions, however, those arising from, and related to, a given individual's ego development are rooted in the *subjective* aspects of personality development. They require a set of explanatory principles that rely on subjective motivational, affective, interpersonal, and value considerations to an incomparably greater extent than is involved in the more objective process of acquiring a psychological structure of knowledge (cognitive structure). Thus, for example, grandiosity, impaired self-esteem, self-derogation, and overly intrapunitive interpretations of failure or acceptance of blame do not primarily reflect faulty cognitive processes or habits of thinking per se, but rather profound disturbances in ego development and functioning.

It is important to distinguish between perception and cognition both as mediating variables and as determinants of ego development. Typically, both terms are unwarrantedly used synonymously and interchangeably. Both processes are obviously similar insofar as their products are significantly determined by relevant aspects of existing cognitive structure. Perceptions differ from cognitions, however, in that they are direct and immediate contents of awareness that do not require prior information processing (with or without problem-solving activity and its attendant logical operations). For example, when a child *first* acquires the concept of "house," this acquisition process is a cognitive phenomenon. Thereafter, however, once this concept becomes clear and stable, subsequent identification of a particular house-like object as an exemplar of the "house" concept is merely a perceptual matter. In more general terms, the *acquisition* of *new* representational, concept, or propositional meanings reflects the operation of cognitive processes, whereas merely recognizing the word, concept, or proposition and thereby comprehending their meanings when they are presented (after having been previously learned) is simply a matter of perception.

The Nature and Acquisition of Biosocial Status

The term "biosocial status" is a convenient abstraction that makes it possible to refer to the generalized aspects of both role and status pertaining to an individual of given sex and functional age level in a relatively homogeneous cultural setting. Its *culturally standardized* attributes are anchored in the organizational procedures, requirements, values, and traditions of social groupings and institutions. Thus, infants, as a group in American middle-class culture, have a stereotyped biosocial status recognizably distinct from that of male and female children, adolescents, and adults. The role aspects of biosocial status consist of significant interpersonal behavior functionally differentiated, in part, by adjustment to the demands and expectations of others; the status aspects delineate hierarchical position vis-à-vis others as defined by relative dominance, control, prerogatives, independence, prestige, and so forth. However, the actual biosocial status that any *individual* enjoys is always a *particular* interactional product that is a *variant* of the cultural stereotype. The latter stereotype serves as an external determinant entering into the formation of personal biosocial status by generating (through appropriate representatives) specific demands and expectations to which the individual carriers of the culture react (as they do to any social stimulus) in terms of existing ego structure, idiosyncratic personality traits, and perceptual maturity.

For the most part, therefore, biosocial status is an *individual achievement* in an interpersonal setting that a person learns by interacting with particular persons who enjoy varying degrees of status and who enact diverse roles. Except for hereditary princes, few persons inherit a ready-made role and status; and except in the relatively rare instances of highly formal and structured situations, roles typically require considerable improvisation in accordance with situational and interpersonal differences in the particular settings in which they are enacted.

As a result of repeated interactions with persons of superior, inferior, and equivalent biosocial status, increasingly stable and more appropriate roles emerge that the individual himself and his opposite numbers have *created*. Each of us must achieve our own biosocial status within the framework of the culturally standardized stereotype. In this learning process, the significance of passively *imitating* stereotyped and hypothetical role models or particular variants thereof has been vastly exaggerated by social learning theorists. The significance of this *imitative* paradigm of role and status acquisition is dwarfed by the active transactional social learning paradigm involving identification (see below). It is only in later childhood, adolescence, and adult life that role modeling becomes a significant factor in structuring initially the role and status aspects of social transactions between persons.

Two Opposite Kinds of Identification: Satellization and Nonsatellization

Whenever group, family, or social life is characterized by differences in role and status and by the objective dependence of one person on another or on the group as a whole, one of the more basic kinds of human interaction that arises under these circumstances is the reciprocal relationship of *identification-acceptance*. This type of relationship includes in varying proportions the elements of "dominance-subordination," "leadership-followership," and "care-dependency" reported for primate and subprimate families and informal groupings.

Much conceptual confusion, however, has resulted in the past, and still prevails today, because of failure to distinguish between two essentially different kinds of identification, each of which involves a reciprocal relationship between a relatively dominant (superordinate) and independent individual (or group) and a relatively dependent and subordinate individual. Naturally this practice has led to incalculable confusion, ambiguity, and self-contradiction; but even worse, it also resulted in failure to recognize certain basic distinctions in parent-child relationships which, in turn, give rise to significant differential consequences in ego development and personality structure, as well as to differential vulnerability to various types of psychopathology or mental disorder.

The more common of these two kinds of human identification, that is, very striking and prevalent in the canine and simian worlds but relatively rare and less intense in the feline world, may be called *satellization*. In a satellizing relationship, the subordinate party acknowledges the dominance and superiority of the superordinate party and accepts a subservient and deferential role; and the superordinate party, in turn, accepts the subordinate party as an intrinsically valuable "retainer" in his or her personal orbit. As an outcome of this type of dependent process and relationship, satellizers acquire a *derived* (i.e., vicarious, attributed, unearned) biosocial status that is: (1) wholly a function of the dependent relationship and is independent of their own competence or performance ability, and (2) bestowed upon them through the fiat of simple acceptance and intrinsic valuation by a superordinate individual whose authority and power to do so are regarded as unchallengeable.

Satellizing children are primarily motivated to perform well at home and in school by anticipating the approval of the persons (e.g., parents, teachers) in relation to whom they satellize. They seek this approval much less to gain *earned* (ego-enhancing) status, or to obtain confirmation of their own competence, than to reassure themselves that they are still intrinsically accepted and valued (i.e., that they still enjoy derived status). Similarly, they accept the values of their preceptors purely out of unselective personal loyalty, in contrast to nonsatellizers who use a criterion of selective expediency or the usefulness of a particular value for the acquisition of earned status.

On the other hand, in the case of the nonsatellizer the two parties to the same "transaction" could relate to each other in quite a different way. The subordinate party could acknowledge his dependency on the superordinate party as a temporary, regrettable, and much-to-be remedied fact of life requiring, as a matter of expediency, various *acts* of conformity and deference but, at the same time, not accepting a dependent and subservient status as a *person*. In turn, as an antecedent relational condition, he or she could either be rejected outright or accorded qualified acceptance, that is, accepted and valued not for intrinsic reasons (as a person for his or her own sake) but in terms of current or potential exceptional competence and usefulness to the superordinate party, that is, as a source of vicarious or reflected status or eminence.

The act of identification, if it occurs at all in the latter case, consists solely in using the superordinate individual as an emulatory model so that the subordinate party can learn the latter's coping and interpersonal skills as well as his methods of "getting ahead," and, thus, eventually succeed to his or her enviable status. Accordingly, the only type of biosocial status that can be engendered in this situation is the earned status that reflects the subordinate's *actual* functional competence, power, or control of situations and other people.

Causes of Nonsatellization

This nonsatellizing type of identification occurs for one of two reasons: either the superordinate party does not or will not extend unqualified intrinsic acceptance (e.g., as in the case of rejecting parents or those who value their children for ulterior self-enhancing purposes), or the subordinate party is unwilling to undergo satellization or is temperamentally incapable of satellizing on a genic basis.

In the more commonly encountered kinds of psychopathology constituting the vast bulk of everyday psychiatric practice, the first-mentioned reason for nonsatellization (i.e., rejection or extrinsic valuation by parents) overwhelmingly predominates. Failure to satellize because of unwillingness or inability to do so, on the other hand, is largely limited in incidence on a psychopathological basis to such relatively rare childhood conditions as Infantile Autism and childhood Schizophrenia, as well as to certain extreme instances of Conduct Disorder in children and of Antisocial Personality Disorder in adults. (It is also found nonpsychopathologically, however, in a modified form [i.e., in less severe types of nonsatellization or in attenuated types of satellization] in children who, on a temperamental [genic] basis, have an inordinate need for volitional independence or hedonistic gratification. In either case it is obviously very difficult for such children to be subservient and deferential to parental direction.)

The primary cause of the psychopathology in all of the latter children's mental disorders that prevent the occurrence of satellization is a prepotent, genically determined difficulty in relating emotionally to others. In cases of extreme emotional and social deprivation or neglect, on the other hand, such as commonly occurred at one time in foundling homes and orphanages, the basic problem is *not* primarily one of inability to relate emotionally to others on genic grounds as, rather, an acquired indisposition or incapacity for such relatedness that results from prolonged exposure to these highly unfavorable conditions of nurturance and child rearing. Under these latter circumstances, also, ego devaluation obviously does not have to take place since the conditions for undergoing the omnipotent phase of ego development never existed in the first place.

Although nonsatellization occurs more frequently by far because of reasons emanating from the parent rather than from the child, inability or reluctance to satellize on the part of children is by no means rare. Lack of capacity for satellization generally occurs in infants and children because of four kinds of factors or circumstances that influence their attachment behavior or ability to relate to others.

First, it occurs infrequently in some brain damaged children where the damage is secondary to congenital, gestational, or perinatal infection, hemorrhage, trauma, or other health problem. Second, it appears in infants under thirty months of age who are not brain damaged; and because these signs of difficulty in relating to others are present in the first few months of life, and also cannot be explained either by neuropathological lesions or by aberrant parenting, the cause may be presumed to lie in prepotent genically determined predispositions. This latter factor is undoubtedly crucial for the development of Infantile Autism and perhaps for childhood Schizophrenia as well.

The third factor, typified by the history of infants with Reactive Attachment Disorder, consists of gross physical and emotional neglect, such as is found sometimes in certain foundling homes (more commonly in the past), and includes, in addition, social and emotional unresponsiveness, apathy, failure to thrive, and disinterest in the physical and social environments. Depending on the onset of the gross neglect, failure to satellize may or may not be preceded by the omnipotent phase of ego development. Lastly, and most commonly, reluctance to satellize is associated with inordinate temperamental assertiveness, volitional independence, or excessive hedonistic needs in the child, and sometimes with extreme overvaluation or permissiveness on the part of intrinsically accepting parents. Under these conditions, however, although satellization is delayed or attenuated, it eventually occurs.

Earned and Derived Status

The wider significance of earned and derived status for personality structure, as we shall hypothesize in detail later, is that each is associated with distinctive patterns of security (freedom from anticipated threat to physical integrity), adequacy (feelings of self-esteem, self-worth, and self-importance), and other ego attributes (level of ego aspirations, dependence and independence, etc.). Corresponding to *derived* status in ego structure are: (1) feelings of *intrinsic* security that inhere in the affectional aspects of a satellizing relationship, and (2) feelings of *intrinsic* adequacy and competence that are relatively immune to the vicissitudes of achievement and position. Corresponding in turn to *earned* status are: (1) feelings of *extrinsic* security that depend upon physical competence, or the possession of a compliant executive arm in the person of an available superordinate figure, and (2) feelings of *extrinsic* adequacy that fluctuate with both (a) absolute level of ego aspirations, power, and control, and (b) the discrepancy between the latter and perceived accomplishment or hierarchical position.

Volitional Dependence versus Executive Dependence[3]

Paradoxical as it may seem at first glance, the omnipotent phase of ego development, when the child's willfulness is at its height, co-exists with the period of his greatest degree of objective helplessness and dependence on parents. Yet this apparent paradox is easily resolved if the nonunitary concept of dependence is divided into its easily discriminable executive and volitional components. When this is done, concomitant self-perceptions of volitional independence and executive dependence during this stage of ego development are not mutually contradictory at all, but are, on the contrary, very compatible with each other under the pancultural biosocial conditions of infancy. Unlike the psychoanalytic doctrine of infantile omnipotence, which unparsimoniously assumes the existence, in part, of a preformed ego and of a sense of volition even before birth, naturalistic ego development theory conceives of omnipotent feelings in infants as a natural and acquired cause-effect product of both interpersonal experience (i.e., experienced parental deference) and of their perceptual-cognitive immaturity.

Viewed in much greater detail, at the same time that infants are developing a functional concept of executive dependence from their gradual appreciation of their own inability to gratify their most elemental needs and of their consequent absolute dependence on familiar and competent caretakers to do so, concomitant notions of volitional independence and omnipotence gradually begin to emerge. This is the case because it is precisely when children are most helpless that, almost invariably in all cultures, they are accorded more indulgence and deference by parents than at any other period of childhood. At this time, parents tend to be most solicitous and eager to gratify the child's expressed needs. In general they make few demands upon infants, since the latter could not respond to them in any case, and usually accede to their legitimate requests. If training is instituted, it tends to be delayed, gradual, and gentle. In this benevolent environment, therefore, much support is almost universally provided by all cultures in external interpersonal conditions for a perception of parental subservience to the child's will, and, thus, for ideas of omnipotence and volitional independence that co-exist with his objective dependence on his parents and his self-perceptions of executive dependence.

Furthermore, it is unlikely that infants are sufficiently mature, perceptually and cognitively speaking, to appreciate the relatively subtle motivations (i.e., love, duty, altruism) underlying this deference. As a result they quite understandably acquire the developmentally autistic misperception that, because of their own volitional power, parents are *obliged* to serve them rather than the true situation that parental superservience is altruistic and practiced out of deference for their extreme helplessness. Hence, their appreciation of their executive dependence does not conflict with, or detract essentially from, their self-concept of relative volitional omnipotence and independence, inasmuch as volitionally powerful persons do not have to be executively competent and independent as long as they have an executively competent and compliant person at their beck and call.

However, as infants' social perception of the actually prevailing power situation and relationships in the family improves, these new and more realistic self-perceptions become an important factor, along with increased parental demands on the child, leading to a sharp decline in their existing self-perceptions of their own omnipotence and exaggerated volitional independence. This paradoxical concomitance of earlier high volitional and low executive independence exists only during the omnipotent stage of ego development for the reasons stated above.

As the child matures cognitively, linguistically, motorically, and socially, parents become less subservient and begin to make greater disciplinary demands, as well as demands for self-help, on him. These changes in the parent-child relationship result in the child manifesting greater executive independence and less volitional independence; in fact, it is pressures such as these that largely lead to satellization itself. Beginning with preadolescence, however, needs for both greater volitional and greater executive independence increase. In a sense, desire and capacity for exercising volitional independence at this time is largely a function of the individual's capacity for exercising executive independence.

Both individual and cultural survival obviously requires that the child acquire a greater amount of executive independence. Growth in motor capacity for self-help is not matched by an equal willingness to assume the burdens which this entails. It is more in accord with notions of regal omnipotence just to will things accomplished and then have others carry out the necessary time-consuming manipulations. This, of course, does not rule out the possibility—and the demonstrable fact—that a child will find pleasure in doing many things for himself; activity is one of the primary sources of pleasure in childhood. (Even in adult life, the king will ask his chauffeur to move over while he takes the wheel.) Frustration of this desire for self-help is in fact one of the more important situational causes of infantile negativism. The important point, however, is that the child's ire is not so much aroused because he is denied the opportunity for executive independence per se but mainly because the frustrated desire for self-help is at the time representative of the broader desire for volitional independence. In other words, he is chiefly angry because his will (as manifested by a desire for self-help) is thwarted, not merely because he is not permitted to do a particular activity by himself. The infant is desirous in the main of retaining his executive dependence that is associated with volitional independence and omnipotence. He becomes more frequently aroused by an attempt to abolish his executive dependence and his habituation to 'baby ways' than by frustrating his attempts at self-help. Much of his 'conservatism' at this stage is actually a frantic effort to perpetuate by ritual the executive dependence characteristic of the earlier phase of ego organization.

The need for executive dependence is compatible with, and reinforced by, the exalted (regal) self-concept of infants and with the benevolent, undemanding environment in which they live. The young child, on the other hand, is coerced by environmental pressures and by the need for derived status both to surrender much volitional independence and to acquire more executive independence. During adolescence the attainment of executive independence is essential for achieving the volitional independence and earned status necessary for adult personality maturation and functioning.

Sources of Psychosocial and Idiosyncratic
Differences in Ego Development

Psychosocial differences in ego development reflect differences in the ways that various cultures institutionalize interpersonal relationships on the basis of age, sex, and kinship—and in the ways that they elaborate basic values and ideals of personality structure. These factors in turn influence such crucial aspects of ego development as the handling and timing of shifts in biosocial status (e.g., explicitness, abruptness, choice of socializing agents), the amounts and kinds of status that individuals are expected to seek, and the degree of personality maturity considered appropriate for different age levels. In our culture, for example, girls are traditionally expected to satellize more than boys, and women are expected to obtain a larger proportion of their current biosocial status than are men from derived rather than from earned sources. Thus, girls more than boys tend to perceive themselves as accepted and intrinsically valued by parents, and are more apt to be relatively docile, to conform to adult expectations, and to be "good."[4] In the areas of self-aggrandizement, personal achievement, possessions, and wishes, emotional responsiveness on the part of boys exceeds that of girls; in the direction of social and family relationships, physical appearance, and personal characteristics girls surpass boys.

Within the normative schema of ego development to be presented below, numerous opportunities also exist for the elaboration of idiosyncratic differences. First, one would expect that children who are temperamentally more assertive, independent, "thick-skinned," self-sufficient, energetic, or resistive to stress, would be less dependent on others' approval, more capable of maintaining self-esteem in the face of less earned or derived status, and, in general, less disposed to satellize than children with the opposite set of temperamental traits. One would also expect that individuals who are genically predisposed to develop strong hedonistic needs would tend to be more resistive to pressures directed toward attenuation of these needs during the course of ego maturation, and that children who are accelerated in motor or cognitive development would be subjected to greater parental demands for mature behavior.

Second, as will be seen shortly, differences in such basic dimensions of parental attitudes as acceptance-rejection, intrinsic-extrinsic valuation, and over- or under-domination, hold important implications for variability in children's satellization, desatellization, needs for achievement, and mode of assimilating values.

A third source of idiosyncratic differences in development lies in variability of perceptual sensitivity. It seems reasonable to suppose, for example, that the perceptually more sensitive child is more vulnerable to the detrimental effects of unfavorable parental attitudes and is more apt to be aware of his own limitations and the realities of the dependency situation.

Finally, once differences in such ego attributes as relative propensity to satellize are established, they themselves serve as important sources of variability in ego development. Thus, we might predict that, everything else being equal, the more intrinsic self-esteem a child enjoys, the less need he has to strive for ego aggrandizement and the more realistically he is able to adjust his current aspirational level downward to accommodate prior experience of failure.

Normative Sequences in Ego Development during Childhood

In this section I propose to outline normative uniformities in the sequential course of ego development during childhood. Most of the evidence for this analysis comes from materials drawn from our own culture. Nevertheless, it is believed that sufficient intercultural commonality prevails in genic patterning predispositions, in individual behavioral potentialities, and in intrafamilial, interpersonal, social, and cultural needs, problems, and conditions of adaptation to make many of the hypothesized general features of ego development applicable to all cultural environments despite culturally induced differences in details. This assumption, however, can obviously only be empirically verified by extensive cross-cultural investigation.

Differentiation of the Self-Concept

Preverbal stage. As a unified abstraction of its essential properties, the self-concept is a complex ideational entity that is slow in developing and usually requires the facilitating influence of language. All the same, the child still possesses a functional preverbal perception of self and of the distinction between that which is within and that which is beyond the borders of his own body, long before he acquires any language. As in the evolution of any new perception, the basic problem is that of defining boundaries between figure and ground. In the case of the self-perception, the boundaries of the self must be delimited from the wider environment of objects and persons with which it is initially fused.

This latter process occurs along multisensory lines as the infant comes into contact with his physical environment. His sense of touch acquaints him with the presence of objects outside himself; kinesthetic sensations make him aware of his own movements in space; and his sense of pain vividly informs him that transgressions of the self-not-self boundary are unpleasant. The visual body image, as manifested by self-recognition of a portrait or mirror reflection, and by correct identification of his own age, size, sex, and skin color (in a series of pictures) first becomes a stable self-percept during the preschool period. Apparently, therefore, in the early years of childhood it serves more as an abstract symbol of self-identity than as a concrete functional datum helping the child to differentiate between himself and the environment.

Self-perception is facilitated further by the infant's reaction to his mother as a person. As early as six weeks he smiles differentially to the sound of the human voice even though it is not associated habitually with care and attention; and in the third month of life he smiles and vocalizes spontaneously in response to the human face. Neonates respond differently to the human voice than to silence, and as early as the first month of life, they respond differentially to their own mother's face than to that of a strange female. Thus, mother's outline serves as an anchorage point for the slowly accumulating self-pattern. It provides a scaffolding for the elaboration of his own self-portrait as a person; and as we shall see shortly, it makes possible a perception of mother as a manipulator of his reality and as a causal agent in the satisfaction of his needs.

Psychoanalytic and family therapists speak of "psychological individuation," meaning by this the establishment of an ego identity separate from that of the mother or from the undifferentiated "family ego mass." However, this is only one dimension of ego development, dealing primarily with the acquisition of individuality and of volitional independence; it is hardly coextensive with all of ego development as described in this chapter, although these authors tend to regard it as the principal significant dimension. Further, volitional independence does not increase linearly with age, but increases from birth to age two, then decreases until preadolescence (with transitory increments at ages two and one-half, four, and six), increases abruptly at adolescence with exaggerated demands for independence, increases less sharply during adult life until middle age, and then begins to decline in senescence.

Perception of other persons also precedes self-perception, as indicated by the self-recognition of body image (as in mirror reflections and photographs) and in the development of language concepts dealing with persons. Perceptual discrimination between self and others is acquired more slowly when others are similar to self, as in pairs of twins.

Perhaps the most poignant experience leading to the consciousness of self develops as an outgrowth of inevitable delays in the gratification of the infant's organic needs. Here the contrast between inner experience and the outside world is highlighted by the juxtaposition of awareness of: (1) painful discomfort and pleasant satisfaction referable to the body, and (2) objects and persons in the environment that lead to dramatic change in the affective quality of consciousness. Later, when a sense of volition develops, the act of willing (as a directed expression of the self as an entity), and the assistance it invokes from other persons, sharpens even more the distinction between self and environment. Further accentuation of the self-environment dichotomy accompanies the appreciation of cause-effect sequences and emerging perceptions of own helplessness, executive dependence, and volitional independence and omnipotence to be described below.

Verbal stage. The abstraction of a unified concept of self from its component percepts (cutaneous, visceral, visual, volitional, etc.) requires the intervention of language. Two preliminary steps precede the final emergence of the self-concept in its most highly developed verbal expression as the first-person singular: (1) the concept of possession, and (2) third-person reference to self. By the eighth month, possessive emotions toward toys are manifested. Between the tenth and twelfth months a positive sense of property becomes observable. By twenty-one months[5] this is conceptualized as "mine," a generalized term that not only includes all personal possessions but also excludes the possessions of others. This concept of possession presupposes a sharpening of the distinction between self and others to the point where objects come to "belong" to the person habitually using them.

A slightly more advanced stage in the acquisition of a verbal concept of self is completed at twenty-four months. At this time, the child becomes aware of himself and others as comparable entities. Before he referred to another child as "baby"; now he uses this same term, or his own given name, in making third-person reference to himself, his possessions, and his activities.

The highest degree of conceptual and nominalistic abstraction in relation to the self appears at twenty-seven months when the child uses the personal pronoun "I." This "I" constitutes a unification and an abstraction of all the separate part-perceptions of self. It implies a genuine conceptual self-consciousness. In contrast to third-person usage, which merely indicates cognizance of himself as a person like other persons, the use of the first-person singular means that his own functions are characterized by the distinctiveness of his own individuality, and that he designates himself as a special and unique kind of personal entity, distinct from all other persons. After this point is reached, a new abstract level of self-reactions becomes possible: identification with persons, goals, and values; incorporation of standards; competitive behavior; and finally, self-judgments, guilt feelings, and conscience.

The Omnipotent Stage

The stage of ego development that follows the emergence of a functional self-concept may be designated as the omnipotent phase (roughly, the period from six months to two and one-half years). As pointed out above, it seems paradoxical and self-contradictory that feelings and ideas of omnipotence and volitional independence should coexist with the period of the child's greatest helplessness and dependence on parents. Yet, as we shall see shortly, this apparent paradox and self-contradiction is easily resolved if the wholistic, nonunitary concept of dependence is first reduced into its differentially perceptible executive and volitional components. When this is done, self-perceptions of volitional independence and executive dependence are easily perceived as quite compatible with each other under the role and status conditions of infancy that prevail in most cultures.

Unlike the psychoanalytic doctrine of infantile omnipotence, which assumes the existence both of a preformed ego and volition at and even prior to birth, naturalistic ego theory conceives of these omnipotent feelings in infants as a very understandable subjective product of actual interpersonal experience (parental deference) and cognitive immaturity. It is self-evident, of course, that the infant's perception of his relative omnipotence cannot be demonstrated empirically prior to the advent of language. And even then, it can be inferred only from the rampant expressions of imperiousness and possessiveness that are so prevalent during the latter portion of this age period.

Development of executive dependence. Although completely helpless and dependent in fact, it is highly improbable that the newborn infant appreciates his helplessness and executive dependence. Before he can conceive of his helplessness, he obviously must first be capable of deliberately willing the satisfaction of his needs and of perceiving in a causal sense his own inability to do so. Similarly, before he can appreciate that he is dependent on another individual for the implementation of his wishes, it is necessary that he is able to perceive both the latter as a person, as well as the succorant acts of this person, as causally related to his need-satisfaction sequences. In the first few months of life, however, it is improbable that crying is volitional, that mother is perceived as a person, and that the child has a conception of causality. It is true, of course, that the mother is always present before and during the act of need-reduction, and that after the first month of life merely holding the infant without offering him nourishment is sufficient to quiet his hunger cry. But at this early stage of development, it is more credible—for the reasons given above—to suppose that mother, by virtue of her habitual association with need-reduction sequences, merely serves as a signal of imminent need satisfaction, and perhaps as a substitute satisfying object in her own right, than that the infant truly perceives his own helplessness and the causal connection between mother's presence and the reduction of his hunger.

From the foregoing analysis, it appears that the development of a sense of volition is a prerequisite first step before a feeling of executive dependence can arise. How this development is brought about, however, must probably remain forever in the realm of speculation. The most plausible hypothesis I can suggest is that volition is a learned outgrowth of the innately determined pattern of general excitement in response to any intense internal or external stimulus (e.g., hunger). This reactive pattern, particularly crying, obviously has adaptive value in that it frequently evokes maternal succorant activity that satisfies the need responsible for the excitement. Eventually, after repeated experiences of the efficacy of crying in relieving the tensions of need (hunger), a causal connection may be perceived between antecedent (crying) and consequent (food, relief of hunger). At this point, crying becomes a conscious, deliberately employed (volitional) device rather than an almost reflex response for relieving unpleasant sensations referable to self.

Once volition is acquired, it reciprocally facilitates the perception of causality, since the act of willing constitutes a vivid content of awareness antecedent in many causal sequences. The child is now in a position to perceive that his expression of will does not in itself lead to need satisfaction through his own manipulative activity (i.e., perception of his own helplessness) but only through the intervention of an external agency (i.e., perception of his executive dependence). In this instance, ability to perceive the mother as a person facilitates the perception of causality inasmuch as it is undoubtedly less difficult to conceive of a person than of an object as a causal agent and manipulator of reality.

Environmental and Perceptual Supports of Omnipotence

All the while that a conception of executive dependence is being developed, a notion of volitional independence and omnipotence is concomitantly evolved. Precisely when the child is maximally helpless in fact, he is accorded, almost invariably in all known cultures, greater deference and subservience by parents than at any other period of childhood. Parents tend to be most desirous and eager at this time to satisfy his apparent needs. They make few if any demands upon him and usually go along with both his reasonable (and not so reasonable) requests. If training is initiated, it tends to be introduced as gradually and as gently as possible. In this benevolent and solicitous interpersonal environment, therefore, much support is provided in actual parent-child interaction as well as in general stimulus conditions for the child's development of a veridical perception of parental subservience to his will.

Additionally at this age children are undoubtedly not sufficiently mature, experientially and cognitively speaking, to appreciate the relatively subtle and covert motivations (i.e., love, duty, altruism) that underlie this parental deference. Nonetheless, the child is mature enough to perceive the overt attitudes and behaviors of individuals in his interpersonal world, for example, he does not seem to expect to receive the same degree of deference from older siblings as from his parents. His perceptual immaturity is manifested rather at the level of perceiving the more subtle, covert, or motivational aspects of attitudes. Thus, in accordance with his notions of volitional independence and omnipotence, the child tends to manifest the quite understandable misperception that the parent is somehow *obliged* to serve him, not that the latter does so altruistically out of deference to his extreme helplessness.

The infant's appreciation of his executive dependence, as pointed out above, does not detract essentially from his self-concept of relative volitional omnipotence and independence. He perceives his helplessness and dependence on others, to be sure; yet when he wills the satisfaction of his needs, they seem to be satisfied nevertheless. Hence, his perception of dependency is limited to the executive sphere. A volitionally powerful individual (e.g., a king) obviously has no basic need for executive competence as long as the executive services of other competent persons are available to him. In fact, it may even enhance the child's estimate of his own power that success in need gratification takes place despite his manifest handicap of executive incompetence. He might, therefore, under the circumstances, legitimately think: "My will must be powerful indeed if a tiny, helpless creature like myself can compel omniscient adults to implement my needs and gratify my desires."

At the very most, perceived executive dependence qualifies or limits the regal scope of the child's will in this stage of ego development by making it subject to the availability of a compliant executive arm. Feelings of executive dependence, thus, become satisfactorily integrated as a subsidiary aspect of the more inclusive self-image of volitional omnipotence. And despite objective biosocial incompetency, the infant's sense of adequacy (self-esteem) at this point—his feeling of personal worth, importance, and ability to control and manipulate the environment to his own ends—is predominantly of the earned type. That is, it depends in part upon perceptual immaturity and a consequent misinterpretation of early parental subservience to his needs and desires, as a result of which he vastly exaggerates his volitional power and independence.

The self-perception of his helplessness, however, understandably constitutes a potential threat to the infant's physical safety and integrity. Hence, it gives rise to an undercurrent of insecurity that can be allayed only by the continued availability of the executive arm (i.e., the mother) upon which he feels dependent. At this stage of ego development, therefore, his sense of security—his level of confidence regarding the future benevolence of his interpersonal environment in providing for his basic needs—is, thus, closely allied with feelings of executive dependence; and inasmuch as a need for security exists perpetually, it generates a parallel need for perpetuating executively dependent relationships.

These dependency needs are reinforced by: (1) the perceived efficacy of such relationships in providing security and in relieving hunger, discomfort, and insecurity, and (2) the perceived frustrating consequences associated with the unavailability of mother, that is, insecurity, hunger, discomfort, the alleviation of which can only be accomplished through the highly canalized device of the dependency situation. Thus, when the dependency needs of infancy are not satisfied because of abrupt separation from the mother, when conditions of succorance become ambiguous or change suddenly, or when demands for executive independence are granted prematurely, there is some evidence that young children later manifest either residual overdependence or overanxiety about dependence on adults. In children older than nine months separation from the mother may precipitate acute anxiety, "anaclitic depression" (acute impairment of physical, cognitive, and social development), and marasmus (severe chronic wasting of bodily tissues).

The Ego Devaluation Crisis

As long as the infant is helpless in fact, parents are content to be indulgent and deferential in treating him, expecting only that he grow and realize the phylogenetic promise of infancy. In part this attitude is indicative of solicitousness and altruism; but it is also the only realistic expectation they can have in the light of his actual incapacity for responding to their direction. They are naturally desirous of being liberated from this subservience as soon as possible and of assuming the volitionally ascendant role that is warranted by the respective relative degrees of competence in the relationship. In addition, they begin to feel the social pressure and the responsibility of training the child in the ways of his culture. But typically in all cultures, they wait until he attains sufficient motor, cognitive, and social maturity to enable him to conform to their direction.

The age deemed appropriate for ending the stage of volitional independence and executive dependence varies between two and four in different cultures. In our own middle-class American culture, it is closer to two than to four. At this time parents become much less deferential and attentive. They comfort the child less and demand greater conformity to their own desires and to cultural norms. During this period, the child is frequently weaned and is expected to acquire sphincter control, approved habits of eating and cleanliness, and to do more things for himself. Par-

ents are less disposed to comply with his demands for immediate gratification, expect more frustration tolerance and responsible behavior, and
may even require performance of some household chores. They also become less tolerant toward displays of childish aggression. In short, all of
these radical changes in parental behavior tend to undermine environmental supports for infantile self-perceptions of volitional independence
and omnipotence.

Increased cognitive sophistication also contributes to ego devaluation
by enabling the child to perceive more accurately his relative insignificance and impotence in the household power structure. He begins to appreciate that his parents are free agents who are not obliged to defer to
him and who satisfy his needs only out of altruism and good will—not
because of his power and control. He begins to see himself as dependent
upon them both volitionally and executively. Now volitional independence is no longer perceived as compatible with executive dependence.
As a consequence of ego devaluation, the situation is precisely reversed:
increased executive independence is now required along with greater volitional dependence. From this point on, perceived lack of executive independence is no longer regarded as a regal perquisite of omnipotence
but as a condition necessitating dependence on the will of others.

The Satellizing Solution to Ego Devaluation

The devaluing pressures described above precipitate a crisis in ego
development that is conducive to rapid discontinuous change. They tend
to render the infantile ego structure no longer tenable and to favor
reorganization on a satellizing basis, since in no culture can the child compete with adults on better than marginal terms. The only stable, non-
marginal status to which he can aspire and still retain a reasonably high
and tenable level of self-esteem requires the adoption of a volitionally
dependent and subordinate role in relation to his parents. Since he cannot
be omnipotent himself, the next best thing is to be a satellite of persons
who are. By so doing he not only acquires a derived status that he enjoys
by the fiat of being accepted and valued as important for himself (i.e.,
irrespective of his competence and performance ability), but also, by perceiving himself as allied with them, he shares vicariously in their omnipotence. His sense of security now becomes less a function of having
competent persons available to satisfy his physical needs than of main-

taining an emotionally and volitionally dependent relationship with stronger, protective, solicitous, nurturant, concerned, and altruistic persons, which implies among other things the provision of whatever succorance is necessary. He is also relieved of the burden of justifying his adequacy on the basis of hierarchical position or actual performance ability, which at the very best is marginal and, in any event, is subject to unpredictable fluctuations.

The satellizing solution to the ego-devaluation crisis is more stable and realistic, and also less traumatic and demeaning than any alternative solution open to the child at this time. Since feelings of adequacy (self-esteem) are largely a function of achieving status commensurate with the level of ego aspiration, the retention of grandiose aspirations of volitional independence and omnipotence, in the face of a reality that would constantly belie them, would obviously tend to make him chronically vulnerable to serious deflation of self-esteem.

On the other hand, there are limits to the degree of ego devaluation that are consonant with the maintenance of feelings of adequacy. If the child's ego aspirations were lowered to the point necessary to bring them into line with his actual ability to manipulate the environment, the resulting abrupt and precipitous trauma to self-esteem would probably be even greater than if the untenable pretensions to omnipotence were retained. By satellizing, he, thus, avoids both unfavorable alternatives and maintains the maximal degree of self-esteem realistically compatible with the role and status of children in our culture.

Prerequisites for Satellization

From the foregoing it is apparent that satellization cannot occur in just any kind of home environment. Before the child can accept volitional dependency and seek a derived status, he must first perceive himself as genuinely accepted and valued for himself (i.e., intrinsically); for, in the absence of these two parental attitudes, the potential advantages of satellization (i.e., the acquisition of a guaranteed and stable derived status and the assurance of intrinsic security and adequacy) are vitiated, and the child has little incentive for relinquishing his notions of, and aspirations for, volitional independence and omnipotence and for becoming subservient to the will of another. Acceptance of volitional dependence on powerful figures is a hazardous venture indeed unless one feels assured in advance of their benevolent intentions. The rejected child also cannot acquire any derived status when his parents, instead of extending emotional support and protection, regard him as an unwanted burden. Rejection is the most extreme method of indicating to the child that the omnipotent and omniscient parents consider him unworthy.

Similarly, the advantages of derived status cannot accrue if the parent only values the child in terms of his potential eminence. Sooner or later the latter realizes that he is not valued for himself but in terms of his potential capacity for providing compensatory reflected glory to relieve the pain and misery of frustrated parental ambitions. In this latter case, however, the infantile ego structure is more tenable and less subject to the usual pressures forcing devaluation: the extrinsic and overvaluing parent obviously has no interest in deflating infantile notions of omnipotence and grandiosity, because he interprets these characteristics as portentous of future greatness; and he continues through indulgence and adulation to provide an environment that helps to maintain for some time the fiction of infantile omnipotence in which he hopes to share vicariously when the child attains adult eminence.

Evidence from a study of children's perceptions of parental attitudes indicates that it is occasionally possible for extrinsically valuing parents to be perceived as accepting (although for ulterior motives). The same evidence, however, supports the logical supposition that the rejecting parent cannot possibly extend intrinsic valuation to his child. In general, acceptance and intrinsic valuation are highly correlated. And since extrinsically valued children are almost invariably overvalued, the latter term alone (i.e., overvalued) will be used henceforth in referring to children who are overvalued for ulterior purposes and perhaps also accepted for similar reasons. It is not rare, however, for accepted, intrinsically valued children also to be overvalued.

Several other factors, related to the personality characteristics of parent and child, tend to make the process of satellization more or less difficult or prolonged but do not affect ultimate outcomes crucially. An unduly submissive or permissive parent who fails to impress his child with the distinction between their respective roles and prerogatives self-evidently tends to prolong the phase of omnipotence. The child is spared the pressure of parental demands for conformity to their will and standards, and hence undergoes less ego devaluation. But if he is truly accepted and valued for his own sake, he may eventually perceive his actual biosocial status and choose satellization nevertheless as the most feasible solution to the problem of maintaining childhood self-esteem in an adult-dominated society. Reference has already been made to the effect of temperamental (largely genically determined personality) traits in the child on tendencies to satellize.

Consequences of Satellization

Satellization has profound consequences for all aspects of ego structure and for the future course of personality development. Part of the satellizing shift in source of biosocial status involves abandonment and devaluation of notions of volitional omnipotence and independence and of the perceived centrality of self in the household interpersonal economy. But to compensate for these losses, the child acquires a guaranteed source of derived status from which he obtains intrinsic feelings of security and adequacy. Thus, children who perceive themselves as more intrinsically valued than average (i.e., who satellize more) tend to undergo more ego devaluation: they correspondingly tend to conceive of their capacities in less omnipotent terms and are less tenacious about maintaining unrealistically high levels of aspiration in a laboratory task after cumulative experience of failure. School children who are ranked high on acceptance by parents also tend to be characterized by "willing obedience" and relative lack of self-sufficiency and ego defensiveness.

Another product of satellization that is related to, but distinguishable from, its devaluing features (i.e., from changes in status, aspiration level, and volitional independence) has to do with the object or content of the child's conformity to parental volitional direction. It encompasses the training goals underlying the new parental demands and expectations to which the child is conforming. These goals may be designated as ego maturity goals since—irrespective of later changes in source of status, independence, and volitional control—they remain as constant parental and cultural objectives of personality maturation throughout the desatellizing and adult period of ego development, as well as the satellizing period. Although there is obviously much intercultural variability in the ideals of personality maturity, the needs of individual and cultural survival require a certain universally common core of changes in personality maturation—that infantile hedonism, executive dependence, aggression, and moral irresponsibility be attenuated in all cultures and that frustration tolerance, perseverance, and resoluteness increase. With respect to all of these components, the infant is characteristically at one pole and the mature adult at the opposite pole. Thus, although there are characteristic fluctuations in ego-status goals throughout the life cycle, there is a continuous increase in ego-maturity aspects of personality from the satellizing stage until senescence when some decline may occur in both spheres.

Hence, as children increase in age beyond the period of infancy, they are expected, in the first place, to grow in ability to develop nonhedonistic goals, and to forego immediate hedonistic gratification in order to gratify more important, long-term aspirations.

Second, they are expected to develop more executive independence. Growth in motor capacity for self-help is not always matched by equal willingness to execute the often tedious and time-consuming manipulations necessary for gratifying needs. However, since parents are unwilling to serve indefinitely as the executive arm of their offspring's will, they demand that their children acquire a certain measure of self-sufficiency in the ordinary routines of living. In contrast to younger children, for example, older children are less apt to request a helping hand in walking a plank blindfolded.

Third, it is expected that children will internalize parental ethical standards, accept the moral obligation to abide by them, and regard themselves as accountable to parents for lapses therefrom.

Finally, almost universally in all cultures, children are expected to become more responsible, to develop greater frustration tolerance, perseverance, and resoluteness, and to inhibit more consistently their socially unacceptable impulses, particularly aggression and sexual experimentation.

During the satellizing period the child is motivated to undergo positive change in these foregoing areas of personality maturity in order to obtain and retain parental approval, since only in this way can he feel sure that the derived status he enjoys will continue. His sense of security and adequacy becomes increasingly dependent upon conformity to parental expectations of more mature behavior. Highly accepted children are judged as willing to exert much "conscientious effort" to hold the approval of "admired authorities"; and children who perceive themselves as intrinsically valued at home are rated by teachers as more executively independent and more able to postpone the need for immediate hedonistic gratification. It has also been shown that task-oriented children, who presumably satellize more and have less need for ego aggrandizement, exhibit more emotional control and make fewer demands on adults.

Finally, satellization has important implications for the mechanisms by which ethical norms and values are assimilated from elders and from membership and reference groups. The essential motivation directing the satellizer's organization of his v˙lue system is the need to retain the acceptance and approval of those persons or groups that provide his derived status. Hence, he develops a generalized set to perceive the world in the light of the values and expectations he attributes to the latter individuals. Children who perceive themselves as most intrinsically valued by parents are least apt to make value judgments deviating from perceived parent opinions. Later, this orientation is reinforced by the desire to avoid guilt feelings that are associated with repudiation of parental values.

Value assimilation is, thus, an unconditional act of personal loyalty in which both considerations of expediency and the objective content of what is internalized are largely irrelevant, that is, from a motivational standpoint. The satellizing child identifies uncritically with the moral values and membership groups of his parents, even when these are only meaningless symbols. Thus, irrespective of his actual experience with black children, the white child of five and six tends to assume his parents' attitudes, favorable or unfavorable, toward blacks.

Negativistic Reactions to Ego Devaluation

Ego devaluation is not usually brought about smoothly and painlessly. Typically, although not invariably, the child first resists the threatened loss of his infantile ego status by more vigorous and aggressive assertion of its grandiose-imperious features before acknowledging that the advantages of a derived status offer him a more tenable biosocial position. This leads to resistive or negativistic behavior that tends to reach a peak between two and three years of age. The sources of resistance to ego devaluation are many: the inertia of existing personality organization; the insecurity and loss of immediate status involved in any rapid transition; the loss of advantages associated with present status and the disadvantages perceived in the new status; and, finally, aggression and counteraggression.

The two- or three-year-old has been accustomed for some time, of course, to living with the prerogatives and immunities of his omnipotent ego structure. Hence, he is understandably reluctant to part with an orientation that places him at the center of his universe and to accept instead the role of dependent satellite. To retain parental approval, he must, among other things, inhibit hedonistic impulses, surrender volitional independence, and conform to parental standards; and until the prospects for satellization are entirely certain, he must contend with the marginality and anxiety of transitional status. Rage, however, is a more conspicuous component of the child's response to ego devaluation than anxiety, providing that the devaluation takes place in a generally benevolent and accepting atmosphere. Such an atmosphere mitigates anxiety by providing a pervasive sense of security, as well as a propitious opportunity to satellize. Finally, negativism during this period constitutes a form of counteraggression against the often aggressive and interfering behaviors that parents use in pressing their training demands. Thus, it tends to be less intense when either parent or child happens to be temperamentally unassertive or submissive.

Issues regarding self-help are frequent excitants of negativism. The child vigorously resists attempts to abolish the executive dependence and "baby ways" that are part of his omnipotent self-concept. On the other hand, denying him the opportunity for self-help is also a common precipitant of resistance. We may hypothesize here, therefore, as we did above, that the child's rage and resentment are aroused not so much because needs for executive independence per se are frustrated, but because of interference with his desire for volitional independence, that is, with his self-perceived prerogative to undertake a particular task by himself if he chooses to do so.

The birth of a sibling is often such a traumatic event because the dethroning and transfer of indulgent attention to a new child comes at a time when the ego is already bearing the brunt of a violent devaluing process. Thus, sibling rivalry tends to be less severe if the younger child is born either before or after (i.e., less than eighteen or more than forty-two months) the crucial stage of devaluation in the older sibling. When firstborn adolescents have siblings who are less than three years younger, they tend to exhibit greater nurturance and affiliative needs than their counterparts with no siblings close to their age.

Girls apparently manifest less negativism at this age than do boys for two reasons. First, because they perceive themselves to be more accepted and intrinsically valued by parents, and also to have a more available like-sexed person with whom to identify, they can acquire more derived status. Second, they are able to obtain more subsidiary earned status than boys can by participating in female household tasks.

In any particular instance of this kind of negativism, specific normative, temperamental, or situational factors are undoubtedly important. Because of volitional immaturity, for example, compliance may be difficult without prior or simultaneous execution of the opposite alternative of refusal. Genuine misunderstanding of requests, disinterest in particular tasks, or requiring the child to exercise control and discrimination beyond his developmental capacity also instigate negativistic behavior. At any rate, children's negativism seems more blatant than that of adults since they lack the latter's language repertoire of polite evasions and circumlocutions when aroused.

The Nonsatellizing Solution to Ego Devaluation

Satellization, for the reasons given above, is hypothesized as the most acceptable and satisfactory solution to the ego devaluation crisis; and hence it is the most frequently chosen way in which children resolve this biosocial crisis in ego development. It presupposes that they can acquire a derived status through the medium of an emotionally dependent, subordinate, and subservient relationship to superordinately perceived parents. In all cultures, however, a variable number of parents are psychologically incapable of, or unwilling to, extend acceptance and intrinsic valuation to their offspring. Some children are also unable or unwilling to satellize. Thus, deprived of the self-esteem provided by the fiat of unconditional parental acceptance, such children, in both instances of failure to satellize, must continue to seek earned status and feelings of adequacy on the basis of their own power to influence and control their environment. There is this important difference, however, from the former stage of ego omnipotence: whereas a previously grandiose extreme status could easily be assumed to exist on the basis of a misinterpretation of parental subservience to their desires, increased cognitive maturity no longer makes this possible. Although the environment may continue to provide some support for notions of volitional independence and omnipotence, these notions must now be related increasingly to actual performance ability (executive competence) and hierarchical position.

If satellization is impossible, two alternatives still remain for resolving the crisis of ego devaluation: ego aspirations can either be maintained at the omnipotent level or else be reduced drastically in order to correspond to actual biosocial competence, unenhanced by the derived status afforded through acceptance by parents and the child's identification with their competence, power, and prestige. In the first instance, no devaluation of ego aspirations takes place; in the second, devaluation is complete. Although the latter alternative (complete devaluation) is conceivable under certain circumstances, it is not very probable.[6] First, it involves an overly drastic, abrupt, and traumatic depreciation of self-esteem. To aim high is in itself an enhancement of self-esteem, whereas immediate capitulation to the most unpalatable ego status available implies defeat and degradation. Second, various factors in the parent-child relationship operate against complete devaluation. An individual who fancies himself omnipotent does not react passively but with counteraggression, bitterness, and vengeful fantasies to the hostility, aggression, and humiliating depreciation of his self-esteem implied in rejection by parents. By setting his sights on power and prestige, he hopes someday to obtain revenge and negate parental judgments regarding his worthlessness.

In the case of the extrinsically valued (overvalued) child, complete devaluation is also an unlikely outcome. The parent who intends to aggrandize his own ego through the child's future eminence does all in his power to perpetuate the fiction of the latter's infantile omnipotence by maintaining a worshipful and deferential attitude toward him.

Thus, only where rejection takes the more passive form of prolonged emotional neglect and deprivation (as in some foundling homes) is the child apt to undergo complete devaluation instead of attempting to retain his omnipotent self-concept and aspirations. If the neglect is thoroughgoing enough, no real need for devaluation exists since omnipotent fancies do not develop in the first place; and in the absence of overt parental aggression as part of the rejection scenario, the maintenance of grandiose aspirations as a mechanism of possible counteraggression and revenge is unnecessary.

Consequences of Failure to Satellize

The child who fails to satellize generally fails also to undergo ego devaluation. The infantile personality structure that is not presented with the prerequisite conditions for reorganization (devaluation) tends to persist despite various shifts in biosocial status. Unable to acquire feelings of security and adequacy on a derived basis, he continues to pursue their extrinsic counterparts. Feelings of adequacy continue to reflect the child's earned status, whereas feelings of security remain a function of the parents' availability in providing for his basic needs until he possesses sufficient power, position, and prestige to feel unthreatened in facing the future more independently in this respect.

Under these nonsatellizing conditions the child is not obliged to relinquish aspirations for volitional independence, renunciation of which is implicit in the self-subordination of anyone who satellizes (i.e., who derives his status from the mere fact of a dependent relationship to, or acceptance by, another). It is true that increased capacity to perceive the social environment more realistically compels him to revise somewhat both his aspirations for interpersonal status and his self-estimate in a downward direction. But even though a chronic negative discrepancy between aspirational level and current status is inevitable for some time, his unrealistically and tenaciously high ego aspirations still tend to persist.

In the absence of satellization, which guarantees a derived (intrinsic) status, the acquisition of extrinsic (earned) status becomes a more compelling necessity. Hence, because of this compensatory need for high earned status, exaggeratedly high levels of ego aspiration remain stubbornly resistant to lowering despite their relative untenability in the present. The child, however, hopes to close the gap in the future; and even in the meantime the steady maintenance of a high aspirational level in and of itself tends to elevate self-esteem. Lending some empirical support to these speculations are the following findings: (1) that children who perceive themselves as extrinsically valued by parents tend to have more omnipotent conceptions of their intellectual and motor capacities, and to maintain a tenaciously high level of aspiration on a stylus maze task despite persistent failure experience on same; and (2) that low acceptance by parents tends to be associated with high scores on self-sufficiency and ego defensiveness in school children, low scores on "willing obedience" in school children, and high need for achievement in college students.

Rejected versus Overvalued Nonsatellizers

Although both rejected and overvalued children can typically enjoy no derived status, and although they both fail to undergo substantial devaluation in terms of aspirations for volitional independence and omnipotence, there are nevertheless important differences between them during the childhood years. In an austere, unappreciative, and hostile home environment, the rejected child cannot possibly acquire a significant degree of earned status or entertain any immediate aspirations for same. Hence, not only does he enjoy little current self-esteem, but he must also project most of his aspirations for power and prestige either outside the home onto school or peer group, or into the more distant future.

The rejected child's potent need for survival also compels a humiliating outward acceptance of an authority and control that he resents. In such generally insecure surroundings, the catastrophic impairment of self-esteem to which he is subjected (because of his worthlessness in his parents' eyes) tends to make him overreact with fear to any new adjustive situation posing a threat to his sense of adequacy. This anticipated fear reaction in response to a perceived future threat to impair his already seriously impaired self-esteem even further is the essence of Generalized or Neurotic Anxiety.[7] Nevertheless, hypertrophied ego aspirations are carefully nurtured within, and there is no inner yielding of volitional independence and no true subordination of self to others. Throughout his life he continues ambivalently to search for an intrinsically accepting parent surrogate (teacher, relative, spouse, friend, mentor, boss) who will enable him to achieve some degree of derived status or intrinsic self-esteem and, thus, enable him to suspend in part his relentless drive for achievement-oriented success.

Nevertheless, fear of further rejection tends to make the rejected individual overcautious in approaching parent surrogates. Further, unable to cope with parental anger and punitiveness, and afraid to retaliate in kind, he fails to learn adequately how to express anger when necessary, how to assert himself, and how to defend himself from the attacks of peers or other adults. He may, thus, let himself be used as a "doormat" for years and then suddenly explode intemperately, thereby jeopardizing his vocational or marital stability.

The environment of the overvalued child, on the other hand, provides an abundant satisfaction of both current needs for earned status and immediate aspirations for volitional independence and omnipotence. The child is installed in the home as a semi-absolute monarch and is continually surrounded by adulation and obeisance. Hence, he suffers no impairment of current self-esteem and has no current cause for Neurotic Anxiety. These latter eventualities first threaten when the protection offered by his unreal home environment is removed and his hypertrophied ego aspirations are addressed to peers and adults who are unbiased in his favor. Because of his obnoxious, egocentric, and overbearing personality, he tends to be rejected by peers—expecting the same deference he receives from parents. Only later, when he recognizes the need for more adequate peer and other interpersonal relationships for furthering his exaggerated ego aspirations, does he make a real effort to become less personally obnoxious.

Motivation for ego maturation. Satellizers and nonsatellizers also differ markedly with respect to motivation for achieving ego maturity goals (e.g., executive independence, attenuation of hedonistic needs, development of moral responsibility). In contrast to the satellizing child who merely assimilates these goals and standards of parental training through a process of value internalization, the nonsatellizer is primarily motivated in his orientation to values by considerations of expediency and attainment of earned status. He responds to the prestige suggestion of authority figures not because he feels any inner needs to agree unconditionally with them, but because he acknowledges their suitability as emulatory models and stepping stones to power and prestige. Children who perceive themselves as extrinsically valued tend to disagree more with perceived parental opinions, and children who fail to identify emotionally with their parents only assimilate the latter's values superficially.

The nonsatellizer, therefore, does not accept an unconditional obligation to internalize and abide by all internalized maturity values, but, rather, tends to be selective in this regard. The basis of this selectivity is the expediential criterion of potential usefulness for ego enhancement.[8] Thus, the curbing of hedonistic impulses and the acquisition of greater executive independence, for example, are regarded as essential for ego enhancement, and, therefore, become invested with moral obligation. Hence, with respect to these attributes of ego maturity, rejected school children tend to be rated just as favorably as their accepted contemporaries; whereas, in relation to these same criteria, extrinsically or overvalued children, who are under little external pressure from parents to conform to standards of mature behavior, are temporarily retarded, probably at least until their status depends more on persons outside the home.

On the other hand, values such as truthfulness and honesty do not always serve and are often in opposition to the interests of self-aggrandizement. In such instances, as suggested by the higher incidence of delinquency in children who are made to feel rejected, unloved, and unwanted, the sense of obligation may selectively fail to operate unless buttressed by either strong convictions of equity or by coercive external sanctions.

The Satellizing Stage

After the negativistic reaction to ego devaluation subsides, the child who finds it possible to satellize is less self-assertive and more anxious to please and conform. He is more responsive to direction and can be bargained with or put off until "later." He perceives his own power and position to be much depreciated, and he feels quite dependent upon parental approval. In their eyes he is a "good boy," that is, relatively docile, obedient, and manageable. But progress toward satellization does not proceed in a straight line. Changing capacities engender new self-perceptions with resulting fluctuations in disposition to remain content with a satellizing status.

Early Fluctuations

The four-year-old is more conscious of his own power and capacity. Marked strides have taken place in intellectual, motor, and social growth, and he is much less dependent on his parents. He learns new ways of manipulating persons and social situations and establishes a modicum of independent status for himself outside the home in the world of his peers. With increased self-consciousness of capacity comes a resurgence of infantile ego characteristics; and possessing still but a rudimentary self-critical faculty, he tends to exaggerate his newly acquired abilities.

This tendency toward self-overestimation is facilitated by the child's intoxication with initial successes, his exposure to competitive cultural pressures, and his history of grandiose thinking only recently left behind. Apparently there are times when he even believes that he is capable enough to regain full volitional independence and to cast aside satellization in favor of seeking an extrinsic (earned) status on the basis of his own competence. Deference to parental authority can become burdensome, especially when it is so obvious to him that he "knows better." Parents are also always interfering with his desires for immediate pleasure.

At the age of four the child, thus, becomes expansive, boisterous, obnoxious, and obstreperous; he is less anxious to please, obey, and conform. His behavior shows resistance to direction and is typically "out-of-bounds." He is "bigger" than everyone and can do everything better. Now for the first time he becomes intensely competitive in his play and in his desires to excel. Everything that he has or can do is compared with the possessions and abilities of others, and the decision regarding relative superiority is invariably made in his favor. He is acutely resentful of the privileges accorded older siblings. His concern with power and prestige is also manifested by his preoccupation with possessions, by interference with and teasing of other children and household pets, and by snatching of toys. With the growth of language his resistance assumes more verbal, subtle, and symbolic forms. Threats, boasts, contentiousness, deceit, and delaying and stalling tactics replace temper tantrums and open aggression.

It is important to distinguish between the negativism present at four from the variety prevailing at two and one-half. The goals of the latter are to perpetuate a highly subjectivistic, unrealistic, and unfounded brand of omnipotence that reflects a very immature grasp of the social reality in which the child lives. The basis of parental subservience is completely misinterpreted and no incompatibility is perceived between executive dependence and volitional omnipotence.

At four, however, omnipotent pretensions are predicated much more upon a more legitimate and realistic basis. Executive competence is partly accepted as a prerequisite for volitional independence; but because of inadequate self-critical ability, a very minimal degree of executive ability is inflated to the point of omniscience and omnipotence. Resistance is provoked when the exuberantly self-confident child tries to capture volitional control from the parent but meets with rebuff. At this age also self-assertion is no longer an end in itself; stimulated by competitive pressures, the child seeks to demonstrate his own superiority and to reveal the weaknesses of others. But despite his bold front, the expression of negativism begins to acquire moral implications that were previously absent. This is revealed by a growing tendency to disclaim responsibility for resistive behavior; to ascribe it to accidental causes, to coercive agents operating on him, or to other persons; and to rationalize it as desirable or as a form of self-defense.

At other times, however, the four-year-old becomes painfully aware that he is only a child. When his bluff is called, his inescapably dependent biosocial position brings him back to reality with a thud. He is, thus, torn between two opposing forces—a longing for volitional independence based on an exaggerated self-estimate of his executive competence, and a frightened desire to return to the protection of his dependent status as he stretches his wings too far and falls. This conflict is generally resolved in favor of the need to retain parental approval and derived status (i.e., in the case of emotionally accepted, intrinsically valued children).

The eventual triumph of satellization is not only aided by the development of a more realistic self-critical approach but is almost an inevitable product of the child's continuing dependent biosocial status in all cultures. The acceptance of parental control is also facilitated by the growing prestige and authority of the parent in the child's unstructured attitudinal field, by the operation of feelings of guilt in the child, by the latter's rationalization of compulsory parental demands as elective desires of his own, and by the liberal application of rewards, threats, and punishment.

Later Aspects

Five, like three, is also a relatively quiet, well-conforming age that succeeds a period of negativism. As the child's self-critical ability improves, his self-exuberance diminishes with a resulting loss of confidence and enthusiasm for his own powers. He is more dependent on adult emotional support, tends to be sympathetic, affectionate, and helpful, and is likely to invite supervision. The parents are idealized and appear more omnipotent than ever. The extent to which the child accepts parental value judgments is indicated by his almost tearful sensitivity to disapproval. A minor threat or mild show of disapproval is remarkably successful in effecting compliance. But until identification with the parent reaches a maximum at about the age of eight, one more major fluctuation in level of satellization still has to occur. It is precipitated by changes in biosocial status occasioned by the child's entrance into school.

The six-year-old tends to be relatively aggressive, expansive, boastful, and resistant to direction. His negativism follows the same pattern met with at age four; there is much of the same cockiness and blustering self-assurance based on an exaggerated notion of a recent gain in competence. But this time there is more real cause for crowing and ego inflation. For the first time he is conceded an official status in the culture that is independent of the home. For several hours everyday he now enjoys— at least in part—an extrinsic (earned) status that reflects his relative competence in mastering the curriculum. In addition, the authority of his parents is undermined by the termination of their reign as sole dispensers of truth and moral values. At the same time, school exerts a sobering influence on the child since it also makes greater demands for mature and decorous behavior. Hence, there is an improvement in such attributes of ego maturity as executive independence and reliability.

School, however, does not have the same impact on all children. The satellizer tends to react to the teacher as a parent substitute, but the approval he receives from her is less unconditional and more related to performance ability than that which he receives from his parents. In the total economy of his personality, also, the earned status he achieves at school still plays a relatively peripheral role in comparison to the derived status provided by his home. The rejected child, on the other hand, finds in school his first major opportunity to obtain any significant status whatsoever, whereas the overvalued child almost inevitably suffers a relative loss in appreciation at the hands of his teacher and classmates.

Satellizing and nonsatellizing tendencies are not mutually exclusive or all-or-none characteristics. Superimposed on the satellizing child's quest for derived status is a greater or lesser striving for subsidiary extrinsic (earned) status. Similarly, rejected nonsatellizers are more or less able to form satellizing-like attachments to nonparental individuals who happen to qualify better for this relationship (e.g., uncles, teachers, scoutmasters).

In addition to these individual differences, typical normative changes also take place in the relative balance between satellizing and nonsatellizing tendencies. Despite periodic fluctuations, the general trend between three and eight years of age is toward greater satellization. Thereafter, rapid strides in social maturity, the new source of status available in the peer group, resentment over exclusion from the adult world, the impetus of sexual maturation, and changing expectations from adults all play a role in undermining the satellizing orientation. But even in adult life, as already pointed out, residual satellizing attitudes continue both to provide a subsidiary source of current status and to influence, in substrate fashion, level of ego aspirations, susceptibility to Neurotic Anxiety, and mode of assimilating new values.

Some Aspects of Ego Functioning

Ego Involvement versus Ego Enhancement

Ego involvement is not synonymous with ego enhancement. It refers merely to the degree of self-implication in a given task or performance, that is, whether or not the outcome is a matter of concern or importance to the individual, but does not in any way make explicit the motives for his concern. Thus, nonego-involved areas in the environment are relatively peripheral and undifferentiated; failure in such areas is easily sloughed off, and success does not inspire elation. As already pointed out, since the magnitude and tenacity of aspirations vary with the degree of ego involvement in a task, the generality of aspirational (as well as of other) "trait" behavior depends upon holding ego involvement constant. Even more than success or failure in performance, the degree of ego involvement also determines the extent to which children find a task attractive. Failure lowers the attractiveness of a task much less when children perceive themselves as "trying hard" to do well than when they are indifferent about performance.

The motivation underlying ego involvement, however, is quite another matter. In many ego-involved tasks the chief object of the activity is ego enhancement, in which case we speak of ego orientation. Here the task is pursued as a source of either derived or earned status. On the other hand, the motivation for some ego-involved activities may be entirely unrelated to ego enhancement, being energized solely by a need to acquire mastery or to discover a valid solution to a problem. Thus, human beings may become intensely ego-involved in tasks in which the outcome per se rather than its relation to self-enhancement is the major focus of concern. In such instances the person is said to be task-oriented. He experiences feelings of success and failure, but not loss or gain in ego status or self-esteem.

It follows that before ego involvement can arise developmentally, the child must first possess a functional concept of self in relation to which various objects and activities in his environment can be ordered hierarchically in terms of relative interest or concern to himself. When this occurs, he is able to experience success and failure whenever ego-involved goals are either gratified or frustrated. The capacity for ego-enhancing motivation, on the other hand, requires, in addition, that the child be able to set ego aspirations regarding the relative competence of his performance, and respond with fluctuations of self-esteem to success and failure experiences related to these aspirations.

In our culture, this latter motivation is illustrated by the competitive behavior that first appears in three-year-old children and becomes increasingly prominent thereafter; such behavior involves minimally one's own and others' performance, appreciation of the concept of surpassing others, and desire to excel. It is also illustrated in the practical setting of aspirational levels for self-help in informal situations; in two- to three-year-olds these aspirations adhere quite closely to level of ability. Consistent levels of aspiration in more formal laboratory situations are not apparent, however, until about the age of five. For this kind of behavior, the child requires additionally a clear notion of the immediate future, some self-critical ability, and acceptance of the cultural value of aspiring to goals that are either less accessible or are somewhat beyond his or her prior level of performance.

Ego-enhancement motivation in our culture tends to have a competitive and self-aggrandizing flavor based upon the proposition that no one can enhance himself without encroaching upon the self-enhancement of others. Children typically work harder in response to prestige incentives than under anonymous conditions, and in response to competitive personal rewards rather than in group contests. But although all ego-oriented motivation is directed toward self-enhancement, this does not necessarily imply a desire for ego aggrandizement. Even in our culture, many children will exert themselves tremendously under conditions that at most allow for private satisfaction with achievement. The Navajo child strives little for individual achievement and seeks to avoid being singled out for superior performance.

The essential feature of earned status is that it is gained through an individual's own efforts (rather than vicariously by virtue of a dependent relationship to others) and depends upon the quality of his performance. It does not necessarily imply individual success, prestige, power, or competitive advantage. It may just as well be based upon personal satisfaction for competence, modest security, and approval for group-mindedness. In noncompetitive cultures self-enhancing status may be best acquired by renouncing individual ambitions and doing a good job of self-effacing, self-denying, cooperative activity directed toward the welfare of others or the group.

Component Aspects of Achievement Motivation

Ego-enhancement motivation in our culture is clearly identified with the achievement motive. The achievement motive in children is characterized by their perception of performance in terms of standards of excellence. Furthermore, this perception of standards of excellence is accompanied by analogous experience of pleasant or unpleasant feelings, respectively, about meeting or failing to meet these standards.

Achievement motivation is by no means the reflection of a unitary or homogeneous drive. It has at least three basic components, of which one is cognitive drive, that is, the need for acquiring knowledge and solving problems as ends in themselves. This drive certainly underlies the need for academic achievement to the extent that such achievement represents to the learner the attainment of the knowledge he seeks to acquire. It is completely task-oriented in the sense that the motive for becoming involved in the task in question (acquiring a particular segment of knowledge) is intrinsic to the task itself, that is, is simply the need to know; and hence the reward (the actual attainment of this knowledge) also inheres completely in the task itself since it is capable of wholly satisfying the underlying motive.

A second component of achievement motivation, on the other hand, is not task-oriented at all. It may be termed ego-enhancing because it is concerned with achievement as a source of earned status, namely, the kind of status that an individual receives due entirely to his achievement or competence level. It is also ego-enhancing inasmuch as the degree of achievement determines how much earned status he enjoys, and, simultaneously, how adequate he feels (his level of self-esteem); feelings of adequacy in this case are always a direct reflection of relative earned status attained. The ego-enhancement component of achievement motivation is, therefore, directed both toward the attainment of current achievement, or prestige, and toward future goals (later sources of earned status) that depend on the latter.

The final, or affiliative, component of achievement motivation is neither task-oriented nor primarily ego-enhancing. It is not oriented toward academic achievement as a source of earned status, but rather toward such achievement insofar as it assures the individual the approval of a superordinate person or group with whom he identifies in a dependent sense, and from whose acceptance he acquires vicarious or derived status. The latter kind of status is not determined as much by the individual's own achievement level as by the continuing intrinsic acceptance of him by the superordinate person(s) with whom he satellizes. Thus, the child who enjoys derived status is typically motivated to obtain and retain the approval of this superordinate adult individual—by meeting the latter's standards and expectations.

Some aspects of each of the cognitive, ego-enhancement, and affiliative components are typically represented in all achievement motivation; however, their relative proportions vary, depending on such factors as age, sex, culture, social-class membership, ethnic origin, and ego structure. Affiliative drive is most prominent during early childhood when children largely seek and enjoy a derived status based on dependent identification with, and intrinsic acceptance by, their parents. During this period, their striving for achievement is one way of meeting their parents' expectations and, hence, of retaining the approval they desire. Actual or threatened withdrawal of approval for poor performance motivates them, therefore, to work harder to retain or regain this approval. Since teachers are partly regarded as parent surrogates, they are also related to in similar but less intense fashion.

Affiliative drive is, thus, an important source of motivation for achievement during childhood. However, children who are not accepted and intrinsically valued by their parents, and who, therefore, cannot enjoy any derived status, are compensatorily motivated to seek an inordinate amount of earned status through high achievement. Thus, high levels of achievement motivation typically coexist with low levels of affiliative drive that are usually more than compensated for, however, by high ego-enhancement drive. Overly high levels of ego-achievement drive may also depress cognitive (task-oriented) drive inasmuch as extrinsic incentives and rewards tend to lower intrinsic interest in a task.

During late childhood and adolescence, affiliative drive both diminishes in intensity and is redirected from parents toward age-mates. Desire for peer approval, however, may also depress academic achievement when such achievement is negatively valued by the peer group. This is a more common occurrence among lower-class and certain culturally deprived minority groups. Middle-class peer groups, as is pointed out later, typically place a high value on academic achievement and expect it from their members.

The importance of satellization versus nonsatellization for early personality development is largely that each personality state is associated with a distinctive pattern of achievement motivation. Generally speaking, the nonsatellizer exhibits a much higher level of achievement motivation in which the ego-enhancement component is predominant, whereas the satellizer exhibits both a lower level of achievement motivation and one in which the affiliative component tends to predominate prior to adolescence.

The satellizer identifies with his parents in an emotionally dependent, subordinate, and deferential sense and is accepted, in turn, by them for himself. He enjoys, by virtue of this acceptance, both an assured derived status and the accompanying feelings of intrinsic adequacy or self-esteem that are relatively immune to the vicissitudes of achievement and competitive position. He has, thus, relatively little need before adolescence to seek the kind of status that will generate feelings of extrinsic adequacy commensurate with his degree of achievement. He does not, in other words, view achievement as the chief basis of his status or as the prime measure of his worth as a person; it is merely a means of meeting the expectations of his parents and of retaining thereby the approval that confirms for him his good standing as a satellizer in their eyes.

The nonsatellizer, on the other hand, is either accepted and valued on an extrinsic basis or rejected by his parents. Enjoying no derived status or intrinsic self-esteem, he has no choice but to aspire to a status that he earns through his own accomplishments. Since his feelings of adequacy are almost entirely a reflection of the degree of achievement he can attain, he necessarily exhibits a high level of aspiration for achievement and prestige—a level that is much higher, and more stable in the face of failure experience, than that of satellizers. This is obviously a compensatory reaction that reflects his lack of derived status and intrinsic self-esteem.

Consistent with his higher aspirations for achievement, the nonsatellizer manifests greater volitional and executive independence than the satellizer, and is better able to defer the immediate gratification of hedonistic needs in order to strive for more long-term goals. Similar personality differences between individuals manifesting ego-enhancement and affiliative drive orientations to learning, respectively, are reported by other investigators of personality development in childhood.

Consistent with the sex differences previously mentioned regarding satellization and intrinsic valuation by parents, female achievement performance is motivated more by affiliative needs, whereas male achievement motivation conforms primarily to the ego-enhancing type.

Other aspects of the parent-child relationship are also implicated in the development of achievement motivation. This kind of motivation tends to be higher in those children whose parents have high aspirations for intellectual achievement both for themselves and for their offspring; whose parents stress independence training and high standards of performance excellence; and whose parents, when present in problem-solving situations with their offspring, exhibit greater participation, instigation, encouragement, and disapproval. Achievement motivation is also apparently stronger in instances where an achievement-oriented mother is dominant in the home. A dominant, demanding, and successful father, on the other hand, is perceived by his sons as providing a competitive standard that is too overwhelmingly superlative to be challenged successfully.

In summary, review of the literature on achievement motivation and parental determinants bears out the prediction that nonsatellizing (i.e., rejected and extrinsically valued) children seek earned status primarily through ego-enhancing motivation. The studies suggest that high levels of active parental involvement, particularly along cross-sex, parent-child lines, provide the basis for achievement-motivation performance on intelligence tests and intellectual-achievement behaviors in free play. In each case, part of that involvement is reflected in such negatively valued parental behaviors or attitudes as rejection, criticality, hostility, or "pushing" the child beyond his ability; and this is particularly true of mothers with achieving children of either sex.

Significant normative fluctuations (as well as individual differences) in the balance between earned and derived status occur throughout the course of ego development. But, as already indicated, initial ways of relating to others tend to persist, especially if they occur at critical periods of socialization. Thus, although it is true that as the satellizing child grows older he increasingly strives for earned status, he will, even as an adult, continue to enjoy the residual sense of intrinsic worth that his parents earlier conferred on him, and will continue to satellize in some aspects of his current interpersonal relationships.

Level of Aspiration

Much insight into ego organization and functioning can be gained by observing the extent to which individuals take past performance into account in setting their level of aspiration for future performance. Children with adequate amounts of self-esteem (well-adjusted, academically successful children) respond to cultural pressure for achievement by aspiring to levels somewhat above the level of prior performance. However, since they do not have compensatorily high ego aspirations, they neither respond beyond the range of present performance capacity, nor cling rigidly to these high aspirations after later failure experience. In these ways, they tend to minimize feelings of failure associated with a marked discrepancy between aspiration and performance levels.

Individuals with relatively little self-esteem (e.g., especially unsuccessful nonsatellizers), on the other hand, are coerced by their high ego aspirations into maintaining tenaciously high levels of aspiration despite realistic considerations to the contrary. They find surrender of their high aspirations more traumatic than the immediate feelings of failure accompanying performance that is below aspirational level; also, merely in the maintenance of their high levels of aspirations, they find a source of ego enhancement. If they can manage to disinvolve their egos from the task, however, they tend to aspire to unrealistically low performance levels that they can always surpass, and, thus, at least spare themselves immediate failure experience. In the long run, however, they fail to achieve either any social recognition or any genuine feelings of self-esteem and succumb eventually either to chronic or acute Neurotic Anxiety.

In support of the above interpretation of level of aspiration behavior are the following findings: (1) boys, since they possess less derived status than girls, generally tend to set higher levels of aspiration and are also more willing to take risks; (2) handicapped or socially stigmatized children who presumably have a greater compensatory need for high extrinsic status—for example, mentally retarded, physically handicapped, and asthmatic children, African American children, individuals of low social and economic status, and children who fail chronically in school—tend more than control groups to aspire unrealistically beyond present level of performance; (3) children or adolescents who perceive themselves as extrinsically valued by parents, who have high prestige needs, and who have unrealistic ambitions all tend to adhere tenaciously to high levels of aspiration in the face of persistent failure experience.

Egocentricity, Egoism, and Subjectivity

By egocentricity is meant the extent to which the individual's self (in contradistinction to other persons, things, and events) is central as an object of attention in his psychological field. At a superficial level of saliency of awareness, it merely connotes preoccupation with self and relative indifference to external events.[9] At a deeper level of value, concern, and importance, that is, as indicative of a very high degree of ego involvement in self and of relative inability to relate emotionally to others, it is more appropriate to speak of egoism or narcissism. Narcissism, along with relative disinvolvement from external concerns, poor interpersonal relations, and extreme introversion are the dominant pre-Schizophrenic or schizoid personality traits that precede withdrawal from adult reality and from mature ego-status and adult ego-maturity goals during Schizophrenic episodes.[10]

Although egocentricity and egoism are probably related positively to each other, they are determined by different kinds of factors. Egocentricity-sociocentricity depends more upon social maturity, social poise and skill, gregariousness, introversion-extroversion, loquacity, and so forth; egoism, on the other hand, is more a function of magnitude of ego aspirations. Thus, it is quite conceivable that an outgoing, sociable person may be sociocentric but egoistic (i.e., superficially interested in others and their affairs, yet not really concerned with their welfare), and, contrariwise, that a shy, introverted person may be egocentric but still capable of genuine concern for and warm attachments to others once he knows them well enough to dispense with his shyness.

In the course of intellectual, social, and personality maturation, both egocentrism and egoism tend to diminish with increasing age. In communicating with others, children gradually grow in ability to perceive, pay sustained attention to, and take into account the feelings and viewpoints of others, and to interchange ideas as well as talk to each other. As they grow older, they tend to become more aware in their play of the presence and needs of others, more cooperative, considerate, and altruistic.

Closely related to, but distinguishable from, egocentricity is the young child's overly subjective approach to the interpretation of his experience, his perceptual autism (confusion between wish and reality), and his marginal reality testing. As he advances in age, he becomes increasingly able to approach questions of equity from a less personal and more detached and objective point of view, to argue from the standpoint of a hypothetical experience or proposition or from the perspective of another. His pictorial representations of reality also come to resemble more and more the model rather than the artist. However, the correspondence in childhood between perceptual, cognitive, and affective perspective-taking in any given individual tends to be relatively low, suggesting that these different dimensions are independently determined.

Narcissism and Ego Hypertrophy

Narcissism or ego hypertrophy is coextensive with: (1) the prevailing normative expression of the omnipotent ego structure of infancy prior to its devaluation in the course of satellization, and (2) the overvalued ego structure of the nonsatellizer. It consists of distorted notions of omnipotence, omniscience, invulnerability, and entitlement; of unrealistically inflated ego aspirations; of grandiose estimates of self-worth, self-importance, and uniqueness; of obnoxious self-assertiveness, exhibitionism, self-dramatization, interpersonal exploitativeness, and pejorative belittlement of others; of high goal tenacity and frustration tolerance; and of exaggerated egocentricity, self-preoccupation, difficulty in relating to others in a genuine, spontaneous, and unaffected manner, and of nonempathic insensitivity to the needs and feelings of other persons.

Although both rejected and overvalued nonsatellizers exhibit ego hypertrophy in the same basic psychopathological sense associated with their respective ego-development histories, it is typically evident overtly only in the overvalued nonsatellizer. This is the case because the rejected nonsatellizer's ego hypertrophy is ordinarily accompanied, and masked, by severe impairment both of self-esteem and of normal self-assertiveness, as well as by Neurotic Anxiety. It is true, of course, that most overvalued nonsatellizers also eventually undergo catastrophic impairment of self-esteem (with attendant development of Neurotic Anxiety), which similarly tends to attenuate and mask the expression of their narcissism.

Hence, the uninhibited overt expression of narcissistic ego hypertrophy is ordinarily found only in child, adolescent, and young adult overvalued nonsatellizers; in the relatively rare older overvalued nonsatellizer who is unusually capable and whose achievements and extrinsic status happen to be commensurate with his inflated ego aspirations; in autistic individuals; in many alcoholics and persons with neurotic defenses against anxiety; in such psychotic complications of Neurotic Anxiety as Reactive Schizophrenia, Mania, Paranoia, and depression (beneath the dysphoria); in many cases of Antisocial, Narcissistic, and Borderline Personality Disorder, and in children with aggressive, undersocialized Conduct Disorder. It is evident, however, that all nonsatellizers may be said to exhibit all or most of the above-listed characteristics of ego hypertrophy, although in many cases these may be masked or partially masked by impairment of self-esteem and self-assertiveness as well as by Neurotic Anxiety and depression. In a sense, then, they may all be said to suffer from Narcissistic Personality Disorder.

Notes

1. Various patterning predispositions and potentialities of genic origin also give rise to intercultural uniformities in ego development. These genic factors, however, in-

fluence primarily those general features of human behavior that set limits to variability in ego development rather than determine the direction of such development in their own right.

2. Perceptual reality considered as a dependent variable is itself an interactional product of stimulus content, cognitive maturity, and ego structure.

3. "Executive" refers to the manipulative activity involved in completing a need-satisfaction sequence, whereas "volitional" refers solely to the act of willing the satisfaction of a given need apart from any consideration as to how this is to be consummated. An infant, for example, displays marked notions of volitional independence and omnipotence, but at the same time may conceive of himself as executively impotent and dependent. In adult life there is greater correspondence between these two aspects of dependence-independence.

4. This is obviously much less true today because of the influence of the women's liberation movement.

5. The Yale norms reported here, and in this chapter generally, were obtained from a very specialized and unrepresentative group of children (overrepresented by middle-class, university-educated, professional, and Yale faculty parents). As used in this chapter they are only intended to convey a rough notion of mean age and sequential order of development in an unrepresentative but relatively homogeneous sample of children in our culture. It is not implied that the same designated mean ages necessarily apply to all children everywhere.

6. Complete devaluation may conceivably occur following the omnipotent stage in the case of children who are subjected to a grossly neglecting emotional and social environment subsequent to the emergence of the omnipotent ego structure. This eventuality is naturally far less common than the failure of ego omnipotence to develop in the first place because of exposure from birth, or shortly thereafter, to such an environment.

7. This anxiety (i.e., Neurotic Anxiety) is chronic in rejected nonsatellizers, with acute exacerbations occurring when they are confronted with novel or threatening new adjustive situations.

8. As will be pointed out later, this factor makes for instability in ego-maturation attributes. Once the nonsatellizer abandons his quest for earned status (e.g., in Reactive Depression or Reactive Schizophrenia), he regresses to childhood levels of ego maturity.

9. When the self, its attributes, and its experiential contents are the focus of psychological self-analysis, the term *introspection* is applicable. It is a prime characteristic of introverts.

10. Actually, shyness and asociality, which, in the past, were typically considered the pathognomonic pre-Schizophrenic traits of children in the United States, are actually associated rarely with adult Schizophrenia, as long as ability to relate emotionally to significant others is not impaired.

2

The Natural History of Ego Development: Desatellization in Preadolescence and Adolescence

Before ego development can be complete, one more important maturational step is necessary: emancipation from the home and preparation to assume the role of a volitionally independent adult in society. But before adult personality status can be attained, ego functioning must achieve a new balance between the dichotomous needs for independence and dependence—a balance that is closer to the volitional independence and self-assertiveness of infancy than to the docility and submissiveness of childhood. This involves largely a process of desatellization: the path away from volitional independence trod during early childhood must be largely retraced. Although the consummatory aspects of desatellization must be postponed until late adolescence, important preparatory aspects are accomplished during middle and late childhood.

In terms of the needs arising out of the child's dependent biosocial status, satellization is the most felicitous of all possible solutions to the crisis of ego devaluation (see chapter 1). However, beginning in late childhood and extending throughout adolescence, a second major shift in biosocial status precipitates a new crisis in ego development—the desatellization crisis—which demands a reorganization of comparable scope and significance. Confronted by changing biosocial conditions and under pressure to become more volitionally independent and acquire more earned status, the satellizing organization of personality becomes just as untenable and unadaptive as the omnipotent ego organization was at an earlier date. But since the home and parents still continue to function as the major status-giving influences in the child's life until adolescence, the actual crisis phase (transitional disequilibrium, disorientation, marginality, and anxiety) is postponed until that time.

Despite much intercultural diversity in the specific content and method of ego maturation, the *general* goals of personality maturation tend to be similar in most cultures. Ego maturation encompasses two essentially different kinds of personality changes: (1) changes in ego-maturity goals, and (2) changes in ego-status goals.

Ego-maturity goals include the attenuation of hedonistic motivation; the acquisition of increased executive independence and frustration tolerance; the development of greater moral responsibility, more realistic levels of aspiration, and more self-critical ability; and the abandonment of special claims on others' indulgence. Beyond infancy there is continuity of cultural expectation regarding the pursuit of these goals for individuals of all ages, the only differences being in the purposes they serve and in the *degree* of development expected.

Thus, progress toward ego-maturity goals is made during the satellizing as well as the desatellizing period. During the latter period, however, the motivation underlying the attainment of these goals tends to shift from the retention of derived status and parental approval to perception of such attainment as prerequisite to the achievement of higher standards of volitional independence and earned status. In deciding whether to assimilate new values, the desatellizing child is more prone than the satellizing child to use such criteria as expediency and capacity for enhancing ego aspirations instead of the criterion of blind personal allegiance (satellizing orientation). This new approach to value assimilation also characterizes the nonsatellizer at *all* ages. It will henceforth be referred to as the rational-objective orientation.

The *status goals* of ego maturation, on the other hand, are discontinuous from early childhood to late childhood, adolescence, and adult life. They include the acquisition of greater volitional independence and earned status; heightened levels of ego aspiration; the placement of moral responsibility on a societal basis; and the assimilation of new values on the basis of their perceived intrinsic validity or their relation to the major goals of the individual.

With respect to these goals, the child is not expected to be a miniature adult. Volitional independence, for example, reaches a high point during infancy, drops to its lowest point during middle childhood, and starts rising again during late childhood. The child obtains the major portion of his status from derived sources and the adult his from earned sources; and although this reversal is not completed until late adolescence, the balance begins to shift during middle and late childhood. Hence, insofar as the realization of ego-status goals is concerned, the stage of satellization represents a period of retrogression rather than of progress.

But even though desatellization restores many of the ego-inflationary features of the infantile period, this doesn't mean that the adolescent is back in the same place he was at the close of infancy; for supporting this gain in ego enhancement is considerable growth in cognitive sophistication and executive competence, much real accomplishment of the goals of ego maturity, and fundamental changes in social pressures and expectations. The concept of maturation can be defined only in terms of a pancultural norm indicating the direction in which certain aspects of personality structure must change if the desired goal of producing an acceptable adult member of society is to be realized. This cultural ideal of personality maturity influences in turn prevailing expectations relative to changes in goal structure during adolescence, the latter being inevitably fashioned in terms of enhancing the former.

The essence of this concept of maturation, that is, acquiring the motivation to achieve greater volitional independence and a more earned source of ego status, is, therefore, obviously incompatible with a relationship of satellization. The satellizing orientation must be weakened before the individual will strive to seek status on the basis of his proficiency in the virtues and competencies valued in his particular culture.

Once these basic maturational goals are internalized, they can be implemented only if a number of other personality attributes are simultaneously modified in the appropriate direction. For example, the enhancement of earned status requires that an individual pay less attention to the immediate gratification of hedonistic needs and concern himself more with planning for long-range prestige goals; that he acquire greater competence in implementing decisions by himself; and that he at least give the appearance of conforming to the moral standards of his social group.

The adolescent is required to give greater self-reference to considerations involving his own competence and his status in the group. Accordingly, he finds it necessary to adopt much more of a rational-objective orientation in the learning of more mature goals and values—because only within the framework of this learning orientation can he efficiently attain the objective of acquiring more earned status. When related to this goal, the criteria of blind loyalty, personal allegiance, and craving for personal approval cannot be very reliable motivations for the acceptance of new values. More efficacious and

TABLE 2.1
Maturation of Ego-Status Goals during Adolescence

A. The Acquisition of Greater Volitional Independence.
    1. Independent planning of goals and reaching of decisions.
    2. Assimilation of new values on the basis of their intrinsic validity or their relation to major goals of the individual, rather than on the basis of loyalty to parents or parent surrogates.
    3. Greater reliance on nonparental (that is, on societal) sources of ego support.
    4. Aspiring to more realistic goals and roles—adopting a level of ego aspiration that is more consonant with ability and environmental possibilities.
    5. Increased frustration tolerance, the ability to withstand more intense and prolonged experience of frustration without marked loss of self-esteem, collapse of aspirational level, or deterioration of performance.*
    6. Emergence of an adequate self-critical faculty—the ability to evaluate one's own performance critically, to perceive deficiencies and inadequacies in this performance, to become cognizant of discrepancies between an objective standard and one's own efforts to attain it.
    7. Abandonment of special claims on others' indulgence.
B. Reorganization or Goal Structure on a Less Devalued Basis.
    1. Greater need for obtaining earned (as opposed to derived) status.
    2. Heightened level of ego aspiration.
    3. Increased self-valuation.
C. Replacement of Hedonistic Motivation by Long-Range Status Goals and Decreased Need for Its Immediate Gratification.*
D. Acquisition of Increased Executive Independence.*
E. Acquisition of Moral Responsibility on a Societal Basis.*

*These ego attributes can also be considered ego maturity as well as ego-status goals.

realistic in this situation are such criteria as expediency and perceived superiority in implementing the gratification of particular status needs. The overt satellizing orientation is also frowned upon socially because it conflicts with the maturational ideal of greater volitional independence which is so crucial for the success of the new approach to status problems.

The preceding is a summary of the characteristic features of adolescent ego-status maturation that appear in related contexts in preceding or succeeding sections of this volume:

Pressures toward Desatellization

No sooner is the dependency of satellization consolidated than new conditions are created that undermine it and alter the shifting balance of dependence-independence. First among the factors impelling change toward personality maturation is the cumulative impact of progress in cognitive and social capacities, which, in turn, induces modification of parental and societal expectations. During the period of middle childhood, there is an unspectacular but steady gain in the child's ability to comprehend abstract relationships, to reason, and to generalize. His level of sophistication in perceiving the attitudes, needs, and feelings of others; the relative status positions of various persons (including himself) in the group; and the distinguishing criteria of social class status are all gradually advanced.

By understanding more thoroughly the nature of the environment in which he lives, the adolescent, thus, feels less awed by its complexity and more confident to navigate alone and unguided. He feels that he now possesses a sufficient fund of social and intellectual competence to qualify for a more mature and responsible role in the affairs of his culture, that is, to engage in the status-giving activities that he formerly regarded as the exclusive prerogative of adults. Hence, he tends to wish, more than younger children do, for such status-conferring attributes as good looks, stature, mental ability, and popularity; to prefer difficult tasks that he cannot complete to easier ones that he can; and to be less hedonistic and authority-conscious in his emotional responsiveness to different situations. But this time, unlike the situation at four (and even at six), he really possesses sufficient executive competence to warrant a serious and legitimate quest for more earned status and greater volitional independence.

Ego maturation in response to parental expectations of more mature behavior may ordinarily be expected to lag initially because of the phenomenon of perceptual constancy in the child. The prepotency of habitual expectations may temporarily force *altered* current parent behavior into *familiar* past perceptual molds despite manifest changes in stimulus content. The rate of ego maturation is also held back by ambivalent feelings in the child, who is naturally reluctant to part with the protection and security of dependency. This ambivalence is probably greater in children with strong needs for hedonistic gratification (who find long-range striving difficult) and in sedentary, shy, "thin-skinned," and introverted children to whom self-assertion comes painfully.

Lastly, ego maturation is a function of cultural expectations and of the availability of mature role-playing experience. These latter factors reciprocally influence each other as well as generate pressure and opportunity for personality reorganization on a more mature basis. Largely for these reasons, when ego maturation in our culture is appraised in a cross-cultural context, the acquisition of ego *status* goals (e.g., volitional independence, greater earned status) is seen to lag markedly behind the acquisition of ego-*maturity* goals (e.g., greater frustration tolerance, greater sense of responsibility, more executive independence, more deferral of immediate hedonistic gratification).

Estrangement of Parent and Child in Urban Cultures

Of course, neither the parent nor the culture is unaware of the growth in cognitive and social competence that takes place during the preadolescent years. In accordance with practical economic needs and the overall cultural training program, therefore, children are expected to acquire a source of extrinsic (earned) status to supplement their role as dependent satellites in the family configuration.[1] Depending on the degree of cultural discontinuity prevailing between children's and adults' roles, children either acquire a subadult, fringe status in adult society or an earned status in peripheral activities (e.g., school, peer group) far removed from the mainstream of status-giving operations in the adult world. In most primitive cultures the home serves as both the source of subsidiary extrinsic status and as the training institution for developing more mature and responsible behavior. The child is assigned responsible tasks of considerable social and economic importance in agriculture, handicrafts, household arts, and care of younger siblings; the tasks that are expected of the child are adapted to its capacity.

In complex modern cultures, on the other hand, children have little opportunity for exercising independence, responsibility, and identification with the world of adult concerns. This necessitates a complete separation of the status, activity, and interest systems of child and adult. Such children are given no responsibility in the workaday world of adult concerns and so evolve a complete set of prestige-giving values of their own. They are obliged to find sources of earned status in peripheral activities and to supplement this with the vicarious status that can be obtained through identification with the glamorous exploits of prominent figures in public and sports life, and with whatever satisfaction can be gained by carrying on covert "guerrilla" warfare with adults and adult standards.

One undesirable consequence of excluding children from *genuine* responsibility in the adult world is that, deprived of this necessary role-playing experience, related aspects of ego maturation tend to lag behind. Study of children in grades 4 through 12 reveals little evidence of marked developmental progress in children's manifestations of responsibility or of any relationship between their sense of responsibility and the number of home duties they assume. The fact that these relationships hold true for rural as well as urban children suggests that the children in our culture have no real opportunity for socially responsible participation. The routine assignments they carry out are so subordinate and expendable that they have little bearing on their earned status or volitional independence.

A second consequence of the displacement of the home as a training center for ego maturation is that children become increasingly dependent on nonparental sources of earned and derived status. In their peer group they are given a chance to obtain the mature role-playing experience from which society excludes them and which their parents are unable to furnish. Identification with this group also provides a substitute source of derived status providing them with ego supports that reduce their dependence upon parental approval. By attributing the prerogatives of volitional independence and moral decision making to a group fashioned in their own image, they effectively demolish their exclusive association of these powers with parental figures, and, thus, pave the way for eventually assuming them themselves. School serves a very similar function. It provides both a new subsidiary source of earned status based upon academic ability and a fresh source of derived status that challenges the parents' monopoly of this commodity and of omniscience as well.

All of these factors—the availability of other sources of derived status, the possession of subsidiary earned status, the need for going beyond the home for sources of extrinsic status, children's own greater competence, exposure to a diversity of family and social climates with resulting awareness of alternative standards and ways of doing things, and the emergence of new claimants of omniscience—tend to break down children's deified picture of their parents. Thus, beginning with late childhood, glamorous figures such as movie stars and sports heroes, attractive visible adults, and composite portraits of admired adults start to displace parents as emulatory models. As the ties of dependency weaken and the perceived omnipotence of the parent diminishes, the latter's power to confer by fiat an absolute intrinsic value on the child begins to wane; and as the parent's glory fades, less vicarious status can obviously be reflected on his satellites.

Systematic observation of eight-year-olds indicates that they are already more outgoing and in greater contact with their environment. They resent being treated as children and cannot wait to grow up. Nine-year-olds are more independent, responsible, cooperative, and dependable. After making a futile attempt to draw adults into their world, they seem to accept the fact that fusion is impossible. They become very busy with their own concerns and do not have time for daily routines or parental demands. There is much planning in great and practical detail. They may prefer work to play. But these concerns are now oriented more toward their contemporaries than toward their parents; and they verbally express indifference to adult commands and adult standards.

Thus begins a long period of estrangement between children and adults that persists until the former attain adulthood themselves. Insurmountable barriers to commonality of feeling, to mutual understanding, and to ease of communication are often built up. This alienation is often accompanied by resentment and bitterness. Although outright resistance to adult authority is usually withheld until adolescence, there is reason to believe that preadolescents' apparent conformity is only a veneer that hides the smoldering rebellion from view. This is suggested by the often contemptuous and sneering remarks they make about adults in their own company; and, perhaps, were it not for compensatory outlets in movies, comics, vandalism, and opportunities for fighting with peers and for bullying younger children, it would come more into the open. Because girls are able, and expected, to satellize more and longer than boys, and can also achieve more earned status at home and in school, they tend to be more conforming to, and less at war with, adult standards and values.

As will be pointed out later, however, it would be a serious mistake to assume either that this alienation is an all-or-none matter or that all adolescents are estranged from their parents and from other adult authority figures. Not only are almost all adolescents influenced by adult values in certain respects (see chapter 3), but in the case of many, parent-youth and adult-youth conflict are minimal, and identification with, and conformity to, adult norms is the rule with only a minimum of intergenerational conflict and intrapsychic turmoil.

The Centrality of Self during Adolescence

There are a number of reasons for believing that the concept of self occupies a more prominent place in the individual's psychological field during adolescence, and that considerable upward revision of self-estimate as well as a heightened level of ego aspiration take place. In contrast to the carefree and extroverted self of late childhood, the adolescent self becomes a more salient and clearly delineated object of awareness. The adolescent appears concerned with a more precise verbalization of his feelings about himself. For all practical purposes, diaries are almost an exclusive adolescent (and feminine) phenomenon. Daydreaming is more common in postpubescent than in prepubescent girls of comparable age. Developmental studies of personality structure using the Rorschach Test agree that adolescents are more introspective and given to fantasy, and also more introverted and concerned with exploring subjective experience than individuals in younger or older age groups.

Increased awareness of and interest in other traditional symbols of selfhood, such as the body, grooming, and one's name, are also characteristic of adolescence. Concern with intellectual status and social relations have considerable self-reference and are important sources of self-esteem in the adolescent. Awareness of one's own sociometric status is also enhanced during adolescence. Finally, adolescent preoccupation with sexual matters can be partly explained by the usefulness of the opposite sex as a contrast medium for self-expression and sharper definition of individuality.

Adolescence is a period of inflation of ego aspirations and self-estimate. In contrast to the early crisis of devaluation, it may be regarded as a time of ego revaluation. All of the maturational tasks of adolescence—the acquisition of volitional independence and earned status; emancipation from parents; working toward the achievement of economic independence; release from dependence on parents in assimilating values; learning a biological sex role; emphasis upon executive independence and long-range status goals; the acquisition of adult body form—have ego inflationary implications. This supposition is confirmed by analysis of the content of adolescent fantasy, which casts the ego in heroic and amorous roles with emphasis upon vocational success and material gain. Analysis of the inferred goals of high-school students and the fact that the vocational goals of adolescents tend to be cast at a higher level than is justified by a realistic consideration of aptitude and job opportunities lead to the same conclusion.

From the foregoing it could be concluded that all of these drastic and far-reaching ego-related changes during adolescence generate an "identity crisis" whether viewed vertically as discontinuity over adjacent age periods of personality development or horizontally as internal inconsistency from one component area of adolescent personality development to another. However, such a characterization of this period of personality development as constituting a crisis in ego identity is little more than an appealing catch phrase and generalization, and does not, of course, enhance our understanding of it unless the particular discontinuities and inconsistencies involved can be specified. It is to this task, therefore, that we shall now direct our attention.

Adolescent Personality Compared with that of Infancy and Childhood

The tasks of adolescent personality development overlap sufficiently with those of infancy and childhood to make a more detailed comparison profitable.

First, the crisis of desatellization, just like the crisis of devaluation, precipitates an extended period of developmental disequilibrium. All of the difficulties and instabilities attending a transitional stage of ego development must be endured again. A secure and established biosocial status is exchanged for a new status that is unsettled, marginal, conflictful, and uncertain of attainment. A highly differentiated and familiar psychological field must be abandoned for one that is uncharted, ambiguous, undifferentiated, and fraught with unknown implications. The quest for orientation must be begun anew. It is no wonder then that resistance to change will come from within as well as from without.

Second, adolescence resembles infancy more than childhood in that a new biological drive (sex) must undergo initial socialization. This emergent phenomenon presents a problem that has not arisen since early infancy, and the control of this new source of hedonistic motivation is comparable in many ways to the early regulation of hunger, thirst, and bladder and bowel evacuation.

Third, there is a reactivation of the issues of dependence vs. independence, of self-assertion vs. subservience, which have lain relatively dormant since the crisis of devaluation. Again violent fluctuations in these dichotomous needs are the order of the day until a new equilibrium is found. But the general trend of change is in the opposite direction. The pendulum swings closer to the infantile goals of volitional independence and mastery of the environment than to the subservient attitude of childhood. This does not mean that the young adult is back in the same place that he left at the close of infancy; for behind this shift in ego development is considerable growth in perceptual ability and executive capacity as well as fundamental changes in social pressures and expectations. Thus, the position that was abandoned as untenable after fierce resistance from three to five is now given a new basis in reality. Henceforth, the tide of battle turns after the turbulent struggles of adolescence and enables the young adult to hold permanently to volitional and executive independence.

Rank and his followers emphasize the shift in the independence-dependence balance during adolescence. This shift, however, is, in and of itself, not coextensive with the process of adolescent personality maturation; it is only one component aspect of the more general constellation of changes occurring in this stage of ego development, and cannot be appreciated properly apart from them. For example, the need for greater volitional independence is accentuated by higher ego aspirations, greater self-valuation, and increased demands for earned status. The adolescent individual who has more modest ego demands, who values himself more modestly, and who is more content with achieving vicarious status can also tolerate considerably lower levels of volitional independence with much greater equanimity than his more ambitious contemporary with a more expansive self-concept.

As in the crisis of devaluation, negativism is a prominent aggressive response of the individual to the insecurities and anxieties of the rapid transition in biosocial status. In ego devaluation, however, the general direction of change is toward a decrease in status, whereas in the new situation the reverse holds true.[2] More important is the difference in the cause of the disproportion between status and capacity that gives rise to much of the conflict-provoking negativistic behavior. In the earlier period, the two- and three-year-old demands volitional freedom far out of proportion to his executive capacity. The adolescent, on the other hand, receives too little volitional independence in relation to his capacity. Status deprivation exists in both instances; in the first case this is attributable to the unrealistic aspirations of the child; but in the second case it is due to the inability or unwillingness of the parents or of the social order to provide the adolescent with status commensurate with his capacity.

The same difference underlies a general similarity between infancy and adolescence in still two other areas. The adolescent, like the presatellizing child, is more concerned with earned (in contrast to derived) status, but has a more realistic claim to it in actual executive competence. Similarly, the adolescent's higher self-valuation is more realistically grounded in environmental supports.

Finally, the adolescent resembles the presatellizing child in owing to personal loyalty relatively little of his feelings of accountability to parental moral standards. But, unlike the situation in infancy, these feelings are based on more abstract propositions, are directed more by societal sanctions and guilt feelings, and do *not* owe their effectiveness to more tangible applications of reward and punishment. Further, they are primarily related to peer-group values and are reinforced by the rewards and sanctions of this group.

On the other hand, adolescence is in several respects more nearly continuous with the direction of personality development during satellization. During adolescence, childhood trends toward greater executive independence, toward increased reliance on long-range goals, toward greater overall moral responsibility (despite the shift in the basis for these), and toward greater conformity to societal demands are further extended, and hedonistic motivation is further attenuated.

But this time the motivation is different. It reflects a need for attaining recently internalized and more mature goals that would otherwise be frustrated by preoccupation with pleasure-seeking activities, rather than a need for gaining parental approval. And although the adolescent shift toward earned status is more reminiscent of infancy, there is a continuation of the childhood trend to seek such status on the basis of actual executive competence.

Preparatory Aspects of Ego Maturation in Adolescence

From the standpoint of *ultimate* criteria of maturity, the satellizing era of middle and late childhood is a period of mixed progress. The attenuation of hedonistic motivation, the gain in executive independence, and the enhancement of feelings of moral responsibility are all steps toward adult personality maturation. But in relation to other, more critical characteristics of mature ego structure, such as volitional independence and reliance on earned status, satellization constitutes at least a temporary setback. It is true that realistic progress toward these goals also occurs; but as already pointed out, whatever earned status is achieved occupies only a subsidiary position in the total *Gestalt* of biosocial dependency.

Childhood may be regarded as a period of apprenticeship in acquiring the *qualitative* aspects of personality maturity that are necessary for individual and cultural survival. Adolescence, on the other hand, is more a period of apprenticeship in attaining the prerogatives and behavioral capacities associated with volitional independence and earned status. Thus, much of the personality development necessary for maturity is achieved before adolescence or exists at a near-threshold level, and is, therefore, a function of the quality of training for maturation provided during childhood.

Factors Bringing about Preparatory Maturation

First among the factors impelling change toward personality maturation in childhood, as pointed out above, is the cumulative impact of progress in perceptual, cognitive, and executive capacities, which, in turn, induces modification of parental and societal expectations. During the period of middle childhood, there is an unspectacular but steady growth in the child's ability to comprehend abstract concepts and propositions, to reason, and to generalize. His level of interpersonal sophistication in perceiving the attitudes, needs, and feelings of others, the relative status positions of various persons (including his own) in the group, and the differential criteria of social class status is gradually advanced. Hence, the first precondition for acquiring more mature behavior patterns—readiness for learning—is satisfied.

But largely as a result of widespread acceptance of the doctrine of Gesell and the advocates of ultrapermissive child education, it is commonly believed that maturation is solely a spontaneous process, generated from within when the child is ready to move on. The application of external pressures is held to be unnecessary, unwise, and productive of resistiveness. But, although the removal of external coercion will prevent negativism, it will *also* preclude the possibility of ego maturation.

Gains in maturity do not arise spontaneously and automatically out of the needs of the child. They are more than a reflection of increased readiness to undergo training as a result of increased capacity proceeding from growth, although this factor must also not be ignored. In every noteworthy maturational advance relative to ego structure there is some change in the expectations of significant persons in the child's environment, a change that is also enforced by some coercive form of pressure.

Just as important for maturation as appropriate revisions in expectations is sufficient opportunity for learning mature and responsible behavior. Without the requisite experience and practice, maturation can evolve no more readily through response to altered external expectations alone than through spontaneous generation from changed conditions of internal readiness.

By inducing personality maturation in the child, parents play a strategic role in the changing environmental expectations. The new demands they set reflect their own needs and desires as well as their changed perceptions of the child's growing capacities for responsible behavior. Also channeled through them are changing cultural expectations of appropriately mature behavior at various stages of development. And in either case, it is they who apply whatever coercive measures are required to effect the necessary degree of conformity. The parent is unwilling to serve indefinitely as the executive arm of his offspring's will. At the termination of infancy, he welcomes the increased self-sufficiency of the child since it frees him for other tasks; he also approves of the shift in ascendance-submission, which gives him greater control and direction of the latter's activities.

To enforce conformity to his new expectations the parent can rely upon reward and punishment, approval and disapproval, prestige authority, and the moral restraints imposed by the child's guilt when he strays from the path of internalized duty. Also at the parent's disposal is the power to extend or withhold the appreciation that chiefly motivates the child's early bids for extrinsic status. Although it is true that external controls and extrinsic sanctions (reward and punishment) generally tend to be replaced by some form of self-discipline, the process of internalization is a very gradual one and, by definition, presupposes the original existence of external controls, since obviously nothing can be internalized that does not first possess an external form. And even after internalization is fairly well established, the presence of external controls in the background has a salutary effect.

In the new face he presents to the child, the parent is for the most part playing the role of cultural representative. Reality training is important among all people who survive. Under an economy of scarcity, everyone must develop certain minimal skills and a willingness to work. When life is more abundant, the child's actual economic contributions to family survival may be deferred until early adulthood, but in any case he is no longer permitted the self-indulgence and irresponsibility of earlier years. At the very least, a large share of self-help is demanded.

Pubescence: Consummatory Factor in Personality Maturation

The preparatory changes in personality maturation catalogued above, as well as the factors bringing them about, are not to be minimized in evaluating the total maturational change from the close of infancy to the beginning of adult life. Yet the transition cannot be consummated merely by the cumulative impact of these same factors, namely, parental and cultural needs for personality maturation; increased executive competence of the child; new sources of derived status and ego support; the weakening of dependency ties on parents; the deflation of parents and the continued progress toward desatellization; and the attainment of an independent, subsidiary source of earned status. This is true even where children are not relegated to a separate and discontinuous world of status opportunity, but contribute to the economic sustenance of the family. The conclusion is inescapable that whatever independence and earned status children acquire before pubescence can play only a subsidiary role in the larger *Gestalt* of biosocial dependency. The gains in these areas are primarily by-products of training in responsibility and in the attenuation of hedonistic impulses that constitute the main maturational business of childhood.

The personality maturity of adolescence and adulthood are *qualitatively* different from the maturity of childhood. In our own culture, this qualitative difference is explicitly recognized in the dichotomy characterizing the types of status activities and opportunities for independence available to children and adults, respectively. In cultures that do not create such dichotomies, this qualitative difference prevails nevertheless as a result of a transcendental qualitative leap that becomes effective at a crucial transitional point on a continuous quantitative scale. This point is reached when, in the total economy of ego organization, earned and derived sources of status exchange positions as subsidiary and dominant (or peripheral and central) figures in the *Gestalt*.

Pubescence plays the role of crucial catalytic agent in shifting the direction of the source of status, and hence in inaugurating the consummatory aspects of personality maturation. It is the cue for reversing social expectations about the major type of status that the child may appropriately seek. Hence, in relation to the pubescent individual, the social value of derived status depreciates while the corresponding value of extrinsic (earned) status increases. The adolescent, thus, not only finds that he is increasingly expected to establish his status through his own efforts, but also that the latter criterion tends to displace the childhood criterion (i.e., of derived status) as the chief measure by which his social milieu tends to evaluate him. Simultaneously, social pressure is put on the parents to withdraw a large portion of the emotional support which they had hitherto been extending to him by way of conferring intrinsic (derived) status.

Generally speaking in our culture, youths who are not pubescent are accepted neither in the adolescent peer group nor in young adult work groups; and in almost all primitive cultures, nonpubescent youths are barred from "rites of passage" that would otherwise lead to junior adulthood in the mainstream of the culture.

Mechanisms of Desatellization

From the foregoing description of the nature and determinants of the desatellizing process, it is apparent that three different kinds of desatellizing mechanisms exist. The first mechanism may be called *resatellization*. It involves gradual replacement of parents by age-mates and others as the essential socializing agents of children and as the individuals in relation to whom the satellizing orientation is maintained. Resatellization follows the same pattern of dependent emotional identification with stronger, prestigeful individuals or groups as did satellization. The identifications are merely transferred in part from parents to teachers, parent surrogates, religious or youth leaders, age-mates, and others on whom the child is dependent for derived status. Values, goals, and attitudes are now acquired from these individuals as by-products of personal loyalty to them.

But although resatellization is a prominent feature of desatellization in our culture, it tends not to occur in most primitive cultures. Here the parents remain the chief socializing agents and the source of standards and derived status; the older child and adolescent merely acquire greater volitional independence and earned status within the family circle *without* revolting against the authority of the head of the household.

Desatellization through the Achievement of Earned Status

More important in bringing about desatellization than the issue of who (parents or peer group) becomes the objects of residual satellizing trends are the child's increased needs for obtaining earned status and the sources from which it is available. The satellizing orientation is abrogated more effectively by the displacement of derived status by *earned* status as the basis of self-esteem than by replacement of parents by peers, teachers, and adult leaders as the source of *derived* status. Hence, the more crucial contribution of these latter individuals to the desatellizing process is the earned status they are able to furnish the preadolescent and adolescent child.

At first, the opportunity of gaining parental approbation constitutes the child's chief motivation to acquire the earned status resulting from independent accomplishment; thus, in the beginning, the acquisition of extrinsic status is largely a modified form of satellization. Later, earned status becomes an end in itself, and accordingly, there is a parallel shift in children's orientation toward value assimilation and in their motivation for achieving the attributes of ego maturity.

Generally speaking, adolescence is less prolonged in cultures in which adolescents gain extrinsic status by participating in the same types of economic activities as their parents. But in cultures characterized by age-mate socialization, parental sources of status are not available to adolescents, adolescence is extremely prolonged, and earned status is achieved in peripheral economic activities far removed from the main economic currents of the social order. We may refer to the latter situation as *interim* status. Although from a long-range standpoint the goals of this type of status have only temporary "stop-gap" significance, they do constitute distinctive objects of striving in their own right during the adolescent period.

Hence arises yet another source of discontinuity between children and adults. Three discrete value and status systems must be learned before adult life is reached. And during adolescence the individual is obliged simultaneously to satisfy the need for immediate age-mate status while keeping an eye toward the more long-range goals of adult status.

In either setting, as indicated above, it is important to realize that earned status does not necessarily mean individual success, prestige, power, or preeminence. It may just as well be competence that is not compared with another's, modest security, safety, approval for group-mindedness, and maintenance of "face." Thus, among the Navajo the youngster is not urged to strive for individual achievement. There is no promise of personal success for the able and hard-working or the good and righteous. On the other hand, a sense of worthlessness is never drummed into a child so that his whole subsequent life is a struggle to justify himself. To accept authority over his fellows or to take initiative in any obvious fashion has for the Navajo the psychological meaning of separating him from the social group to which he looks for both support and regulation. But a sense of responsibility is none the less real for being divided and shared, for being—to the white person—vague and unfixed. The majority seem to be only interested in safety. They themselves will sometimes say, "All we want is enough to eat for ourselves and our families." The predominant drive is for moderate material well-being.

We may, therefore, reach the following conclusions: (1) that the magnitude of residual intrinsic adequacy feelings available to adolescents and adults is partly a function of a societal norm, the mean value of which varies from culture to culture, with considerable room for individual family differences; (2) that the drive for extrinsic status is inversely related to the magnitude of these residual feelings of adequacy; and (3) that the particular orientation of the goals toward which earned status is directed— whether competitive and individualistic or cooperative and group-related—is conditioned by the prevailing value system of a culture or subculture.

In both types of socialization patterns (age-grade and parental) a transitional variety of earned status is evident. That is, the child's initial quests for extrinsic status are largely bids for parental approbation, and, as such, must be considered modified manifestations of satellization. If they elicit appropriate signs of appreciation from parents, their continuation as ends in themselves is encouraged.

Desatellization through the Exploratory Orientation

Two modes of assimilating values have already been discussed, the satellizing orientation and the rational-objective orientation, as characteristic of childhood and adulthood, respectively. The latter orientation is naturally an accompaniment of the quest for greater extrinsic status since it utilizes a criterion of ego enhancement as the preparatory set in reacting to new value experience. The satellizing orientation, on the other hand, is predicated upon personal loyalty and the need to retain parental approval or at least to avoid the guilt engendered by repudiation of parental standards. Common to both orientations, however, to a greater or lesser degree, is a subjective bias favoring the generation and perpetuation of a given type of status (earned or derived), and a relative indifference to objective considerations impinging on the empirical or logical validity of the value in question.

A third type of learning orientation (exploratory) is not status-oriented in either sense, but is directed toward objective problem-solving regardless of the status implications involved. We have earlier referred to it as "cognitive drive," and as "intrinsic" or "task-oriented" motivation or value assimilation. In every person's psychological world there is a sphere of value-laden, ego-involved learning experience in which the task itself and not its relation to ego status is the primary focus of concern. Where task-oriented goals or values are concerned, levels of aspiration operate, success or failure is experienced, but self-esteem is not necessarily affected since ego status is not at stake. This task-oriented approach to motivation and value assimilation stresses such criteria as objective validity, logic, and equity, and deemphasizes the status considerations, both derived and earned, that underlie the satellizing and rational-objective orientations, respectively.

The utilization of the exploratory orientation is obviously limited during childhood, for as soon as the implications of independent objective investigation are pursued to their logical conclusion, the danger always exists that they will conflict with values tied to primary allegiances, and hence precipitate an avalanche of guilt feelings. But as subservience to parental values wanes, the exploratory orientation can be used more freely, and continued use promotes desatellization by deemphasizing considerations of personal loyalty in value assimilation.

Unfortunately, however, the development of the exploratory orientation is severely curtailed in the course of age-mate socialization. The adolescent's marginal status and his dependence on the peer group for both earned and derived status permits very little deviation from group values, and hence little opportunity for independent exploration. The adolescent who ventures beyond certain strictly circumscribed limits is quickly ostracized from peer society. On the other hand, when the adolescent owes his opportunities for earned status to his elders, there are similar pressures to make him conform to traditional values. In both instances the exploratory orientation tends to be sacrificed because of the adolescent's need to conform to the standards of the agents who control the sources of his status. The very operation of this factor, in other words, is just another manifestation of the rational-objective orientation.

Facilitating and Retarding Factors in Desatellization

Desatellization is a stressful and conflictful phase of ego development. Children are expected to become more volitionally independent and self-assertive; and in achieving this goal, they have to combat ambivalent tendencies both within themselves and in their parents. If they are too submissive and dependent they lose face in their own eyes and in the eyes of their peers. If they are too independent and aggressive they feel guilty for excessive repudiation of their parents. Whether or not maturation actually occurs depends on the ways in which various factors of parental behavior, child temperament, and cultural expectations facilitate or retard the mechanisms whereby desatellization is effected.

The central developmental task of desatellization is the regaining of the volitional independence surrendered in the course of satellization. Hence, desatellization can best be implemented by: (1) encouraging the rational-objective and exploratory orientations and by discouraging the satellizing orientation in the assimilation of values; (2) developing multiple sources of intrinsic security and adequacy through satellization with persons and groups outside the home; and (3) developing skills in independent planning and goal-setting by providing opportunities for practice and appropriate conditions for learning realistic roles and goals, adequate frustration tolerance, and realistic self-criticism.

Desatellization, for example, is facilitated if the child (in contradistinction to his or her behavior) is accepted unconditionally, that is, if obedience and conformity are not made the price of acceptance. This requires that they be allowed to accept the values of our culture rather than having them crammed down their throats, with withdrawal of parental emotional support as the ever-threatening penalty for disagreement. But even if unconditional acceptance is assured, disapproval must still be used reservedly since it tends to precipitate feelings of guilt in the child. Hence, parental disapproval should not be administered automatically whenever the child's attitudes or behavior deviate from the parents'—as if disagreement per se were evil. It should be reserved for instances of serious deviancy that would lead, if left unopposed, to personality distortion or maladjustment. Disapproval and feelings of guilt, as already indicated, can be used to discourage blind and uncritical reflection of parental viewpoints; and the praise that is usually reserved for this situation can be administered when evidence of independent and critical thinking is presented. Similarly, the more impersonal the basis on which obedience and conformity are required, the less likely is the desire for independence to be inhibited by feelings of personal loyalty and guilt.

The dependent aspects of satellization can also be minimized if the child can find derived status in multiple sources rather than in his parents alone. Under these circumstances the one source is no longer so precious. He need not tread so warily to avoid arousing disapproval. Fortified by the ego support he receives from friends, grandparents, older siblings, teachers, group leaders, and others, he can afford more often to assert his independence and risk arousing parental ire. Even if these additional sources of intrinsic status play only a subsidiary role in relation to that of parents, they may often spell the difference between complete subservience and occasional defiance.

It also seems reasonable to suppose that if children are to develop executive independence and frustration tolerance, they must have firsthand experience in coping with frustration and must be confronted unambiguously with the expectations and limitations defining their biosocial position. Overly permissive parents fail to develop frustration tolerance, executive independence, and nonhedonistic motivation in the child, both because they fail to demand independent accomplishment and because they yield excessively to children's demands for hedonistic gratification, frustration intolerance, and help whenever they encounter difficulty.

Overly permissive parents fail also to structure realistically the limiting and restrictive aspects of the child's world, thereby making difficult the setting of realistic goals and the accurate perception of self-role and the boundaries of acceptable behavior. Extremely underdominated children, therefore, tend to be aggressive, rebellious, and disobedient. They may develop the notion that they are very precious and privileged persons and that their parents and others *have* to do things for them because they have a special claim on their indulgence. Insofar as the desire to protect the child from all frustration leads to similar kinds of parental behavior, comparable developmental outcomes may be expected in the overprotected child. School phobia is, thus, relatively common in overprotected, underdisciplined, and overvalued children because in the school environment they have no special claim on the indulgence of teachers or peers as they do on parents at home.

Ego maturation in response to parental expectations of more mature behavior may ordinarily be expected to lag initially because of the phenomenon of perceptual constancy in the child. The prepotency of habitual expectations may temporarily force *altered* parental behavior, as noted earlier, into *familiar* perceptual molds despite manifest changes in stimulus content. The rate of ego maturation is also held back by ambivalent feelings in the child, who is naturally reluctant to part with the protection and security of dependency. This ambivalence is probably greater in children with strong needs for hedonistic gratification (who find long-range striving difficult) and in sedentary, shy, "thin-skinned," and introverted children to whom self-assertion comes painfully.

Last, ego maturation is a function of cultural expectations and of the availability of mature role-playing experience. These latter factors reciprocally influence each other as well as generate pressure and opportunity for personality reorganization on a more mature basis. Largely for these reasons, when ego maturation in our culture is appraised in a cross-cultural context, the reaching of ego-status goals (e.g., volitional independence, earned status) is seen to lag considerably behind the achievement of ego-maturity goals (e.g., executive independence). Parents in our culture expect much executive independence and conformity to adult standards but allow children relatively little opportunity to fend for themselves.

Overpermissiveness (Overindulgence)

The necessary conditions for developing personality maturity have been grossly violated by the present-day fetish of permissiveness in child rearing.[3] The tremendous vogue enjoyed by this doctrine can in part be explained as a reaction to the rigid and authoritarian parental practices that were fashionable in the preceding two decades. In part also, it is a by-product of the recent overemphasis placed upon frustration as an etiological factor in the behavior disorders and an invariable and unqualified evil. More specifically it has been rationalized on the basis of evidence that has applicability to young infants only, and by reference to the analogy of the more permissive and democratic approach to the learning of values advocated above and practiced in the more progressive schools.

However, it is one thing to advocate self-demand feeding schedules because of the low frustration tolerance of infants, and their recognized exemption from stringent social demands, and quite another matter to suggest the indefinite prolongation of this policy into the early and later years of childhood. Similarly, there is no incompatibility between granting children greater freedom in accepting values, on the one hand, while insisting, on the other, that their behavior be confined within certain broad limits imposed by the social expectations and prohibitions relative to their age group.

It seems unreasonable to expect that a child can ever orient his goal structure realistically in relation to obstacles and barriers without some direct and firsthand experience with frustration. In order that he acquire sufficient frustration tolerance to persist (despite inevitable setbacks in the pursuit of long-range goals), in maintaining his essential independence, and in avoiding an excessively lax and uncritical self-appraisal of his accomplishments, he must learn the meaning of failure and the means of grappling with it. Exposing the child to unnecessary or pointless frustration or to frustration beyond his developmental capacity for coping with same will no doubt only impede the growth of this tolerance. But the extreme and doctrinaire permissive viewpoint, often embodied in the underdominating parent—who conceives of her "parental role as intended to insure the fact that her child suffers not the slightest" impediment in implementing his desires lest he become "emotionally insecure"—leads to the very same result.

Purposeful and persistent avoidance of frustration creates for the child a conception of reality that is so distorted that he becomes exclusively conditioned to living in a hedonistic environment. Under these conditions, maturation, which involves adjustment to a reality fashioned in good part from the fabric of frustration, becomes an utter impossibility.

The development of frustration tolerance, therefore, requires that a child be encouraged to solve his own problems and learn through his mistakes, that his course through life not be continually smoothed by systematic elimination of all of the problems that confront him. He must learn to take responsibility for the consequences of his behavior when mistakes are made and failure ensues. Parental "whitewashing" does not develop frustration tolerance but reinforces the immature tendency to cope with failure and misbehavior by rationalizing, disclaiming responsibility, and abandoning even minimal standards of self-criticism.

Another undesirable outcome of indiscriminate permissiveness is that a child finds it difficult to perceive self and self-role realistically, to deal adequately with the child-adult relationship, and to evolve goals that are realistically related to the probability of success and the amount of motivation at his disposal. The conditions under which self-role can be realis-

tically learned require a clear appreciation of what can be included legitimately within the appropriate age-sex-subculture role and what must per-
force be excluded from it. The attitude of unvarying permissiveness fulfills
neither condition. By advocating unrestricted freedom for the child in
setting his goals, by refusing to impose limitations on behavior that is
socially unacceptable, and by denying the legitimacy of status differences
between children and adults, the overly permissive parent or teacher makes
it impossible for the child to perceive the boundaries of his role.

In some extreme cases, exposure to this variety of child rearing leads
to complete unrealism regarding the demands that an individual can legitimately make on others and on their moral obligation to help him (the
"Prince" or "Princess" complex). The child perceives his biosocial incompetence, and satellizes in the sense that he accepts a derived status
and a dependent position in relation to his parents. But the latter cater
excessively to his dependency needs, indulge his desire for executive dependence, fail to impose or enforce any demands or restrictions, and scrupulously avoid making any distinction between child and parental roles.
As a result of this extreme underdomination, he develops the notion that
he is a very precious and privileged person: his parents *have* to do things
for him and *have* to help him—not because his will is omnipotent or irresistible, but because he has a special claim on their indulgence. Eventually this orientation is extended to the world at large: "The world owes
me everything I need. People are obliged to help me; it is my natural due.
After all, they can not let *me* fend for myself or suffer pain and deprivation. In the case of other people, yes, but not *I*. In *my* case it is different. it
would be too cruel, too unfair." Such individuals approach even complete strangers with the unabashed plea, "I'm in a terrible fix, you've simply *got* to help me, or I won't be responsible any longer for what I do."

In no culture can the distinction between parental and filial role be eradi-
cated. The parent is required to be more dominant and ascendant in the
relationship than the child. His judgments must be given more weight
and his demands more authority. The welfare and safety of the child require that he sometimes defer completely and comply immediately with
parental requests. The parent has a right to expect unconditional obedience in times of danger without offering explanations for his demands.
Where differences are irreconcilable, and issues of parental responsibility or social principle are involved, the parent's view should prevail. But
the adherents of unqualified permissiveness refuse to face these issues

squarely because to do so would mean repudiating the theoretical basis of their child-rearing doctrines. On the other hand, they cannot ignore these considerations completely, because the practical pressures of meeting everyday situations and occasional crises, and of minimally satisfying cultural demands, require the adoption of more directive and authoritarian attitudes than are consistent with their underlying philosophy. What results, therefore, is an unsatisfactory compromise that only adds to the ambiguity of the learning situation.

This compromise approach is reflected in many different attitudes of the overly permissive parent. He persistently refuses to define or clarify the acceptable limits of child behavior and handles each situation as it arises according to the demands of expediency. In this way he feels that he remains true to his doctrines while still in a position to cope with special situations. But the child exposed to this treatment cannot generalize in any consistent fashion about the limits of behavioral acceptability. The parent, for example, fails to make clear that his demands upon the child have a different status than the child's demands upon him, but on occasion acts as if this were the case by using force or threats. The child who has been indoctrinated with the principle of equality of status is thereby justified in concluding that either the general principle still holds but was unfairly violated by the parent, or that he, too, can exercise the same prerogatives as the parent with respect to the employment of force and threats. The same parent may permit his child to participate in activities far beyond his developmental capacities, but will cut them short on some pretext, if embarrassing or unfortunate consequences ensue, rather than let him learn the fitting generalization that he is not yet equipped to handle certain situations.

The ambiguity surrounding the limits of unacceptable behavior is further enhanced by the parental tendency to avoid issues, which might arise from opposing the child's desires, by resorting to distraction. While this technique is occasionally defensible—when the child is ill, unduly fatigued, hungry, or excessively irritable—it effectually prevents him from learning what constitutes out-of-bounds behavior if used habitually as the path of least resistance. Much less objectionable is the widely accepted practice of saying, "You can't do this, but you *may* do that." This tactic avoids the error of ambiguity and is a feasible method of handling many difficult situations. But if used compulsively (as implied by the popular permissive dictum, "Say 'no' to a child as infrequently as possible, but if you must, always offer him a positive alternative"), it conditions him to an environment that is highly unrealistic in terms of the actual social prohibitions that will inevitably limit his behavioral freedom.

The restrictions imposed in most real-life situations have only a negative aspect. This does not mean that positive alternatives cannot be found or that the child should not be encouraged to search for same; but if they are available or can be applied, it should be made clear that in most cases they originate as a product of the frustrated individual's resourcefulness and are not inevitably given in the prohibition itself.

Two other favorite techniques of the overly permissive parent are self-insulation and empty verbalism when an occasion for discipline or restraint arises. Obviously, if a parent cannot see or hear anything objectionable he cannot be expected to interfere. If, on the other hand, the behavior is so flagrant that self-insulation is impossible, half-hearted verbal disapproval is often given. The parent then feels that merely by voicing his objections he has discharged his parental duty even if the child continues this behavior during and after the time that the reproof is being administered. Actually, however, unless he takes active measures to halt or punish the objectionable activity and to prevent its occurrence in the future, he is really condoning it.

The child under these conditions perceives that the disapproval is only verbal since the parent does not feel strongly enough about the matter to enforce his demands, an option that is obviously within his power were he disposed to use it. Hence, all the while that the latter stands declaiming against the unacceptable behavior and doing nothing about it, reinforcement is continually provided by the assurance that the misbehavior is condoned and that the rewards motivating it will not be taken away. Unenforced verbal commands become in effect stated guarantees of immunity from interference and punitive action. The upshot of this situation is that the child becomes positively conditioned to verbal disapproval, and not only ignores its purported intent but also feels encouraged by it to continue exhibiting the unacceptable behavior.

The conclusion is, thus, inescapable that the important goal of consistency in discipline cannot be achieved unless the child understands unambiguously what his environment demands and expects of him. This absence of ambiguity can be realized only if reinforcement is provided at both ends of the range of behavioral acceptability. It may be true that reward and approval are more efficacious in motivating the learning of acceptable behavior than are punishment, restraint, and disapproval in discouraging undesirable behavioral patterns. Nevertheless, neither is sufficient by itself.

From a developmental standpoint, it is naive and unrealistic to assume that in the early and middle years of childhood the learning of desirable rewarded behavior *automatically* endows its logical opposite with negative valence. Each valence must be separately established in order to encourage activity at one pole and discourage activity at the opposite pole; for until such time as the negative valence is established by active measures of reproof, the unacceptable behavior has a natural positive valence in the eyes of the child and competes in attractiveness with the benefits adhering to approved behavior. He will, therefore, be constantly tempted to sample the advantages of the former; and if not discouraged by disapproval, he can legitimately interpret tolerance as license to continue.

In due time, of course, interaction, synthesis, and mutual reinforcement ensue when only one of the reciprocal pairs described above is either rewarded or punished as the case may be. In the case of older children and adults, endorsement of the "good" alternative carries with it an implied condemnation of the "bad." But this implication is never as thoroughgoing as the advocates of the self-consistency theory of personality would have us believe. Tennyson's dictum that a man must hate evil before he can love the good is true in the sense of absolute logic, but implies a level of logical consistency that is rare in the typical person's organization of values and attitudes. The temptation to test the limits of tolerance for unacceptable behavior, to see how much one can "get away with" before incurring retribution, to take advantage of laxness, certainly declines with maturity, but nevertheless is present in all of us irrespective of whether a generally wholesome conscience is operating. Hence, consistent and unambiguous discipline requires explicit definition of the limits of unacceptable behavior, reinforced by tangible evidences of disapproval, especially in the early years of life when ability to generalize values is limited.

The same need for explicit restraint holds true for similar reasons when we consider the growth of internalization of social prohibitions in relation to the problem of consistent discipline. It is true that the only effective and enduring type of discipline we can hope to establish is a self-discipline based upon internalization of external restraints. The control that relies primarily upon constant supervision, force, fear, or threat contributes little to ego maturity.

This does not mean, however, that in order to promote self-discipline external prohibitions must be completely removed. The process of internalization occurs only gradually and is never complete. Other controls, therefore, must be visible enough in the beginning, can be relaxed somewhat as maturity increases, but must always be held in readiness in the background to reorient goals when the child strays from the path of reality. In this sense, external controls serve not as the chief supports of realistically oriented and socially acceptable behavior but as limiting factors that restrain impulsive flights toward caprice and fancy. Like policemen on the corner, they are hardly responsible for the usual decorum of the law-abiding citizen but are convenient reminders that ill-considered mischief and out-of-bounds behavior will not be passively tolerated but may, on the contrary, lead to painful consequences.

Apart from the deleterious effects on maturation that will be described more fully in later sections, there is little reason to believe (contrary to the views expressed by indulgent parents) that excessive permissiveness makes for a happy childhood or adolescence. Quite the contrary, it leads to the insecurity that follows from adhering to any unrealistic, ambiguous, or inconsistent frame of reference.

Unrealistic goals usually prove to be unsuccessful. Undue demands on persons other than parents ordinarily meet with a cool reception. Expectations of receiving special consideration outside the family circle are seldom realized. Ordinary frustrations cannot be borne with equanimity but lead to the precipitate abandonment of goals, petulance, and temper tantrums; and at this point another source of insecurity arises from the child's dependence upon his own inadequate control of aggressive impulses. In the absence of suitable external restraints, he has good reason to fear the consequences that his uninhibited rage may bring upon him. He might even blame his parents: "It's your fault for making me so mad"; or "Why didn't you stop me from doing that?"

But he may also blame himself for these excesses of aggression and suffer more than his share of guilt feelings. Since punishment is not forthcoming from parents, there is not infrequently the necessity for self-punishment. Much of the wild, reckless, and unconventional behavior of the overindulged child may be attributed to his demands for punishment; and his behavior becomes so extreme only because his overindulgent parents are slow in taking him to task. For this reason the overindulged child may frequently be so extremely rebellious and aggressive that his behavior necessitates punishment by a somewhat hesitant parent.

The entire complex of absent self-control, selfish unreasonableness, importunate demands for immediate gratification, unrestrained aggressiveness, rebellious self-assertion, refractoriness to routine, irresponsibility, and lack of consideration for the needs of others forms such an unattractive, unlovable portrait that social acceptance by teachers, neighbors, and agemates is difficult indeed. Thus, even this last desperate defense upon which the advocates of extreme permissiveness are thrown back—that the child is happier in such a setting—is open to serious question.

Perhaps now after four decades of overenthusiastic and uncritical endorsement of rampant permissiveness as a panacea—as a virtue per se, as the epitome of the "psychological" orientation to interpersonal relations—this unorthodox but doctrinaire approach to discipline has suffered a serious decline. Parents, teachers, and clinical workers are now more able to appraise its values and consequences more objectively. A more rational, consistent, and common-sense theory of discipline has emerged that recognizes the necessity and the legitimacy of placing limits on child and adolescent behavior.

Overprotection and Overdomination

For children to develop the skill and confidence necessary for competent exercise of volitional independence, they require opportunity for practicing self-direction, making plans and decisions, actually participating in mature role-playing experience, and learning from their own mistakes. Overdominated children, although mature in such respects as "conscientious effort" and "orderly production," tend to be shy, submissive, lacking in self-confidence, and deficient in the volitional aspects of independence. The latter outcome also holds true for overprotected children whose parents withhold the opportunity for independent decision making lest it lead to injury or frustration.

Similarly, the more impersonal the basis on which obedience and conformity are required, the less likely is the desire for independence to be inhibited by feelings of personal loyalty and guilt. Navajo parents do not demand obedience as a personal right or regard disobedience as "bad," but point out "the advantages of obedience [and] the value of taking advice and instruction from more experienced persons." Threats are not warnings of personal reprisal for insubordination but objective predictions of disaster for children who fail to heed prudent admonition. The authority for discipline is impersonalized and referred either to supernatural forces or to agencies "outside of the immediate family circle." If a plea for good conduct is made by appealing to shame avoidance, it is from the child rather than from the parent that the plea for deflection of shame is made. In all of these ways, the overly dependent and personal aspects of satellization are minimized.

Even when parents are not overprotective or overdominating, inherent factors in the parent-child relationship make the latter ambivalent toward the child's emancipation. They tend to fear the loss of love that removal of his dependency creates.

Parents have a vested interest to protect in dependency situations—the satisfactions, the ego supports, and the feelings of power and importance that go with having another individual dependent upon them for guidance and direction. Emancipation requires much sacrifice by parents. They must relinquish authority and learn the patience and restraint required to develop the capacity for self-direction in the child. This is naturally a much more difficult task for parents who are exploiting the dependent aspects of the child's attachment for them as a substitute source of status and affection in instances of vocational or marital maladjustment. Such feelings of ambivalence naturally give rise to parental inconsistencies in behavior and expectations that confuse the child and compound the retarding influence the ambivalence exerts on maturation.

Feelings of rivalry, often only dimly perceived, also complicate the parents' attitudes toward the child's maturation. They cannot help comparing their waning powers and motivations with the child's growing competencies and naively sanguine aspirations. If these are a source of pride, they also represent a threat, which, with each passing day, brings the shadow of eventual displacement closer. "Unconsciously," therefore, they may be motivated to slow the progress of maturation. The resentment that these attitudes provoke in the child, however, may bring about the opposite effect (desatellization) by deepening the estrangement that already so frequently exists.

Not to be ignored in this picture is the possibility of serious lag between alteration of attitudes and appropriate modification of related behavior. It is a commonplace observation that underlying attitudes may remain unaltered despite formal changes in outward behavior. Less frequently recognized is the equally important tendency for old behavior patterns to persist out of sheer inertia despite modification of the attitudinal substrate. It takes time to learn the appropriate gestures, mannerisms, and inflections of a new role even if one has mastered the required shift in feeling tones. And even then the phenomenon of perceptual constancy in the child may force altered parental behavior into the same perceptual molds because of the prepotency of habitual expectations.

Hence, the child frequently fails to respond appropriately to changes in parental expectations of greater maturity, despite manifest changes in stimulus content, because he cannot reorganize into a new *Gestalt* what to him can only have a fixed and constant perceptual meaning. He, thus, withdraws from parents for no other reason than the fact that they are the ones to whom he has always *been* a helpless child.

Personality maturation also suffers from the ambivalence of the child. He is naturally reluctant to part with the protection and security of dependency and of a familiar biosocial role for the anxiety and insecurity inevitably associated with any transition in development. And, unfortunately, sufficient ambiguity prevails regarding the biosocial role considered appropriate for adolescents to provide some support also for ambivalent behavior. Additionally, the period of transition is sufficiently prolonged to offer considerable support for the yearning to return to the "good old days" of childhood. This regressive alternative has a more powerful attraction both for children who have strong needs for hedonistic gratification and find long-range striving difficult, and for sedentary, shy, "thin-skinned," and introverted individuals for whom self-assertion is difficult.

Desatellization, therefore, is, even under the best of circumstances, a difficult and inevitably conflictful stage of ego development. The child must contend with ambivalence, rivalry, and the inertia of habitual attitudes and behavior patterns in his parents at the same time he confronts his own ambivalence and perceptual constancy. If he becomes too independent, he provokes parental resistance and internal feelings of guilt. On the other hand, if he remains too dependent and submissive, he loses face in his own eyes and in the eyes of his peers, feels inadequate for failure to gain extrinsic status, and develops feelings of hostility and resentment toward parents for thwarting his growth.

Adult-Youth Alienation

The alienation of youth from the standards, status-giving activities, and training institutions of adult society, plus their compensatory immersion in a peer culture of their own making is a characteristic feature of adolescence in our culture. How is this alienation brought about and what are its effects? But first, in order to appreciate how adult-youth alienation occurs, it is necessary to understand the universal changes in personality structure that take place at adolescence. It is also necessary to appreciate why these changes do *not* typically result in such alienation in most primitive or traditional cultures but *do* result in alienation in modern Western cultures such as our own.

Everywhere, in all cultures, the metamorphosis of children into physically and sexually mature individuals, and the concomitant growth of their intellectual and social capabilities generate, or set in motion, powerful pressures for certain changes that will equip them for more equal status and responsible membership in the adult community. These pressures consist of the adolescent's own recognition of the significance of his gains in physical, sexual, social, and intellectual maturity; of diminished parental and social acceptance of the appropriateness of a dependent status for more competent, adult-appearing individuals; and of the social urgency of transforming these persons into a new generation of adults capable of perpetuating the culture.

Universally, therefore, these pressures result in three major kinds of changes in the personality structure of adolescents so that they can qualify for their enhanced new role in the culture. First, they develop a need to strive more for an *earned* status based on their own efforts and competence and to strive less for an *attributed* (derived) status based on their dependent identification with and intrinsic acceptance by parents. Earned status, thus, becomes a more important source of their self-esteem and displaces attributed status as the principal determinant of their feelings of adequacy as persons.

Second, they develop a need for volitional emancipation from their parents, that is, for exercising independence in formulating their own goals, for making their own decisions, and for managing their own affairs.

Third, they are gradually expected to acquire, through appropriate training procedures, those mature personality traits and those basic skills and values that are necessary for implementing their needs for greater earned status and volitional independence. Hence, they are under greater pressure to persevere in goal striving, despite serious setbacks, to postpone immediate hedonistic gratification in favor of achieving long-range objectives, and to display greater initiative, responsibility, executive independence, and respect for the demands of reality.

Finally, they are expected to learn vocational skills, their appropriate sex roles, the basic norms and values of the culture, and the proper way of comporting themselves socially as adults.

In Primitive Cultures

Now, in primitive and traditional cultures, these new personality needs of adolescents can be satisfied, and these new traits, norms, and skills can be acquired, *not* without some difficulty and conflict, but without serious alienation from adult society. Adolescents can acquire earned status as junior adults by participating in status-giving activities within the *mainstream* of the adult culture, and can also achieve a significant degree of volitional independence and emancipation from parents while playing more mature and responsible social, economic, and sex roles in family and community life. Thus, because they both acquire earned status and exercise volitional independence within the *adult* culture, and also simultaneously receive their training in the course of doing both these things in the same adult context, they are not alienated from adult status-giving activities, are not resentful of adult training institutions, and do not reject adult standards and authority. And since they also continue to identify emotionally with parents and other adults, they continue to receive some measure of attributed status from such identification and from adult acceptance of their membership in the wider culture. This, in turn, establishes a basis for implicit loyalty to the culture and for implicit acceptance of its values.

In Our Culture

Adolescents in our culture, naturally, have the same needs for greater earned status and volitional independence. But the greater complexity of our technological society necessitates an extended period of education and economic dependence on parents, prolonged vocational training, and the postponement of marriage until well beyond the age of sexual maturity. Under these circumstances, the adolescent cannot experience any *real* volitional independence in the *adult* sense of the term, and can obviously acquire only a token earned status outside the mainstream of the adult culture. He not only resents his exclusion from adult spheres of independence and status-giving activities, but also tends to resent such adult-controlled training institutions as the home, the school, and various youth organizations because they conduct their training functions entirely apart from any opportunity for him to exercise volitional independence, or to acquire earned status within the context of the adult culture. Hence, he is alienated from adult status-giving activities, from adult training institutions, and, accordingly, from adult standards as well.

Two Consequences of Alienation

This alienation from adult society, coupled with the accompanying resentment and prolonged frustration of his needs for adult volitional independence and adult earned status, have two serious consequences, namely, the generation of aggressive anti-adult attitudes and the compensatory formation of distinctive peer groups with distinctive standards, status-giving activities, and training functions of their own. Let us consider each of these consequences in turn. The aggressive anti-adult orientation not only promotes further retaliatory rejection of adult standards, but also makes it more difficult for adolescents to identify with adults, to obtain any attributed status from such identification, and currently to accept adult values implicitly. The formation of peer groups, on the other hand, increases the existing adult-youth alienation, reinforces the aggressive anti-adult orientation, and facilitates its overt, antisocial expression. Precisely how it does these things deserves more detailed scrutiny.

Role of the Peer Group in Adult-Youth Alienation

Because all adolescents are in the same boat, so to speak; because they share the same deprivation of their needs for adult status and independence, the same alienation from adult society, the same resentments, and the same anti-adult attitudes; because they feel they are not wanted, do not belong, and are excluded from the larger scheme of things, they reach out toward each other for mutual support and for providing in *concert* the things that they want but cannot get *individually*.

Thus, since the modern urban community is unable to provide teenagers with the kind of earned status, volitional independence, and training in social skills that they desire, the adolescent peer group is constituted to gratify, in part, these crucial needs. It is the only cultural institution in which their position is not marginal, in which they are offered earned status, volitional independence, and social identity among a group of equals, and in which their *own* activities and concerns reign supreme. The peer group is also the major *training* institution for adolescents in our society. It is in the peer group that by *doing* they learn about the social processes of our culture. They clarify their sex roles by acting and being responded to; they learn competition, cooperation, social skills, values, and purposes by sharing the common life. The peer group provides regularized media and occasions for adolescents to gratify their newly acquired desires for increased social contact with the opposite sex as well as a set of norms governing adolescent sex behavior.

By virtue of performing these essential functions, the peer group also displaces parents as the major source of attributed (derived) status during adolescence. By identifying with and acquiring acceptance in the group, by subordinating himself to group interests, and by making himself dependent on group approval, the adolescent acquires a measure of intrinsic self-esteem that is independent of his achievement or relative status in the group. This "we-feeling" furnishes security and belongingness, and is a powerful ego support and basis of loyalty to group norms.

How does all this increase adult-youth alienation? In the first place, the adolescent's very membership in a distinctive peer group, with its own status-giving activities, standards, and training functions, puts him in a *separate* subculture apart from adult society. Second, since the peer group is composed of *his* kind of people, and since he is largely dependent on it for his volitional independence, for his earned and attributed status, for his sense of belongingness, and for his opportunities to acquire social skills and practice his social sex role, he accordingly tends to assimilate its standards. As he becomes progressively more responsive to its approval and disapproval, he becomes increasingly more indifferent to adult norms and values, to adult suggestion, and to adult approval and disapproval. Lastly, the peer group's exaggerated needs for rigid conformity to its norms—as well as its power to exact conformity from its members in return for its unique ability to satisfy their needs—further accentuate the adolescent's alienation from adult society.

Factors Reducing Adult-Youth Alienation

But adult-youth alienation is also not an all-or-none matter. That is, operating simultaneously with the various factors causing adult-youth alienation in varying degrees, there are also two general factors within each adolescent that maintain or increase his or her identification with adult society. One of these factors stems from ultimate aspirations for the future; the other is a legacy from childhood. Both serve to counteract the severity of anti-adult attitudes.

Thus, we must not lose sight of the fact that at the same time adolescents, particularly those from middle-class backgrounds, are alienated from adult standards and preoccupied with achieving *vicarious* forms of adult status and independence in the peer group, they are *simultaneously* engaged in, and intensely concerned with, educational and other pursuits that serve as stepping stones to *genuine* adult status and independence and to full membership in adult society.

They know that their *ultimate* goal is not high status in the peer group but rather attainment of economic security. They realize that this attainment requires long-term striving, self-denial, postponement of immediate hedonistic gratifications, the approval of persons in authority, restraint of aggressive impulses, and avoidance of an unsavory or delinquent reputation. Furthermore, the assimilation of new peer-group values does not by any means imply complete repudiation of previously assimilated adult values.

Many middle-class adolescents in post-World War II society appear to have rejected the materialistic rewards of middle-class status because their elders have seemingly betrayed the underlying values (such as competence, hard work, self-fulfillment, moral uprightness, responsibility) leading to these rewards, in favor of outright expediency. In the process many adolescents coming from conservative families in the 1960s and 1970s had also rejected their underlying social-class values and had become hippies, whereas youngsters of liberal parents often found expression in the student activist movements in the same time frame. Although students of the 1970s and beyond were still concerned about these issues, their main focus of concern, however, was related to the uncertainty and outcome of their schooling and the possibility of obtaining a job.

Thus, it greatly overstates the case to claim that adolescents are ever entirely oblivious of adult approval, that they completely reject adult values, standards, and aspirations, and that they manifest no feelings of moral obligation to abide by earlier assimilated norms of conduct. This much is clearly evident when we pause to consider that one of the principal functions of the peer group, in addition to providing its own distinctive set of standards, is to transmit from one generation to the next the appropriate social-class values, aspirations, motivational patterns, and character traits that adolescents are often unwilling to accept from parents and teachers, but *are* willing to accept from their age-mates. It is easy, therefore, to exaggerate the existing degree of adult-youth alienation. As a matter of fact, both parties to the alienation tend to perceive it as greater than it actually is. Indeed, where conditions are propitious, the norms of the student peer group include the same intellectual concerns and excitement that prevail among the college faculty.

It must be admitted, however, that the progressive moral deterioration characterizing our culture since World War II has tended to undermine the counterbalancing effect of these two factors (aspirations for genuine adult status and previously assimilated adult values) on adult-youth alienation. First, since adolescents perceive adults as being able to "get ahead" without fully exemplifying the traditional middle-class virtues, they naturally are led to believe that (1) they too can achieve the adult status and independence they crave without thoroughly acquiring these same virtues, and (2) adults are not really concerned whether or not adolescents acquire these virtues. Thus, they are not as highly motivated as pre-World War II adolescents were, either to develop such traits as self-restraint, willingness to work hard, a sense of responsibility, impulse control, self-denial, personal integrity, and respect for the rights and property of others, or to seek adult approval for so doing. Further, the middle-class peer group, which has the responsibility for transmitting middle-class standards to its members, can transmit only those adult standards that *actually* exist.

Second, the realization that adults do not actually live up to the standards that adolescents had implicitly accepted in childhood as axiomatically right and proper tends to undermine implicit belief in these standards and feelings of obligation to abide by them. When children become sufficiently mature to interpret adult behavior for what it actually is, they are impressed more by example than by precept.

Finally, awareness of the grievous lack of moral courage in the adult world and of the premium that adults place on conformity and expediency furnishes adolescents with a very poor model for holding fast to their moral convictions in the face of group pressure.

Conformity and Individuality in Adolescence

As a reaction to overconforming tendencies in our society since World War II, it has become fashionable to decry conformity as an unqualified evil in and of itself. The issue, however, is not nearly that simple. In the first place, a certain desirable degree of conformity is necessary both for the viability of small groups and for the development and perpetuation of culture. Second, it is evident that nonconformists who deviate from the norms of their culture typically conform even more rigidly than the average person does to the norms of his particular reference group. The reasons for this will become clear shortly. Third, conformity to certain group pressures can also reinforce and support individuals in preserving their moral scruples in opposition to other negative group pressures operating on them.

Conformity Aspects of the Peer Culture

From the preadolescent to the adolescent period of development, as the child's dependence on, and stake in, the effectiveness of the peer group increases, the latter's power to exact conformity is concomitantly enhanced.

This conformity assumes exaggerated patterns and proportions, particularly relative to conspicuous aspects of behavior, such as musical tastes, fashions in dress, and fads, to such an extent that for the adolescent there can be no stronger argument for having or doing a thing than that "all the others are doing it." Opinions, prejudices, beliefs, likes, and dislikes are also determined by the group; and boys or girls who differ are made to feel the force of group ostracism unless they have sufficient strength to gather their peers around them. The adolescent turns increasingly toward age-mate groups and sets. Even though his parents are loved and valued, the result is reduced emphasis on parental capability and overestimation of the worth of age-mate capacities.

The tendency to conform to group opinion is greater the more attractive group membership is perceived to be. In general, particularly during the adolescent period, girls are more conforming than boys. And, as one might anticipate from the data on authoritarianism, conforming tendencies are greater among lower-class and religious adolescents.

In a review of several related studies conducted over a period of ten years, it was concluded that the most peer-oriented and gang-involved children tend to come from either high permissive or high punitive homes, and that adult-conforming children tend to come from homes with optimum combinations of adequate but not smothering support, firm but not rigid control, and moderate but not excessive punishment. There were also indications that these practices, from moderate ranges of parental behavior, are related to autonomy in children.

Conformity to group standards depends, for the most part, on the internalization of shared expectations and of a set of norms that the group members themselves help to formulate. Overt pressures and sheer physical force are relatively minor factors. The group norms that seem most coercive and most significant in the members' hierarchy of values are the ones that regulate group solidarity among members and that determine norms of conduct with respect to the motivational factors that attract them to the group. The groups that are most closely knit are precisely those whose members have the fewest and weakest ties with other groups and institutions, and hence whose membership in the group is highly important to them.

Group solidarity is, therefore, highest in low-rank neighborhoods. In all groups, however, the range of acceptable behavior exhibits least latitude for the leader and high-status members. With regard to behaviors affecting the maintenance of group activities and of loyalty to the group, the leader is expected to be the emulatory model.

It is necessary, for two important reasons, that the peer group demand considerable conformity from its members. First, no institution, especially if it has status-giving functions, can exist for any length of time without due regard by its members for uniform, regular, and predictable adherence to a set of avowed values and traditions. Hence, in its efforts to establish a new and distinctive subculture and to evolve a unique set of criteria for the determination of status and prestige, the peer group must do everything in its power to set itself off as recognizably distinct and separate from the adult society that refuses it membership. If this distinctiveness is to be actually attained, widespread nonconformity obviously cannot be tolerated.

Second, conformity is also essential to maintain the group solidarity that is necessary to offer effective and organized resistance to the encroachment of adult authority. If an appeal to precedent or to a prevailing standard of adolescent behavior is to be the basis for exacting privileges and concessions from adults, a solid and united front with a minimum of deviancy must be presented to the world.

Because of the adolescent's marginality of status, the peer group is in an excellent position to demand conformity from him or her as the price of its acceptance. Much more so than children or adults, adolescents are desperately dependent on the peer group for whatever status and security they are able to achieve during these hectic years of transition. The group implicitly and explicitly makes clear that it expects conformity to its standards, interests, activities, and value systems in return for the moral support, the feeling of belongingness, the attributed status, and the opportunities for earned status that it extends. Adolescents, in turn, like any people with marginal status, are excessively sensitive to the threat of forfeiting what little status they enjoy as a result of incurring the disapproval of those on whom they are dependent. Thus, to allay the anxiety from the threat of disapproval, they tend to conform more than is objectively necessary to retain group acceptance or to avoid censure and reprisal.

After adolescents win an assured place in the group, still other factors reinforce conforming tendencies. They learn that group approval brings a welcome reprieve from anxiety and uncertainty. If the group approves, these individuals can feel absolutely certain of the correctness of their position. Feelings of loyalty, belongingness, and indebtedness also influence conformity—to be rendered automatically as a voluntarily assumed obligation. Finally, if these implicit group pressures and internalized restraints and dispositions are insufficient to keep an individual in line, explicit sanctions are imposed. Depending on the seriousness of the offense and the functions and nature of the group, the punishment may vary from ridicule, censure, and rebuff to physical chastisement and complete ostracism.

It is clear, therefore, that the marginality of adolescent status makes teenagers prone to overvalue the importance of conformity and to exaggerate the degree of conformity required for acceptance by the peer group. Sociometric studies show that adolescents consistently *overestimate* the status of popular individuals and correspondingly *underestimate* the extent to which deviant or low-prestige persons are accepted by the group. These studies also point to the conclusion that apparent disregard of the group's approval tends to enhance an individual's sociometric status by making him or her appear above the need for currying favor with others.

Hence, many perfectly safe opportunities for the expression of individuality and the defiance of conformity are obviously lost.

In the light of the structural properties of their peer group and of prevailing overconforming trends in the culture at large, it is small wonder that American adolescents tend to overvalue conformity and expediency and to avoid independent thinking and ideological commitment. In the adolescent peer culture of Prairie City, it was found that accepting generally approved stereotypes was one outstanding characteristic of most beliefs. Individual positions deviating from generally accepted beliefs were typically avoided. This was demonstrated by reluctance in expressing minority views contrary to generally held beliefs, and by approving behavior that one considered wrong if most of one's associates were implicated in it. Individual opinions tended to be subordinated to both adult and peer-group views even when the latter were held to be ethically wrong.

Other expressions of these same conforming tendencies include the approved attitude of "coolness" toward, and emotional detachment from, moral and controversial issues, and the low status accorded intellectuality and intellectual status in most peer groups. During the 1960s and early 1970s, however, many adolescents deviated from the norms of the culture at large and from many age-mates by engaging in antiwar and civil rights movements.

Qualifications and Positive Aspects

Lest we tend to take too dim a view of the seemingly negative features of adolescent conformity, it is important that we now consider some of the more positive aspects of this phenomenon. The transfer of allegiances from parental to peer-group standards constitutes more than an exchange of one type of slavish conformity for another. By providing a new source of values and standards, as well as experience in behaving as a sovereign person, the peer group plays an important role in devaluing parents and promoting desatellization.

In switching their basic loyalties to the peer group, adolescents take great strides toward emancipation. They find a new source of basic security to supplant the emotional anchorage to parents that had hitherto kept them confined within the dependent walls of childhood. By vesting in their peers the authority to set standards, they affirm their *own* right to self-determination since they are patently no different from them. They no longer need to implicitly subscribe to the belief that only parents and adults can determine what is right. The peer group also serves as a bulwark of strength in combating authority. By pooling their resistance in groups and throwing up barriers of one kind or another against adult interference, adolescents manage to exclude adults and protect themselves from the coercions that adults are prone to use.

The peer group's desatellizing influence also carries over into the sphere of ideas and moral values. Its norms provide the adolescent with a new and stable frame of reference for moral judgment and conduct. It furnishes relief from uncertainty, indecision, guilt, and anxiety about proper ways of thinking, feeling, and behaving. Because the peer group is never dignified by the same halo of sanctity surrounding parents, adolescents can experiment more freely with functional concepts of moral principle and with a more impersonal and logical approach to value judgments. To be sure, full exploitation of this new active, independent, and critical approach to moral values is obviously limited by their marginal status and their need to conform to peer-group norms. The difference, however, is that now they conform to external standards because they consciously recognize the *expediency* of so doing rather than because they *implicitly* accept their validity.

Finally, the dreary picture of adolescent conformity must be qualified by certain limiting factors. In the first place, its existence tends to be restricted to the particular developmental requirements of the adolescent period that induce it. One of the surest signs of approaching adulthood is a resurgence in the legitimacy of deviancy. Second, along with their conforming tendencies adolescents display a "concomitant urge to be unique, to achieve individuality and 'separateness.' After the young adolescent has submerged himself in the group to the point where he cannot be criticized for nonconformity, he ... then proceeds to gain recognition for himself as an individual." Adolescents must be careful, however, to keep their urge for uniqueness and creativity within the narrow framework of acceptability recognized by the group.

As we know from the history of innumerable youth movements, there is among many adolescents a vigorous strain of exuberant idealism and impatient dissatisfaction with many outmoded traditions and features of contemporary life. For example, this was reflected in dramatic ways by student activism in the 1960s. The war in Indo-China, with its accompanying draft, along with the dehumanizing pressures of a highly technological society, turned students into an independent political force. In addition, civil rights organizations in the early 1960s crystallized community action in the latter part of the decade and engaged the participation of youth. Critical of the values of a technological society, students created new life-styles (for example, preindustrial life became fashionable); they affirmed the rights of each individual above utilitarian goals and technological efficiency; and they substituted self-fulfillment in place of a professional career. This aspect of adolescent personality, when channeled intelligently, constitutes a most strategic means for effecting social change.

Conformity and Individuality: A Prescription for Adolescents

Where do all of these developmental and cultural considerations regarding conformity and individuality leave us in proposing a feasible and morally defensible prescription for adolescents?

The crucial role of the peer group as a socializing agency and as a source of earned and attributed status counsels a certain minimal degree of deference to its standards during the self-limited period when such an exaggerated premium is placed on the value of conformity. During adolescence deviants are not in an enviable position. In varying degrees they all face social ridicule, abuse, and isolation. The fortunate ones achieve some measure of status and security by forming warm attachments to age-mates of their own kind. Sometimes a sympathetic adult friend or teacher will offer them affection, direction, and encouragement. Often, however, they are left to flounder uncertainly, to drift further and further away from group living, to develop feelings of anxiety and inferiority, and to withdraw deeper and deeper into themselves or into a compensatory world of unreality.

As far as the wider community is concerned, the adolescent should be encouraged to adjust satisfactorily to the kind of world that currently exists, not the kind adults wish existed but as yet have been unable to create. Even while endeavoring to change them it is necessary to recognize established laws and customs, irrational or otherwise. This does not imply that the status quo must be implicitly accepted for what it is, but rather that a mature attitude toward social change be adopted, an attitude that does not encourage the adolescent to batter his head against the wall of custom simply because these customs are inconsistent.

However, this minimal and desirable degree of conformity to peer-group standards and social custom is still a far cry from advocating a policy of "hunting with the hounds." Those who counsel adolescents would be remiss in their responsibility if they failed to appreciate the importance of nonconformity for the optimal differentiation of personality structure, for self-realization, and for the development of moral courage and the ability to stand alone without group support.

Counselors must also be sensitive to individual differences in the need to conform. Highly self-assertive teenagers, for example, can only restrain their individuality up to a point; and introverts inevitably draw a line beyond which they refuse to participate in out-of-bounds behavior. Adolescents who have a highly developed set of moral or religious convictions may refuse to condone the practices of their group. Other individuals may have all-absorbing interests that are regarded with scorn by their agemates. Finally, as has already been pointed out, the mental hygiene dangers of nonconformity and social unpopularity have been vastly exaggerated. Even the peer group tolerates much more deviancy than the adolescent's anxiety and marginality of status lead him or her to believe.

Cultural Factors Affecting Adolescent Ego Maturation

There is no doubt but that the cultural availability of extrinsic status is the crucial variable affecting the rate, the duration, and the difficulty of adolescent maturation. Almost all of the distinctive characteristics of adolescent development in Western civilization are derivatives of the fact that pubescent children's greater executive competence can receive no social recognition in terms of adult status-giving activity. On the other hand, in primitive rural cultures such as the Navajo, there is no period of several years when an individual is neither a child nor an adult as the adolescent in white American society today. The Navajo's physical maturity and social maturity are more nearly coincidental. Our adolescents must customarily look forward to an eight-year period of subadulthood that provides a marginal, interim status in peripheral activities, and a good deal of uncertainty regarding the eventual attainment of adult status.

Such a situation is more or less inevitable in any complex culture requiring extended education and apprenticeship. The peer group is obliged, then, to provide compensatory sources of status and to assume responsibility as the major training institution of adolescence. But this dichotomy need not be as absolute as it is at present. With some intelligent social engineering, adolescents even as apprentices can be provided with a good deal of status-giving experience and responsibility in projects involving the community as a whole.

The reasons for the prolonged adolescence in our culture and its grosser behavioral consequences were already discussed at some length. Here we shall be concerned only with what at first glance seems to be a purely self-evident phenomenon, namely, the precise nature of the mechanisms whereby socioeconomic conditions necessitating a prolongation of the transitional period of subadulthood becomes translated into an actual process of retardation in the sphere of psychological development. The relationship between social status, on the one hand, and ego valuation on the other is a fundamental problem of ego psychology.

The most important intervening factors in this process of transmutation—"the level of social expectations regarding rate of maturation and the availability of mature role-playing experience"—are intimately related. The former, in fact, is almost completely a function of the latter, which depends upon socioeconomic factors influencing the need for adolescent manpower. In accordance with the fluctuations in this need, society keeps shifting its view of the urgency with which adolescent maturation should take place. This relationship is never a one-to-one affair since a minimal level of status change is anticipated on the basis of pubescence alone, and a certain amount of time lag is inevitable between the onset of changed economic conditions and the evolution of new social attitudes. Nevertheless the correspondence is quite close; and in the more usual type of economic situation in our culture, conditions are such that little sense of urgency is felt regarding the rapidity of maturation. Thus, although the adolescent may desire to gain status more rapidly than he is allowed to, he feels no pressure to do so—at least from the adult segment of society.

Having no other frame of reference as a guide than prevailing social expectations, his level of aspiration with respect to the proper rate of maturation generally corresponds to the relative urgency with which society regards the problem. Most adolescents would believe any other course to be virtually impossible, since, like children, they tend to believe that prevailing social arrangements are absolutely given and hence immutable.

Why do adolescents base their levels of aspiration regarding maturational progress on cultural expectations? First, as in any unstructured field, these expectations undoubtedly exert considerable influence in the form of prestige suggestion. Second, they have motivational properties emanating from their capacity to generate *transitional anxiety*. The mere existence of these expectations constitutes a threat. Adolescents are expected to mature at a certain rate or else face the possible loss of status advantages otherwise accruing from successful maturation. The feelings of anxiety and insecurity instigated by this threat can only be reduced by suitable evidences of maturation, thereby giving rise to appropriately pitched motivations (levels of aspiration).

When culturally induced, low levels of aspiration for maturational progress actually result in developmental retardation. They do so by making the adolescent disinclined to seek out role-playing experiences propitious for personality development. And the most proximate factor involved in this chain of events, the one directly responsible for the lagging rate of maturation, is deprivation of the necessary experience required for personality growth.

When the cultural unavailability of adult status becomes very extreme, it retards personality maturation even more directly. By ruling out access to needed experience to individuals who would otherwise obtain it through high endogenous motivation (despite social discouragement), it exerts a leveling influence negating motivational variability of other origins.

In addition to status deprivation, other social factors largely idiosyncratic to our culture, such as various types of cultural discontinuities and discrepancies in attaining adult status, also tend to retard adolescent personality maturation.

Later Impact of Nonsatellization on Ego Maturation in Adolescence

As already indicated, the nonsatellizer never really surrenders his aspirations for volitional independence and exalted earned status during childhood. Hence in a sense the ego-status goals of maturation are already accomplished in advance; and since the main function of most ego-maturity goals is the enhancement of self-esteem through the acquisition of earned status (by implementing elevated ego aspirations), these ego-maturity traits tend to be acquired with little difficulty. The chief exception here relates to the development of realistic goals, which is largely precluded by the nonsatellizer's insistent need to maintain high ego aspirations irrespective of the reality situation or his level of ability.

It would also be reasonable to question under certain conditions the stability of values that were never implicitly internalized on the basis of personal loyalty but solely for the expediential purpose of relevance for achievement and ego enhancement. The obligation to abide by all internalized moral values, for example, is attenuated by the fact that many such values are often in conflict with the ends of ego enhancement. As will be pointed out in chapter 5, these children are also particularly vulnerable to Neurotic Anxiety by virtue of their lacking an inner core of intrinsic self-esteem to protect their egos from the vicissitudes of life and because of their tendency to compensate for this lack of intrinsic self-esteem by internalizing only high levels of aspiration.

As represented by the tasks of acquiring greater volitional independence, of striving primarily for extrinsic status, of raising the level of ego aspiration, and of adopting the rational-objective and exploratory learning orientations, desatellization is ordinarily the main business of adolescent maturation. Since in nonsatellizers these tasks are, so to speak, accomplished in advance, it follows that maturation involves a less comprehensive change and is more likely to be successful. The nonsatellizer, with his high ego aspirations and his exaggerated needs for earned status, has always regarded dependence disdainfully, as symbolic of retreat and defeat in his quest for these goals. Volitional independence had also never been really surrendered, and hence does not have to be regained.

Other aspects of maturation take place for the express purpose of implementing the acquisition of earned status—provided there are no overwhelming contraindications emanating from the nonsatellizing situation itself. For example, goal frustration tolerance, self-critical ability, executive independence, and long-range goals are acquired easily enough. But the imperious need for superior accomplishment and preeminent extrinsic status effectively prevents the setting of realistic goals in many cases. Although level of ego aspiration is uniformly high in nonsatellizers and is extremely resistant to lowering in the face of failure and frustration, there is no reason for believing that the distribution of ability in this group is uniformly high. Aspirational level will, therefore, be persistently and unrealistically high except in the small minority of individuals whose abilities happen to be commensurate with their ambitions.

It would be reasonable to expect that the attenuation of immature personality traits mainly on the basis of expediency (ego enhancement) is a much less stable outcome than attenuation on the basis of satellization. In satellization there is implicit and unquestioning acceptance of the desirability of this change. In the case of nonsatellization, on the other hand, "where changes are made with specific ends in view," (1) abandonment of ends leads to reversal of change, and (2) incompatibility of the change with underlying ends often leads to sabotage of change. Thus, should either the goals of ego enhancement be abandoned (as in periods of psychosis or severe personality disorganization) or should any of the goals of ego maturation be perceived as in conflict with the ends of ego enhancement, maturational regression can easily take place. The most vulnerable aspect of this type of maturation lies in the stability and durability of feelings of moral accountability under conditions that are prejudicial to personal gain and advantage. Lacking the satellizer's implicit acceptance of the duty to abide by all internalized moral values, the nonsatellizer is sorely tempted to let these values "go by the board" if the stakes are sufficiently high and the chances of apprehension and retribution sufficiently low.

If maturation is more successful in nonsatellizers, it is also more stressful. The satellizer's extrinsic self-esteem is damaged by status deprivation during adolescence, but this injury tends to be peripheral because of a residual core of intrinsic self-acceptance. The nonsatellizer's self-esteem, on the other hand, is wholly a creature of the environmental vicissitudes that deny or gratify the exalted ego aspirations on which he has "staked his value as a human being." Hence, the absence of intrinsic feelings of adequacy makes the damage wrought to the only type of self-esteem he knows, (extrinsic) central rather than peripheral. And, in addition, it is only when intrinsic self-esteem is lacking do threats to extrinsic self-esteem have the power to induce Neurotic Anxiety.

The destructive impact of status deprivation on self-esteem and potential for anxiety responses is greater in nonsatellizers for still another significant reason besides lack of intrinsic adequacy. Because of their exaggerated needs for ego enhancement (which are highly resistant to discouragement), they find the same degree of status deprivation much more deflating to self-esteem. They are also denied the current source of derived status that adolescent satellizers enjoy by maintaining in part a satellizing orientation toward peer group, teachers, and employers.[4] They are unable to experience the ego support and "we feeling" that is derived from the act of dependent identification with and self-subordination to group interests.

Ego Maturation of Rejected Adolescents

Although rejected children generally find adolescent status deprivation more stressful than do satellizers, adolescence often presents quite a few more opportunities for acquiring earned status than does childhood. The decreased importance of the rejecting home in comparison with the importance of school and peer group is in itself an ego-inflating factor. The fact of parental rejection itself becomes less catastrophic as the salience and importance of these rejecting figures in the psychological world of the rejected individual diminishes. Also, in comparison with childhood, many new opportunities of achieving extrinsic status present themselves.

Rejected children also have a latent capacity for forming satellizing-like relationships to benevolent and nonthreatening superordinate individuals. Their original failure to satellize was due to the absence of suitable parental figures in the home rather than to any inherent disinclination. When removed from the home, the possibility of satellization is increased, although fear of repetition of rejection makes them move cautiously in this direction.

Neurotic Anxiety is almost invariably present in rejected children from the very beginning. Self-esteem is sufficiently impaired, both by (1) the absence of intrinsic feelings of adequacy and by (2) the catastrophic injury to extrinsic adequacy feelings implicit in the rejecting situation, to constitute the major source of threat in any adjustive situation.

The socialization of the rejected child is made difficult by his inability to assert himself adequately and to protect himself from the aggression of others. This is a consequence of a learning deficit acquired in the course of having to submit so long and helplessly to parental aggression that he cannot master emotionally the roles necessary for expressing adult self-assertion. Aggression by others typically evokes a habitual response of helpless submissiveness. What other persons usually fail to recognize, however, is that this aggression and domination are only outwardly accepted; that quite unlike the overdominated satellizer who genuinely accepts the subservience to which he is subjected, the overdominated nonsatellizer gradually accumulates a reservoir of resentment and hostility that eventually overflows with such violence as frequently to jeopardize or rupture existing relationships beyond repair.

Typically, the rejected child tends to be taken advantage of, appears to accept the situation meekly, and then to the amazement of others erupts violently and impulsively. To avoid this sequence of events, he often prefers to withdraw from conflictful situations and to intellectualize his aggression. Either course of action, however, does little to promote effective interpersonal relationships.

Ego Maturation of Overvalued Adolescents

In contrast to its effect on the rejected child, adolescence usually brings a marked *loss* in extrinsic status and self-estimate to the overvalued child. He can hardly expect the same flattery and adulation in school and peer group that he was accustomed to receiving at home. In fact, adolescence frequently marks the onset of his Neurotic Anxiety; for only now is the impairment to his extrinsic self-esteem sufficiently catastrophic to predispose him to this personality and emotional disorder. But unlike that of the rejected child, the anxiety is not offset by the possibility of obtaining some derived status (and, therefore, some intrinsic self-esteem) through the belated establishment of satellizing-like relationships.[5] His failure to undergo ego devaluation and satellization was less a compensatory reaction of self-defense than an outcome of the parent's active fostering of his omnipotent ego organization. Thus, he tends to find satellization too degrading, and is often too obnoxiously selfish, self-centered, and narcissistic, especially in early adolescence, either to inspire genuine love in others or to be capable of relating himself emotionally to them.

The overvalued child also differs from the rejected child by manifesting no incapacity for self-assertion and aggression. In fact, his socialization is hindered by an excess rather than by a deficiency of these qualities. He tends to alienate associates initially by his overbearing, egocentric, domineering, insensitive, narcissistic, and importunate behavior. But in his case the motivation is available to modify the strategy of his interpersonal relationships and to learn more acceptable social behavior, since he recognizes the importance of good social relations in the struggle for vocational success and power. Through assiduous study and intelligent application of self-control, he is typically able to acquire an agreeable set of formal manners and a superficial veneer of good fellowship to mask his formerly offensive aggression and self-seeking. Hence, he is eventually able to learn a highly effective form of self-assertion in interpersonal relationships that does not alienate others.

Because of his excessively permissive upbringing, the overvalued child also experiences more initial difficulty than the rejected child in acquiring goal frustration tolerance, long-range goals, self-critical ability, and executive independence, and in relinquishing the need for immediate hedonistic gratification. But unlike the underdominated satellizer, his lack of intrinsic self-esteem, his exaggerated need for ego enhancement, and his genuine volitional independence motivate him more strongly eventually to acquire these attributes of ego maturity.

Under certain unusual circumstances, ego-maturity goals may be rejected by nonsatellizers despite the importance of these goals for their ego aggrandizement. For example, overvalued preadolescents or adolescents (especially girls) may reject the goals of adult personality maturation in retaliation for the later paradoxical increase in parental domination, restrictiveness, and control that is often related to parental fears about their daughters' precocious involvement in heterosexual experience. Such adolescents (particularly girls) frequently drop out of school, marry unsuitable mates, become hippies, or use drugs just to revenge themselves on parents—even though it frustrates their hypertrophied ego needs as nonsatellizers. In later adult life, however, they may either belatedly mature or experience Reactive Depression or Schizophrenia because of their underlying low self-esteem and predisposition to Neurotic Anxiety.

The Ego in Adult Life

Consistent with my decision not to write a separate chapter on ego development during adult life and senescence is my view that developmental changes in the ego tend to be quantitative or continuous rather than qualitative or discontinuous in nature after the desatellization of adolescence. This by no means implies that all significant personality development ends at the close of the adolescent years but rather that such growth does not constitute a distinctive qualitative stage (or stages) of ego development in terms of basic reorganization of ego structure such as, for example, takes place in early childhood and adolescence (ego devaluation and desatellization crises).

This is the case despite the fact that the young adult, the middle-aged, and the senescent individual constitute socially recognized age groups in all cultures. Thus, there are no orderly sequential changes or developmental regularities as individuals, for example, move from young adulthood (with new vocational, marital, and parenting experiences) to middle age (with children "leaving the nest," their own parents becoming older and more dependent, a possible "mid-life crisis," etc.). Rather, there is only a characteristic chronological sequence of life-cycle problems or events through which most adults pass as they grow older; and these successive life-cycle phases neither constitute separate and distinct stages of ego development, in and of themselves, nor give rise to such stages by inducing qualitative reorganization of ego structure. As we shall see later, this is as true for the cognitive as for the ego aspects of development.

Another way of expressing the same view is to say that ego development in adult life is largely characterized by the accentuation of cumulative individual differences or idiosyncratic traits (both personality and cognitive), rather than by clearly defined normative trends or age-level changes. Over time, therefore, relatively small differences between individuals tend to increase or accumulate, resulting in progressively greater interindividual divergence in personality trait profiles. Increments in certain aspects of personality and social sophistication probably occur from the end of adolescence until death, but for the most part they are *horizontal* rather than vertical in their impact on personality functioning in that they do not involve any basic restructuring of the core elements of ego structure (e.g., source of status or self-esteem; relative need for earned ego status; volitional independence; ego maturity traits; mode of assimilating new values). Not even in beginning middle age is there any *general* or *consistent* pattern of emotional-social disengagement from social and vocational roles, as hypothesized by some investigators. Rather, numerous patterns of altered degree of involvement or interaction with the social environment are found in aging persons—from decreased, more passive and constricted, to more active and increased, both interindividually and between sex groups. In fact, the only consistent personality change that is uniformly correlated with aging is increased introversion.

So-called "life-cycle" studies focusing on adult personality development tend erroneously to identify successive life-period phases in adult life, and their attendant major adjustive problems and "crises," with genuine stages of personality development. In addition, their validity and generality are flawed by one or more methodological deficiencies, such as cross-sectional rather than longitudinal design, only male subjects, exclusively middle- or professional-class representation. This same latter limitation, of course, also applies to Gesell's studies of ego development in infancy and childhood but is self-evidently less serious because the impact of these social-class differences is operative mostly for several years rather than for virtually a lifetime.

As adult life approaches, exaggerated demands for volitional independence from parents give way to more temperate needs for autonomy. The adolescent's independence is now an established fact; he has no more need to be strident about demanding it. He satellizes less in relation to the peer group, reestablishes his own individuality, is less dependent on it for his status (earned or derived), and thinks more in terms of, and also begins to acquire more, earned status in the mainstream of the adult culture. Rapprochement with parents typically occurs.

Satellizers continue to acquire some secondary derived status in relation to their bosses, spouses, and glamorous public figures; and rejected nonsatellizers continue to search for "safe" persons (i.e., persons who will not reject them) with whom to establish a satellizing relationship so as to acquire some supplementary derived status and, thus, have an intrinsic source of self-esteem independent of their compensatorily high and typically unrealistic needs for achievement. Their success in this endeavor usually depends on how successful a marriage they can make and on whether they can find a mentor who takes a *personal* as well as a professional interest in their careers. Overvalued nonsatellizers rarely satellize in adulthood and typically seek vicariously in their children the ego aggrandizement that they are seldom able to achieve themselves unless they are unusually able individuals. Thus, this vicious cycle is perpetuated from one generation to the next.

The drive for earned status and recognition tends to peak in the middle forties for most people. Motivation, adaptiveness, venturesomeness, flexibility, creativity, self-discipline, hard work and self-denial, physical stamina, intellectual acuteness, and problem-solving ability—all required for successful achievement—start to decline. Many nonsatellizers begin "to see the handwriting on the wall" at this time, and their self-confidence and self-esteem accordingly begin to wane. With time running out, and death approaching, they begin to realize that they will never gain the success and recognition they crave in terms of their exaggerated and unrealistically tenacious needs for self-aggrandizement. This often precipitates the "crisis of middle age," exacerbates the level of chronic anxiety, and may even precipitate panic states or a Reactive Schizophrenia or depression.

In some cases there is preoccupation with death. More typically, however, this inevitable end to their strivings is relegated to a "back burner," and the individual seldom comes to terms, psychologically or philosophically, with the problem of his own demise. Thus, most people in Western culture die by default, so to speak, without ever evolving a deliberately formulated set of attitudes about death or coming to terms with its implications for ego identity.

At the very least, middle age requires some stock taking and self-reappraisal, some revised reality testing and discarding of cherished but improbable aspirations, and much reordering of priorities in terms of probabilities of realization prior to death rather than of absolute preference. Many persons in their fifties begin to appreciate seriously for the first time the finiteness of life and the reality and inevitability of their own deaths.

As senescence sets in with physical frailty, ill health, and frequently slow or more precipitate deterioration of intellectual faculties (due to organic causes of dementia) and of physical stamina, a reverse process of satellization often takes place. Old people may renounce their own strivings and tend to live in the reflected glory of their children's accomplishments. Ego-status goals decline inasmuch as opportunities for earned status diminish, and older persons in our culture are more the objects of poorly disguised derision than of veneration. Self-esteem thus gradually begins to ebb until much volitional independence is surrendered; and the senior citizen often returns to the emotionally dependent status of childhood. At best he is typically accepted on sufferance in Western culture and often has little to look forward to except death. His interest in life and events begins to flag, and this, in turn, accelerates his physical and intellectual deterioration.

Notes

1. Achievement motivation tends to be relatively high in children whose mothers make early demands for and reward independent accomplishment highly. There are also marked intercultural and social-class differences in achievement motivation.
2. However, the status of the infant is heading toward greater biosocial stability and security in childhood, whereas the transition from childhood to adolescence involves a comparable loss in these areas.
3. For purposes of highlighting the chief issues involved, this critique of permissiveness is based upon the most extreme presentation of this philosophy of child rearing and of its basic underlying rationale that can be found in books on child care and school discipline. The reader should bear in mind, however, that all shades and degrees of permissiveness short of authoritarianism exist. In fact, the author would regard his own position as a limited endorsement of permissiveness if judged against the impersonal, overstrict, and rigid Watsonian (behavioristic) criteria of child rearing popular in the interval between World Wars I and II.
4. It might be noted here that adolescent nonsatellizers also use the rational-objective and exploratory orientations almost exclusively in value assimilation.
5. Neurotic Anxiety may be allayed in the rejected child by his attainment of intrinsic (derived) status per se, and by the reduction of frustration that this permits through a lowering of level of ego aspiration.

3

The Natural History of Ego Development:
The Development of Conscience

Modern psychology and psychiatry have tended to drift away from concern with problems of ethics and moral values. The "moralizing" orientation in psychotherapy is treated with scorn in present-day textbooks of psychology; and if the directive and nondirective schools of thought agree on any one thing it is that there is no room for moral judgment in the therapeutic situation. The focus is on adjustment. The therapist, we are told, cannot say that behavior is good or bad; he can only express an opinion on the quality and efficacy of an adjustive mechanism. When he can divorce himself completely from ethical judgments, and can concern himself only with understanding the psychopathological origins and adjustive significance of deviant behavior, it is alleged that he has attained the ideal therapeutic attitude. The thesis that will be presented below is that not only is it impossible for a psychotherapist to ignore the question of moral judgment but also that it is undesirable and artificial for him to attempt to do so.

Behavior and Ethics

Far from being unrelated, the problems of behavior and ethics are inextricably bound together. To appraise a man's personality and ignore his moral character is equivalent in many respects to evaluating the setting of a ring while overlooking the diamond. True, the psychologist has a ready explanation for this apparent paradox. Moral values, he contends, are subjective and unverifiable. Every man to his taste and to his opinion; no objective psychological criterion is possible. We can only describe a man's personality traits with the aid of existing measuring instruments, hazard a guess as to how they developed, try to evaluate their adjustive value, and provide a plausible explanation for their antisocial components.

The same psychological abhorrence of ethical judgment can be seen in our modern orientation toward antisocial conduct, crime, and delinquency. Criminality is regarded as either a psychological or a social disease. There are no delinquent individuals, only delinquent parents or delinquent social systems. When one really understands why a criminal behaves as he does, the psychological evaluation is complete. Whether he is good or bad or whether he is morally accountable are arbitrary value judgments, matters of social policy or legal philosophy that do not concern the psychologist. To the latter, the delinquent is a product of his heredity and environment, an individual who allegedly had no other choice but to act as he did; and in the light of this psychological determinism, moral responsibility and retribution are necessarily irrelevant, inconsistent, and illogical. Behavior can be appraised as unfortunate or antisocial but never as evil. As long as it can be explained in psychological terms, it cannot be perceived as evil, since such an evaluation implies a value judgment that lies beyond the scope of scientific behavioral assessment.

In the history of psychology, this absolute separation between morality and behavior is a comparatively recent development. Aristotle, Spinoza, and Dewey, for example, all held that ethics can only be based on a science of human behavior, and that "objectively valid value propositions can be arrived at by human reason." And whether the psychologist chooses to recognize it or not, most purposeful human behavior has a moral aspect, the psychological reality of which cannot be ignored.

Problems of Moral Development

The investigation of the moral development of the human being provides one of the main cornerstones for an objectively and logically verifiable psychology of ethics. By means of a developmental approach it becomes possible to: (1) determine the limits that define man's capacity for acquiring moral behavior and the sequential steps involved in moral growth; (2) predict the various types of delinquent behavior that may arise as a consequence of aberrant moral development; and (3) determine under what conditions individuals shall be held morally accountable for their misdeeds.

Looked at in this light the learning of moral values is only a component aspect of ego development. It obeys all of the principles regulating the assimilation of any ego-related value, except for the understanding that an issue of good or evil is involved. When in addition, a notion of obligation and the possibility of inhibitory control arise, and a self-evaluative attitude is adopted towards one's own behavior in areas that impinge upon moral values, the collective term *conscience* is employed. It should be realized, however, that *conscience* refers to a class of ego-related value judgments and possesses no more substantive properties than a generalization such as *ego*. An illusion of substantive identity, however, is provided by the association of conscience with the highly specific and identifiable self-reaction of guilt, with its familiar psycho-physiological response pattern.

From a developmental standpoint, therefore, we can see no theoretical advantage in separating moral development from any other aspect of ego development involving the learning and assimilation of values. It only confuses the issue to postulate a separate layer of personality as embodying in a reified fashion the properties associated with conscience reactions, and arising in an inevitably predetermined manner in relation to a single aspect of psychosexual development.[1] In our analysis of the development of conscience, therefore, we shall be concerned with the same type of variables that determine the outcome of other aspects of ego development, namely, the biosocial competence of the individual, the demands of his social environment, his capacity to perceive himself and his environment realistically, the various dimensions of the parent-child relationship, and other personality characteristics of parent and child (e.g., dominance, strength of hedonistic motivation, introversion-extroversion).

The Role of Values in Conscience Development

Values, of course, refer to ways of striving, believing, and doing, and also to questions of good and evil, whenever purpose and direction are involved or choice and judgment are exercised. Values are implied in the relative importance that an individual attaches to different objectives and activities; expresses in his moral, social, and religious beliefs; and shows in his aesthetic preferences. They underlie sanctioned ways of behaving and interacting with people in a given culture and the kinds of personality traits that are idealized or condemned. Values, therefore, are important factors in determining goals and goal-seeking behavior, standards of conduct, and feelings of obligation to conform to such standards and to inhibit behavior at variance with them. They help to order the world of the child differentially in terms of degree of ego involvement (i.e., to determine his interests), orient him to his cultural milieu, influence the content of his perceptions, and sensitize him selectively to perceive certain classes of objects and relationships.

Values, thus, have a more *general* role in personality organization and functioning, as indicated above, but *moral* values also have a special role in the formation and development of conscience: the internalization of values, performed differently by satellizers and nonsatellizers (see below) constitutes the first step in conscience formation; it determines to *which* (if any) moral values the individual feels a sense of obligation to conform.

The Transmission of Values

Three component problems are involved in the intracultural transmission of values. First, we must consider the external patterning factors to which the child is exposed and which influence him selectively to interiorize certain values in preference to others. Second, we must identify the mechanisms through which the external standards are interiorized. Third, we must reckon with the sanctions (both internal and external) that maintain values in relatively stable form once they are internalized.

External Patterning Factors

The young child's world of value judgments is largely unstructured for lack of relevant experiential frames of reference and hence is very susceptible to the influence of prestige suggestion from significant figures in his environment. First through his parents and later through other socializing agents, he is exposed to both explicit and implicit indoctrination. The latter occurs insidiously through recurrent and unobtrusive exposure to the underlying value assumptions of family and culture. Thus, young children tend to identify with the value symbols of their parents' membership and reference groups long before they are sufficiently mature to comprehend the meaning of these symbols.

However, the question of whether suggestibility can be considered a general personality trait is still unsettled. Evidence from studies with adults indicates that degree of suggestibility is inversely related to self-sufficiency, self-assertiveness, and relative indifference to others' approval. In accordance with a social sex role, which includes being more docile, conforming, and submissive to adult authority, girls tend to be more responsive than boys to prestige suggestion.

Mechanism of Interiorization

We may distinguish, on the basis of the degree of motivation involved, between two essentially different ways of interiorizing the values of other persons or of groups. As an individual simply habituates to a given set of norms, the values underlying these norms may acquire an aura of axiomatic rightness and may be accepted as self-evidently valid. Here no particular needs of the individual are satisfied. A simple mechanical type of imitation belongs in the same category; the expressed values of one person serve as a stimulus instigating acceptance of comparable values by another. This process is facilitated in group situations and is very similar to behavioral "contagion."

However, whenever such imitation involves a more active *need* to be like other persons or to conform to their expectations (apart from fear of punishment), it is more proper to speak of motivated interiorization or *identification*. Identification, therefore, is a motivated form of imitation in which both the *interpersonal relationship* (direct or fantasized) between imitator and imitated, as well as the imitated act itself, are highly significant for the learning that ensues.

Although identification implies an underlying motive in one person's acceptance of another's values, the term itself without further qualification does not specify the type of motivation that is operative. In order to designate more precisely the individual's motivational orientation to value assimilation, the terms *satellizing* and *rational-objective* (nonsatellizing) have been used above. In each case the child responds to prestige suggestion but does so for different reasons. The nonsatellizer (in contrast to the satellizer) does not accept prestige authority blindly and uncritically from a person or group out of personal loyalty or desire for derived status, but because the authority of the suggester is respected as relevantly influencing the outcome of his quest for earned status. The purpose of his hero worship is not to be a loyal and devoted camp follower but to emulate and displace the hero, and to use him as a guide and stepping-stone for his own ego enhancement. Conformity to group norms in his case is more a matter of expediency, and of obtaining the status advantages of group reference or membership than a reflection of a need for a self-subservient sense of belongingness or "we-feeling." The *exploratory* orientation to value assimilation, on the other hand, is a more task-oriented, problem-solving approach that ignores considerations of both earned and derived status and places major emphasis on objective evidence, logical validity, and equity in determining the acceptability of different value positions.

Component Aspects of Conscience Formation

The term "conscience" has been employed in a collective sense to refer to that aspect of ego structure concerned with the cognitive-emotional-motivational organization of moral values and to other psychological processes involved in keeping conduct compatible with internalized moral standards. As the outcome of an elaborate developmental process, a set of internalized moral standards is built up in relation to the interpersonal relationships of the child's life. In this process of conscience acquisition, the child is more than a passive recipient. It is true that he accepts values from those who discipline him; but in the process of internalization, the norms he adopts are modified by his own individuality and are endowed with qualities that they originally did not possess. Functionally, therefore, the rules and the role of the disciplinarian do not necessarily operate as the latter sees them, but as they appear in the eyes of the child who projects them into reality.

Considered in this reciprocal light, the operation of conscience can be seen to depend upon a number of underlying and component psychological processes. Since these component processes mature at different rates and vary in relevance and importance during the various developmental stages of conscience formation—even failing to evolve at all in certain cases of aberrant development—it is not possible to regard all of them as indispensable for the functioning of conscience. Conscience also is rarely a completely consistent and coherent system of behavior.

To begin with, the operation of conscience presupposes a capacity to *anticipate unpleasant consequences*. Regardless of whether the deterrent is punishment, insecurity, anxiety, or guilt, it would not lead to inhibitory control of behavior if the child were not able to project the consequences of his actions into imagination in advance of their execution. However, once this power to anticipate is acquired, it cannot become very effective in the functioning of conscience until *self-restraint* becomes possible. The acquisition of *inhibitory self-control* is a very gradual process which parallels the growth of the ability to endure postponement of immediate hedonistic gratification. Implicit in the development of self-control is the proposition that there is a counter-need potent enough to enable learning to occur in a direction opposite to the motivational influence exerted by hedonistic needs. In the course of ego development the nature of this need varies from avoidance of pain and disapproval to insuring the continued basis of derived status and the avoidance of guilt feelings.

Conscience formation also implies the ability to internalize values, by which is meant the capacity to assimilate external standards, or to evolve new standards which in either case exert a relatively stable *internal* directional influence on behavior. Such internalization can occur either through the satellizing, rational-objective, or exploratory orientations. The process of internalization in relation to conscience development differs from the internalization of any other value only in the fact that a moral issue is involved.

The assimilation of moral values, however, does not necessarily mean that these values will influence behavior in any stable and systematic fashion until a sense of *obligation* or "oughtness" evolves. The sense of obligation refers to the individual's feeling of duty or responsibility to conform to or abide by his internalized code of moral values in his own personal conduct. Developmentally this step appears after the internalization of other values. The child believes that certain actions are good or bad before he feels that he "ought" not do them himself. The key to moral conduct then is the feeling of obligation, the recognition of imperatives in thought and action. It is the sense of obligation that transforms mere behavior into conduct.

The basis of the sense of obligation also changes with age and personality development. In the satellizing era, it is a component function of a generally subservient attitude of sharing in, and desiring to retain, derived status, loyalty, unilateral accountability, and a need for approval. Thereafter these aspects of obligation acquire a residual substrate function, and more abstract cognitive factors divorced from the parent-child relationship become more prominent, that is, concepts of justice, equity, and reciprocal duty; of responsibility to group, social class, and society. Like every other moral value, the sense of obligation also acquires more or less stability and effectiveness in regulating behavior in accordance with the degree of internalization it undergoes.

The feeling of obligation provides the central cognitive-emotional strand of the fabric of conscience. It is the unifying factor welding together the various moral values of the individual into an organized system of behavior. It gives generality and genotypic consistency to moral conduct by entering into every moral decision he makes. Whether or not he refrains from committing a particular immoral act depends on more than the relative strengths of the particular moral values involved in this act and of their deterrent influence. The *total inhibitory* control that can be employed in this situation is rather the strength of the particular moral values multiplied by a general factor represented by the effectiveness and stability of the sense of obligation. It is the association of inhibitory control with this general feeling of moral obligation that gives to conscience its apparent substantive properties, and provides the individual with a powerful regulatory mechanism over his behavior that is very similar to the philosophical concept of "free will" in the moral sense of the term.

The final psychological process involved in the operation of conscience is the self-critical faculty. Without this capacity for realistically appraising one's own intentions and behavior in the light of internalized moral principles, it is neither possible to inhibit immoral actions nor to experience guilt after they are executed. The importance of the self-critical faculty in the development of conscience can be seen in the fact that the latter remains in a rudimentary state until the former is reasonably well advanced (ages five to eight). When self-criticism can be employed, feelings of culpability and guilt become possible since these are a reaction to the perception of a discrepancy between one's own behavior and the internalized normative moral standards in relation to which a sense of obligation exists.

Feelings of guilt, therefore, are not only in a general sense a psychological process underlying, or necessary for, the operation of conscience but are also a cognitive-emotional reaction of the individual to the perceived disparity existing between behavior and obligation in particular moral situations. The core ingredient of guilty feelings is the sense of shame, which is evoked in these situations when he anticipates the reactions of others (especially authority figures) to the discovery of this same disparity in his behavior. In addition to shame, guilt includes feelings of self-reproach, self-disgust, self-contempt, remorse, and various characteristic visceral and vasomotor responses.

Through the processes of retrospective association and anticipation, guilt tends to be incorporated into the behavioral system of conscience, providing it with some of its most distinctive identifying features and apparent substantive qualities. Behavior leading to guilt typically evokes the anticipation that retribution will be inevitable either through the suffering inherent in guilt feelings, the seeking out of social punishment as a means of guilt-reduction, or through the medium of a supernatural agency. The sense of the inevitability of punishment, therefore, is one of the characteristic properties of conscience reactions.

Importance of Conscience in Socialization

Moral obligation, as a key component of conscience, is one of the most important psychological mechanisms through which an individual becomes socialized in the ways of his culture. It is also an important instrument for cultural survival since it constitutes a most efficient watchdog within each individual, serving to keep his behavior compatible with his own moral values, and thereby with the values of the culture in which he lives. Without the assistance it renders, child rearing would be a difficult matter indeed.

If children felt no sense of accountability to curb their hedonistic and irresponsible impulses, to conform to accepted social norms, or to acquire self-control, the socializing process would be slow, arduous, and incomplete. The methods of sheer physical force, threat of pain, deprivation, and punishment, and withholding of love and approval—all used in combination with constant surveillance—would be the only available means for exacting conformity to cultural standards of acceptable behavior. And since the interests of personal expediency are not always in agreement with prescribed ethical norms, since the maintenance of perpetual vigilance is impractical, and since fear alone is seldom an effective deterrent against antisocial behavior, a social order that is unbuttressed by a sense of moral obligation in its members can enjoy precious little stability.

In the more mature forms of ethical conduct, however, the sense of moral obligation stems more from a reasoned judgment based on some personal ethical principles rather than from simple conformity to prevailing cultural norms. The cultural basis of conscience development in the individual, on the other hand, may be found in the potent need of both parents and society to inculcate a sense of responsibility in the child. Not only the physical survival of its members but also the perpetuation of its selective way of life is contingent upon the parents' and the culture's degree of success in this undertaking.

Thus, in this latter sense, the attenuation of infantile irresponsibility might be considered part of the necessary process of ego devaluation and maturation that presumably characterizes (ego) personality development in all cultures. Socialization requires the learning of self-control and self-discipline, the subordination of personal desires to the needs and wishes of others, the acquisition of skills and self-sufficiency, the curbing of hedonistic and aggressive impulses, and the assimilation of culturally sanctioned patterns of behavior. Moreover, in its most mature aspects, socialization also requires that the individual govern his behavior by *rules* that he arrives at rationally before conforming to them. It seems highly unlikely that any of these prerequisites for socialization could be adequately stable before conscience itself is firmly established. Additionally, the very concept of *character* formation assumes adherence to the directive role of conscience in moral behavior.

Related Changes in Ego Development

Our discussion of ego development in a moral context rests on the assumption that moral development is a subset of general ego development which can be conceptualized independently. The essential similarities between moral- and ego-development theory are seen in the three-stage developmental process that all theorists embrace. This three-level process in moral and ego development implies: (1) a first level at which rules and the expectations of others are external to the self; (2) a second level at which the self is identified with, or equated with, the rules, stereotypes, and expectations of others, especially authorities; and (3) a third level at which the self is differentiated from conventional rules. In our ego-development framework, level one is the presatellizing stage, level two involves early and late satellization, and level three is the desatellizing stage. The reason for discussing ego development here is that the *cognitive-judgmental* component of conscience development is incomplete without considering its *executive aspects* that are closely related to ego development considerations. The following discussion will, therefore, consider "conscience" development under *general ego development* sequences, described in chapters 1 and 2.

Developmental Stages in Conscience Formation

The investigation of conscience development offers us considerable encouragement for establishing an empirical and objectively valid psychology of ethics because of the implications that the knowledge of such development holds for the understanding of socially delinquent behavior and for the assessment of moral accountability. But we can only hope to understand the development of conscience as an integral component of ego development. It shifts with changes in the parent-child relationship, in social expectations, perceptual ability, and cognitive organization, and with maturational advances in biosocial competence and goal structure; and in turn it has an important influence on all of the latter aspects of ego development.

Normative Changes in Conscience Development

Although none of the conditions necessary for the emergence of conscience can ever be satisfied at birth, all human beings are potentially capable of acquiring conscience behavior under minimally favorable circumstances. Culture may make a difference in the form that this behavior takes and in the specific kinds of stimuli that instigate it. But the capacity itself is so basically human and so fundamental to the sanctions by which social norms are normally maintained and transmitted to the young in *any* culture that differences among individuals within a culture would probably be as great as, or greater than, differences among cultures.

Thus, despite the probable existence of many important, culturally conditioned differences in children's acquisition of conscience behavior, there are presumptive grounds for believing that considerable commonality prevails in the general patterning of sequential development. Such commonality would be a product of various uniformities regarding: (1) basic conditions of the parent-child relationship; (2) minimal cultural needs for socialization of the child; and (3) certain growth trends in cognitive and personality development from one culture to the next.

Normative growth in conscience development reflects both gains in cognitive maturity and age-level changes in personality organization. Significant personality factors include alteration in dependency relationships, ego-status needs, and mode of assimilating values. Significant cognitive factors include increased capacity for perceiving social expectations and

the attributes of social roles, and increased ability to discriminate, generalize, formulate abstractions, take multiple perspectives, and make moral
judgments. Growth in self-critical ability and in capacity for a less egocentric and more objective approach to values involves both cognitive
and personality variables. Interaction between these two sorts of variables
is responsible for most developmental changes in the basis of moral obligation and in notions of moral law, justice, and culpability; because of
the many psychological components of conscience, however, it is entirely
conceivable that some aspects of moral development are influenced more
by one type of factor than by another.

The Presatellizing Stage

Needless to say, the infant enters the world completely irresponsible
in a moral sense and remains this way for the first few years of his life.
This does not mean that his moral future is wholly uncharted. By virtue
of his latent capacity for assimilating ethical values, acquiring feelings
of obligation, evaluating his own behavior, carrying on cognitive processes, and so forth, the broad sequential outlines of conscience formation are already predetermined in terms of process, but not in terms of
specific content.

Presatellizing conscience, for the most part, involves little more than
the development of inhibitory control on the basis of learning to anticipate and avoid punishment. Previous experience with a given type of unacceptable behavior leads the child to expect pain, deprivation, isolation,
or disapproval if such behavior is repeated, and hence leads to feelings of
insecurity in contemplating same. Inhibition of such behavior, therefore,
is rewarded since it reduces insecurity.

Thus, in the presatellizing era the child is aware of his parents' demands, standards, and values, but does not truly internalize them. He is
primarily concerned with satisfying his own immediate needs and asserting his volitional independence. The parent can compel conformity only
by arousing feelings of insecurity in relation to forbidden acts, which
means associating the latter with pain, restraint, threat of isolation, or other
negative acts. Such control, however, is stripped of any moral implications since it only indicates submission to authority on a discomfort-re-
duction basis rather than inhibition of misbehavior on the basis of any
genuine acceptance of moral norms. Before guilt can be experienced not

only must moral values be internalized, but also a feeling of obligation to conform to them, as well as sufficient self-critical ability to recognize disparity between the standards and the actual behavior.

Early Satellizing Conscience

When the needs of the parents and the culture coincide with sufficient growth in the child's biosocial competence to make him responsive to training demands, a new stage in conscience development is reached. As the child perceives his actual volitional impotence and his dependence upon parents for volitional direction, and agrees to accept a satellizing role in relation to them, ego devaluation is accomplished; and with satellization comes a need to assimilate parental values and the gradual emergence of a feeling of obligation to conform to them. True conscience appears for the first time, since inhibitory control becomes predicated upon acceptance of the satellizing situation (with its concurrent need for maintaining the conditions under which derived status can be enjoyed) rather than upon anticipation and avoidance of punishment and the reduction of feelings of insecurity.

The development of a satellizing conscience, however, is a very gradual matter. It does not unfold spontaneously but in response to the parents' new authority role and training demands. Before internalization and self-discipline can be acquired, external forms of control must be maintained, especially in the initial phases. The self-evidence of this proposition is especially apparent in the first period of negativism, which accompanies the crisis of devaluation. As parental training demands become insistent and threatening enough to the prevailing ego organization to elicit negativistic behavior, the child's grandiose self-esteem is challenged.

Gradually, however, under propitious conditions, negativism becomes supplanted by a satellizing attitude that carries over into the sphere of value assimilation. Typically this assimilation occurs as a by-product of the general attitude of subservience, and hence takes place on a highly uncritical level. It is reinforced by: (1) the child's need to retain his derived status, which, therefore, causes him to react with anxiety whenever it is threatened by parental disapproval; and (2) his acceptance of the moral obligation to abide by the standards that he has internalized. This latter step is accomplished by acquiescing to the proposition that disobedience or personal nonconformity to parental standards is "wicked," disloyal, and hurtful to the supreme authority figures whom he has accepted as his models. At this point a basis for feelings of guilt is established. When the child perceives disparity between his own behavior and his internalized standards, this complex psycho-physiological response is set into motion. It consists of the subjective elements of shame, anxiety, remorse, and self-disgust, and the autonomic reactions of vasomotor instability, sweating, visceral giddiness, and inhibition of ordinary vegetative functions.

As soon as guilt feelings can occur, another powerful motive arises for interiorizing and abiding by parents values, namely, the need for guilt avoidance. The possibility of experiencing guilt makes punishment inevitable, since in addition to the anxiety that it evokes by threatening self-esteem, the intense reactions of self-condemnation and reproach, shame, self-disgust, and remorse are generally more punishing and inescapable than external punitive agents.

The interplay of factors leading to early conscience formation is also dependent upon various other aspects of the parent-child relationship and upon other personality characteristics of the two principals. Unconditional acceptance and intrinsic valuation of the child by the parent (following upon an initial history of parental altruism) are necessary preconditions for the development of a satellizing conscience. The firmer and more consistent a parent's discipline is, the more easily are his standards assimilated. If there is marital discord, the child can identify with either parent only at the risk of alienating the other. Children of both sexes find it more difficult to accept the father's authority because of the relatively negligible male influence in the ordering of home and school life.

With respect to personality factors in the child that influence the course of conscience formation, ascendence, volitional independence and viscerotonia are perhaps the most crucial. The more independent and self-assertive a child is, the more likely he will be to resist the imposition of parental standards upon his behavior. Similarly, the greater his need for visceral satisfactions the more reluctant he will be to accept the obligation of conforming to standards aimed at minimizing these satisfactions.

Late Satellizing Conscience

The cardinal feature of this stage of conscience development is the stabilization and internalization of the sense of moral obligation as a result of gains in self-critical ability. As long as the child can uncritically view

himself as capable of managing his own affairs and as entitled to volitional independence, feelings of moral obligation are bound to be unstable,
since he finds the authority role of the parent distasteful and provocative
of hostility and resentment. However, after he learns to appraise himself
and his situation realistically enough to accept the dependent biosocial
status that is inevitably his in any culture, he is able to make a satisfactory satellizing adjustment to parental authority, which he can now regard as self-evident and unquestionable.

In the late satellizing stage, reinforcement of the sense of moral obligation is provided primarily by guilt feelings. These become a powerful deterrent to unacceptable behavior; they are much more threatening and
anxiety-producing than external punitive agents. In the first place, remorse
is more perseverating and recriminating than pain or deprivation. Second,
guilt is more inevitable since detection cannot possibly be avoided. Last,
and most important, the punishment dispensed by one's own conscience
does not significantly reduce guilt or confer absolution at this stage. In contrast, punishment by parents (because of continual occurrence in the sequence of misbehavior, guilt, punishment, forgiveness, and reacceptance),
acquires highly important guilt-reducing properties for the child.

As a symptomatic variety of anxiety, guilt is unmatched in its potential disruptive influence on self-esteem. Hence, both guilt avoidance and
guilt reduction serve as extremely potent motivators of human behavior.
Fear of guilt reprisals plays the central role in the moral inhibitory control characteristic of this age period, and for that matter, as we shall see
later, of all subsequent periods as well.

Conscience in the Desatellizing Period

As the satellizing orientation begins to wane in the middle and preadolescent years of childhood—until it becomes but a subsidiary source
of current status in the adolescent period—marked changes in a corresponding direction occur in the organization of conscience. Nevertheless,
in the same way that the impact of childhood satellization leaves a permanent residue in adult personality structure, the satellizing conscience
becomes the only firm foundation upon which a stable, rational conscience
can be built.

Five main lines of development in conscience formation can be noted
at this time:

1. There is a decline in moral absolutism. The self-evident rightness of moral propositions tends to be replaced by a more empirical, exploratory, and rational approach based upon functional needs in interpersonal relationships.
2. Conscience becomes less authoritarian and more reciprocal in nature. "Constraint and unilateral respect" give way to "mutual respect and cooperation."
3. Moral principles acquire greater generality and abstractness.
4. The child's moral viewpoint becomes less egocentric.
5. The sense of moral accountability (the feeling of obligation or responsibility to abide by internalized ethical values) is placed on a societal basis instead of remaining a function of the child-parent relationship. These changes are produced by modifications in the parent-child relationship, shifts in the child's needs for, and source of, status, alterations in his group experience, and maturation of his perceptual and cognitive processes.

The first break in the authoritarian conscience occurs when the child enters school. A new source of moral authority enters the picture challenging the omniscience and infallibility of the parents. And the mere fact that he becomes aware of the existence of alternative ethical values— even if he does not accept them—undermines his parents' claim to uniqueness as the sole law givers. As long as more than one alternative exists, as long as he is required to exercise choice and discrimination, a given set of values can no longer be completely accepted as self-evidently true. With increasing age, more and more of the child's store of axiomatic truth acquires the status of hypotheses needing external verification.

As the child escapes from the constraining uniformity of the family hearth into the more variable practices of the culture at large, the prepotent influence of his initial models begins to decline. Not only is he confronted by many conflicting value systems, all of which dispute the parents' early monopoly of moral authority, but eventually he also becomes part of a peer group that sets itself up as a moral authority in its own right. He becomes less awed by adults and older children and more inclined to search for moral values that reflect the principles of cooperation and reciprocal obligation and serve a functional purpose in regulating group life. This desire for equality and reciprocity in interpersonal relationships also increases with age.

Various changes in the organization of the peer society also facilitate transition to a more functional and reciprocal moral law. Groups become larger, less isolated, and more stable. Children experience membership in several different groups exhibiting a variety of rules, practices, and values. As formal hierarchical relationships are established and individual roles are differentiated, the need for cooperation and mutual obligation increases, as illustrated by the development of "certain features of solidarity such as not cheating or not lying between children." The child's attitude toward the group also changes in terms of his status needs. The older he becomes the more he looks to the group as a source of extrinsic status rather than as an adjunctive source of intrinsic security and adequacy. It is for this reason, and also because the group is never dignified by the same halo of sanctity surrounding his parents, that the child can adopt the exploratory orientation in his peer group long before he dares to do so at home. It is not until adolescence that the omniscience of parents becomes sufficiently devalued to permit full and objective criticism of their practices.

Growth in ability to generalize, to think more in terms of abstractions, and to reach logical conclusions in more complex types of problems also tends to promote the development of a more consistent and rational moral code divorced from situational rules and regulations.

Conscience During Adolescence

Most of the material in the previous section applies here too, since adolescence must be regarded as a period of desatellization. The main differences between preadolescence and adolescence are in terms of the intensity and completeness of the underlying desatellizing processes, which bear the relationship of preparatory and consummatory stages to each other.

For many reasons, the adolescent is both more strongly disposed and in a better position than the preadolescent to employ the rational-objective and exploratory orientations. The parents by this time are devalued to the stature of ordinary mortals and are unable to extend derived status by fiat. Furthermore, their disposition—which reflects the expectations of the culture—is to withdraw derived status and compel the adolescent to seek a greater measure of extrinsic (earned) status; but since they themselves cannot provide what they advocate, they must yield authority and allegiance to the peer group which can.

A reshuffling of loyalties takes place on the basis of this shift in status-giving power. The adolescent looks to his peer group primarily as a source of feelings of extrinsic adequacy; but the group, as the chief moral authority of adolescence, also becomes the major object of his residual satellizing attitudes in value formation. The increased importance of the rational-objective orientation is a reflection of his greater concern with achieving extrinsic status; and the greater prominence of the exploratory orientation reflects his enhanced needs for independence, equality, and self-assertion that lead to emancipation from parents. In making this transition, feelings of guilt are inevitable, since repudiation of loyalties to parents is necessary in accepting these new value systems.

Adolescence in our culture also provides an extended period of time during which experimentation with a functional morality is possible. Our culture is unique in that the adolescent is not absorbed soon after the termination of childhood into an adult world of absolutistic moral standards. Strict conformity to the adult culture is not demanded, although this does tend to occur anyway, since despite overt rebelliousness the moral values of adolescents resemble those of adults more and more closely as they grow older.

Adolescents do take an active role in elaborating new moral standards to fit the needs of the group, although in this role they are not uninfluenced by the prevailing standards of the socioeconomic class to which they owe allegiance or by career considerations controlled by the latter. We have already seen that adolescents tend to share the major values of their class reference groups, and that the peer culture itself takes the responsibility of enforcing these standards. Furthermore, despite greater flexibility in the group evolution of new values, once these are determined, more complete conformity is demanded than in the adult culture. In conclusion, it must be admitted that the freedom to choose between moral alternatives in adolescence is present but is much more apparent than real.

The modern adolescent, therefore, by virtue of living in a heterogeneous society, also apparently has the opportunity of choosing between a multiplicity of alternative moral standards in contrast to the single code confronting the adolescent in primitive cultures. Thus, it is undeniable that the availability of alternatives greatly facilitates the development of a rational and functional conscience; it is problematical, however, whether it can be regarded as a *sine qua non*.

Moral beliefs of adolescents show several interesting trends when compared to preadolescent beliefs: a trend toward expediency and conformity which reflects the greater concern with extrinsic status; a trend in the direction of cynicism which is indicative of the same factor plus aggression toward adults; and a trend toward greater tolerance and flexibility.

Aberrant Conscience Development

In Nonsatellizers

The type of relationship that the child develops with his parents (satellizing or nonsatellizing), thus, becomes increasingly important for moral development after the devaluation crisis. Conscience development among nonsatellizers differs markedly, both in process and in outcome, from that of satellizers, considered above as more or less constituting the norm. However, even among nonsatellizers conscience development can hardly be regarded as being of one piece. It is very different, for example, in rejected than in overvalued children.

Nonsatellizers obviously fail to undergo the various changes in conscience development associated with satellization and, similarly, the changes resulting from desatellization. Their moral development, however, is less discontinuous than that of satellizers. During early and middle childhood, nonsatellizers continue to conform to parental standards for the same expediential reasons as during infancy; they fail to develop a sense of moral obligation in relation to a general attitude of subservience, loyalty, and need for approval and retention of derived status. Fear of deprivation and loss of succorance rather than guilt avoidance keep them in line and check the overt expression of their hostility. Moral obligations are assimilated on a selective basis only, that is, if they are perceived as leading to ego enhancement. In moral judgment the saliency of this ego-enhancement criterion is seen in the adoption of a rational-objective orientation. The nonsatellizer's conformity to moral rules is, therefore, based on the principle of expediency; those moral obligations that lead to the acquisition of earned status are selectively assimilated. His moral value system is, thus, functional and based on mutual obligations leading to ego enhancement.

During late childhood, nonsatellizers become capable of internalizing moral values and obligations on an exploratory orientation basis. Unhampered by satellizing loyalties, they find it easier to grasp functional concepts of moral law based on equity and reciprocal obligations. In this way they too may acquire the prerequisites for a guilt-governed conscience.

But the stability of moral obligations that circumvent a preliminary history of satellization is highly precarious for two reasons: (1) infantile irresponsibility had never been attenuated by strong, emotionally charged feelings of obligation toward significant figures in the child's interpersonal world, and (2) powerful needs for ego enhancement are often in conflict with the content and goals of ethical norms. Under these conditions, nevertheless, moral obligations are seldom repudiated outright, since this would result in direct and inexpedient vulnerability to cultural sanctions.

However, two less drastic alternatives are available: (1) indirect evasion of the demands of conscience and the punishment of guilt when the needs of ego aggrandizement are too strong to be denied, and (2) buttressing conscience by the mechanism of reaction formation when moral obligations are too solidly entrenched to be circumvented.

Moral obligation may be evaded by either: (1) selectively inhibiting the self-critical faculty so that, when expedient, even glaring discrepancies between precept and practice cannot be perceived, or (2) claiming superior status so that one is perceived by oneself as *above* the law for *ordinary* people.

Reaction formation rigidly suppresses motives that are at variance with internalized moral obligations and substitutes more acceptable motives in their place. Nevertheless, many loopholes for surreptitious circumvention are still present. Antisocial trends can often be expressed under the guise of lofty ideals. At the very best, the moral behavior of the nonsatellizer becomes unspontaneous, stereotyped, and unduly circumscribed. Awareness of the underlying strength of unacceptable motives encourages the erection of exaggerated defenses.

Overvalued children who have never felt much pressure to conform to parental standards frequently regard themselves as exempt from ordinary moral obligations. Rejected children, on the other hand, are not likely to claim such unique exemptions, since they have been subjected to rigorous discipline. In most instances they will acquire a strong rational conscience buttressed by reaction formation and permitting occasional moral lapses through impairment of the self-critical faculty.

However, the concomitance of harsh rejection and extreme self-assertiveness in the child may result in the latter repudiating the entire fabric of parental moral values; the resulting personality structure and correlated type of delinquency is known as aggressive, antisocial psychopathy.

When rejection is expressed by parental neglect, hostility, self-love, or inordinate injustice, children displace the hostility they feel for their parents onto others. Such behavior is reinforced by the parents' tendency to condone it as long as they themselves are not disturbed. On the positive side, rejected children possess a latent capacity for forming satellizing-like relationships that enable them to experience the type of guilt feelings that occur in satellizing children.

In Satellizers

Among satellizers, aberrations in conscience development are generally less severe. The more serious problem is presented by underdominated children who have great difficulty acquiring a sense of moral obligation. To begin with, they are not required to inhibit hedonistic motivations or to curb aggressive impulses. The limits of unacceptable behavior are poorly defined and inadequately or inconsistently enforced.

Second, like overvalued children, they are sometimes treated as specially privileged persons, exempt from usual responsibilities toward others and are not encouraged to develop a realistic self-critical faculty.

Capricious and inconsistent parental discipline is associated with lack of self-discipline in children and is more characteristic of delinquents than of nondelinquents. Fortunately the motivation for immoral behavior is more likely to lie in hedonistic self-indulgence than in unprincipled ego aggrandizement at the expense of others.

A reciprocal, interactive relationship between children and parents is more likely to promote moral responsibility than is an underdominant or overdominant relationship. The chief difficulty in moral development for overprotected and overdominated children, on the other hand, lies in transferring feelings of moral obligation from parents to society and in arriving at independent value judgments. Even when delinquent behavior does occur in such children, self-critical capacity and guilt are still substantially correlated with more mature moral judgment levels. This situation has less serious consequences if the parents are alive and do not subscribe to antisocial attitudes. If the parents are moral deviants, however, uncritical loyalty on the part of the child can lead to delinquent behavior, whereas the death or removal of the parents can create a vacuum in moral responsibility.

Personality Factors in Children

Ascendence and visceral drive are probably important temperamental factors influencing the course of conscience development. The more self-assertive and volitionally independent children are, the more likely they will be to resist the imposition of parental standards upon their behavior. Similarly, the greater their need for hedonistic satisfactions, the more reluctant they will be to accept the obligation of conforming to rules aimed at minimizing these satisfactions.

Dishonest children tend to be impulsive, emotionally unstable, and suggestible. Delinquents may also be more prone, for temperamental reasons, to utilize aggression as a defense or status-gaining mechanism. In contrast to nondelinquents, they have been described as more restless, active, impulsive, and danger-loving.

Cognitive Factors

Since values and moral behavior obviously have a cognitive aspect, we could reasonably anticipate that they would be influenced by both intelligence and moral knowledge. A minimal degree of intelligence is required for acquiring abstract principles of moral value, for perceiving the moral expectations of the culture, for anticipating the consequences of behavior, and for appreciating the advantages of conforming to social norms. Thus, it is not surprising that most theorists agree that intelligence and moral behavior are related. However, although the correlations between them have consistently been found to be positive, the degree of correlation has typically been quite low.

Moral conduct also presupposes moral knowledge. It seems, however, that intelligence and moral knowledge are only significantly related to moral behavior when they fall below a certain critical level. Beyond this point, personality and motivational factors are probably the crucial determining factors. Moral behavior is not simply a matter of the intellect but involves the total personality. However, it would be a mistake to equate moral knowledge with moral judgment and moral reasoning with moral behavior.

Tests of moral reasoning correlate positively with intelligence. Moral judgment is only moderately correlated with IQ but quite highly related to age, with intelligence controlled. Intellectual development, then, is an important condition for the development of moral thought, but level of moral thought can be clearly distinguished from general intellectual level.

Substantial correlations between moral *conduct* and intelligence have also been obtained. Further, intellectually "superior" children surpass their "average" contemporaries in such traits as conscientiousness, perseverance, prudence, and truthfulness.

The following factors, therefore, probably contribute to the positive relationship found between intelligence and certain kinds of moral traits:

1. Brighter children are better able to perceive the expectations of their culture and to learn appropriate forms of conduct. They can also perceive more accurately which character traits are required for academic and/or vocational success.
2. The personality traits that correlate most highly with intelligence are also most highly prized by middle-class homes, and as already pointed out, intelligence test scores are positively related to social status.
3. Highly motivated children tend to be persistent, stable, and responsible and to make the most of their intellectual endowment by continually exercising their cognitive capacities and by performing maximally on intelligence tests.

The moderately positive relationship between intelligence and honesty can, therefore, be largely attributed to such extrinsic considerations as having less reason to cheat in order to do well in schoolwork and being shrewd enough to avoid detection or inadvisable opportunities for cheating. This interpretation is supported by the fact that intelligence correlates more highly with moral conduct than does moral knowledge.

Evidently then intelligence affects moral conduct less by influencing moral knowledge than in some extraneous fashion. Mental deficiency occurs more frequently among delinquents than nondelinquents, and the mean IQ of the former is also somewhat lower.

Scores on moral knowledge are not highly correlated with moral conduct and fail to differentiate between delinquents and nondelinquents. Thus, low IQ per se cannot be an important etiological factor in delinquency, but may constitute one of the larger constellation of factors associated with depressed socioeconomic conditions that contribute to the development of delinquent behavior. Intellectual deficit, for example, increases suggestibility, the tendency to take unwise chances, and the probability of apprehension.

Guilt Reduction as Motivation

It will be recalled that the individual's recognition, acknowledgment, or admission that a behavioral act of his has violated both one of his particular internalized moral values, and a sense of obligation on his part to conform his behavior to all of the internalized moral values embodied in his conscience, typically instigates uncomfortable, and even emotionally painful, guilt feelings.

Of course, the person's anticipation that these guilt feelings will occur, if he submits to the temptation of committing the immoral act in question, may be sufficient to enable him both to avoid the latter act (by inhibiting the misbehavior) and the guilt feelings that would otherwise follow it. Thus, guilt feelings may, in a sense, be both a form of endogenous punishment for immoral behavior, as well as an effective and a highly prevalent deterrent for same. Both this emotionally distressful part of these guilt feelings and their potential deterrent effects are integral component aspects of conscience considered as a process or mechanism, the function of which is the internal or self-regulation of moral conduct.

Assuming that the immoral behavior is actually committed despite the deterrent effects of the anticipated and resultant guilt feelings and their associated concomitants (anxiety, culpability, remorse, feelings of disloyalty, diminished self-esteem, regret, humiliation, self-reproach, self-disgust, etc.), how can these feelings of guilt be reduced or minimized so that the individual suffers less emotional discomfort, and that the moral blemishes disfiguring his ethical self-image can be removed as efficaciously as possible?

In the everyday behavior of human beings, self-justification constitutes an impelling and ubiquitous motivation. The picture of self as shameful and contemptible is highly threatening to self-esteem and is productive of considerable anxiety. Hence, we can expect that guilt-reduction mechanisms will, for the most part, parallel those involved in anxiety reduction.

Specific Guilt-Reduction Mechanisms

The most commonly used mechanism of guilt reduction is repression. However, repression of guilt is not the primary cause of even symptomatic anxiety, but is mainly a consequence of it. Conscious guilt is repressed because it is anxiety-producing. This repression, in turn, intensifies the anxiety because repression obviates the possibility of punishment, confession, expiation, and other guilt-reducing mechanisms. It is true that repression can never be complete, as demonstrated, for example, by the appearance of repressed guilt feelings in dreams. This incompleteness of repression, however, does not provide a convincing explanation for the conversion of guilt into anxiety since we know: (1) that conscious guilt can be productive of anxiety; and (2) that repression interferes with the development of guilt-reduction mechanisms.

Projection of guilt is a still more effective means of guilt reduction, since in this fashion accountability is not merely repressed but is actually *disowned* by perceiving the moral blame elsewhere. This, of course, involves distortion of evidence similar to what happens in rationalization. Through dissociation, depersonalization, amnesic states, and states of multiple personality, it is possible to divorce segments of behavior from the sense of personal identity and thereby to disown all connection with the associated guilt. Obsessions displace concern away from the genuine source of guilt feelings and monopolize the field of consciousness with relatively innocuous material, whereas compulsions may often symbolize a form of expiation. In another type of displacement, a person may feel consciously guilty for not pleasing authorities, while "unconsciously" he feels guilty for not living up to his own expectation of himself.

More direct forms of guilt reduction include punishment, confession, and expiation, all of which are extensively employed by various religions. Social punishment, namely, that form of punishment imposed from without or made known to others, can confer almost complete absolution. Confession involves the preliminary phase of punishment: self-culpability is exposed to others so that their condemnation can be secured in place of self-condemnation that has less guilt-reducing properties. A variant of this mechanism is found in the self-accusatory, auditory hallucination. However, it is obviously more guilt-reducing for a latent homosexual ostensibly to hear "external" voices accusing him of being a "loathsome fairy" than to accuse himself of the same tendency. A patient of the author ceased hearing such voices after gaining insight into this mechanism, but soon began to hear motors humming. When in turn this symbolic substitution was understood, the motors vanished only to be replaced by overt symptoms of anxiety.

Expiation is a form of punishment emphasizing restitution or exaggeration of the particular moral trait or virtue in relation to which a sense of guilt is experienced. A typical example of the latter variety is the adjustive mechanism known as reaction formation, for example, the mother who feels excessively guilty for rejecting tendencies may become inflexibly oversolicitous toward her child.

Various formal and culturally stereotyped varieties of guilt reduction are also available, such as verbal magic, pseudoremorse, and hypocritical religious devotions. Thus, many persons tend to believe that if they make a formal, verbalistic show of remorse, confession, and self-castigation, their guilt is absolved. The insincerity of this maneuver is revealed by the fact that their remorse is often offered as a preface to the actual execution of the behavior that is otherwise verbally condemned.

The more morally bankrupt certain people become—the more incapable of experiencing genuine feelings of guilt—the more they seek out the formal moral respectability that comes with ritualistic observances. They wish to continue their immoral practices and still enjoy a reputation for righteousness. Sometimes, of course, they must suffer continuous chastisement by hearing their hypocrisy berated by the clergy. But even this does not faze them. Furthest from their thoughts is a desire for genuine reforms; and at the same time they are too shameless to be offended by moral reproach. What happens, therefore, is a sentimental orgy in which tears of pseudoremorse and self-pity are shed as their immorality is exposed; and once having shed these tears, they are convinced that they are both morally acquitted and entitled to pursue all over again the same unprincipled path. This kind of orientation to religious observance is sometimes referred to as pietistic.

Tolerance for Conscious Guilt

It is not necessary to believe, however, that all guilt feelings are intolerable and must somehow be repressed, disowned, rationalized, confessed, expiated for, and so forth. In the same sense that there is tolerance for conscious anxiety, there is tolerance for conscious guilt, the degree of tolerance, of course, being subject to wide individual differences. Man's portrait of himself need not be free of all moral blemishes. Hence, a good deal of ordinary guilt can be acknowledged on a conscious level and taken in stride without any efforts made toward guilt reduction. There is reason to believe that the intrinsically secure person who is moderately self-sufficient possesses more guilt tolerance than either the insecure or the overly dependent individual.

In our culture we tend to underestimate man's capacity for moral depravity.[2] We tend to assume that people could not conceivably be guilty of certain immoral intentions and practices because if they were, "How could they possibly live with themselves?" And even if we do admit such a possibility, we reveal the impact of psychological determinism, psychoanalytic doctrine, and moral relativism on our thinking by blaming "unconscious motives" and by absolving the individual from moral accountability on the grounds that he is the innocent product (victim) of his heredity and environment. "How could he have possibly acted in any other way?"

Several alternative explanations, however, should be considered. First, most people can tolerate more conscious guilt than we are willing to concede; we have exaggerated man's need for perceiving himself as completely untainted in a moral sense. Second, many times when we think that a person should be experiencing guilt feelings he really is not for one or both of two good reasons: (1) no real internalization of moral values or of moral obligation to conform conduct to same has taken place; or (2) self-criticism is inhibited to the point where no discrepancy can be perceived between behavior and obligation, regardless of how flagrant the disparity may appear to others.

It is necessary to differentiate this latter situation from instances in which: (1) guilt is actually experienced but wrongdoing is still denied because of pride, inability to admit being in the wrong, and outright intellectual dishonesty; (2) guilt occurs but is rationalized away without conscious awareness of distortion or misrepresentation of facts; and (3) very little guilt is actually experienced because either a double standard of judgment is used—one for himself and another for everyone else—or else the individual claims a "special entitlement" to commit the category of immoral acts in question.

The Special Roles of Ideas of Culpability and Entitlement

In the sequence of cognitive-emotional conscience processes culminating in guilt and related feelings, it is clear that acknowledgment of a discrepancy between (1) an internalized moral value and (2) an obligation to conform moral behavior to it is prerequisite to experiencing feelings of culpability. These latter feelings of culpability are, therefore, crucially important because if they are not present all of the other internal consequences of moral misconduct (e.g., shame, guilt, anxiety, remorse, etc.) cannot be experienced.

Ideas of special entitlement are an especially pernicious, conscience-less, and guilt-reducing mechanism used by predatory, antisocial personalities and by self-designated members of fanatical hate groups. Because of their membership in these groups, they feel specially privileged to violate certain moral and criminal laws without incurring any moral or criminal culpability or liability for their actions.

The mental-hygiene value of keeping guilt on a conscious level parallels the advantages of dealing with anxiety on the same basis: The possibilities of evolving constructive solutions are greatly enhanced. In the case of the former, this means learning to bear and live with one's quota of guilt while taking such realistic preventive and restitutive measures as are indicated. Where legitimate compromises with moral principles are clearly necessary, the reasons for same should be unambiguously perceived and acknowledged as such rather than rationalized on a more acceptable basis. In this way it is possible to retain one's moral code intact under the most trying of circumstances. Unless the reasons for unavoidable moral expediency are kept clearly in mind, habituation to and corruption by convenient deviations from moral responsibility tend to occur; and what may start out as a reluctant maneuver under duress ends up by becoming an individual's characteristic mode of ethical behavior.

Lapses of Conscience

Although conscience, as thus formed and constituted (as indicated above), appears to function reasonably well in most psychosocial and interpersonal settings and instances, in keeping individual conduct within the bounds of moral and legal propriety, many reasons exist both for serious and/or habitual moral delinquency in some persons and for only occasional and less serious lapses of conscience in others: (1) weak internalization of moral values or of the moral obligation to conform conduct to same, because of defective child-rearing attitudes (e.g., rejection, overvaluation, valuation for ulterior motives, overpermissiveness, overdomination, etc.); (2) inordinate temperamental needs of the child for autonomy and volitional independence; (3) identification with delinquent parent values; (4) overidentification with the lax and deviant moral values and practices of the peer group; (5) persistent denial or refusal to perceive the existing discrepancy between conduct and internalized moral values (i.e., to acknowledge culpability); (6) undeveloped or impaired self-critical ability and excessive extropunitiveness (the general tendency to blame others rather than oneself for wrongdoing); (7) the use of double standards of judgment, that is, a lenient one for oneself and a stringent one for everyone else; (8) ideas of special entitlement, that is, beliefs that one is specially privileged to violate certain moral and criminal laws without incurring any moral or legal culpability or liability for their consequences; and (9) minimization or rationalization of the seriousness of the offense in question.

Thus, it is quite possible for even sincerely moral persons seeking justice and equity to evade the strictures of conscience and then to delude themselves into believing that their consciences are "clear," when to the objective and disinterested observer, this is actually very far from being the case.

People frequently express shock and amazement in questioning how it is possible for someone to live with a particular "mortal sin," or with the weight of guilt for same, on his conscience. In part this is because they often lose sight of the many different ways in which culpability and guilt can be evaded, even by persons with apparently sound consciences.

Actually the answer to this latter question of how it is possible for someone to live with a very large burden of sin or guilt on his conscience is not that difficult: (1) some people have never developed functional consciences or the capacity for experiencing genuine guilt feelings at all; (2) in the case of many more others, one or more of the nine reasons listed above are operative in explaining why the dictates of whatever semblance of conscience they may have developed tend to be effectively circumvented; and (3) more people can live comfortably with a very high burden of conscious and warranted guilt feelings than is generally appreciated or thought to be the case. Hence, the frequently heard assertion that an individual's conscience is clear should not be taken too seriously or at face value. For the reasons already given, the conclusions reached by almost all persons with consciences regarding culpability and guilt are quite fallible, at least in part.

People frequently tend to defend themselves against a charge of malice by saying, "I did not *mean* to hurt you." Actually this says very little about their actual intent or motives in this regard because in our culture most individuals tend to overlearn the interpersonal principle that "nice" persons do not deliberately intend to hurt others or at least are not aware of any such intention. Thus, they will either repress hostile intentions and hence be consciously unaware of these intents, or else resort either to sins of omission (which are less obviously hostile) or to more indirect or disguised sins of commission.

Cultural Factors Influencing Moral Development

Cultural and social-class factors affect the development of conscience and account for intercultural differences (or intracultural uniformities) by influencing the particular moral values that are assimilated and their mode of transmission, the kinds of internal and external sanctions that are imposed, and the ways in which guilt feelings are instigated and expressed. The effects of these types of factors are exceedingly pervasive but differ in that individuals are typically influenced by the norms of other social classes but only rarely by the standards of other cultures. Although conscience is commonly reified or personified in folklore and colloquial discourse, it is not an "inner wee voice" telling us what to do and what not to do. We are not born with a conscience but rather only with a potentiality for developing one from our genic constitution (genotype) and from our interpersonal and cultural environments.

Because man's potentiality for acquiring a conscience is largely a function of his human genotype, its acquisition and distribution are universal, that is, it occurs in all cultures; and it is fortunate indeed that it does do so, because without the existence of individual consciences, few if any cultures could survive very long. It is only because most men want to conform most of the time to the general mores, as well as to the more specific norms of their own cultures (because they have consciences), and are monitored and policed for the most part by their own consciences in so doing, that cultural institutions, traditions, customs, and norms as well as interpersonal relations, transactions, and agreements can function reliably and predictably enough to sustain the division of labor and the cooperative living and working arrangements on which cultural existence depends. Otherwise total surveillance or some other form of purely external control would be necessary to enforce the necessary compliances; and this would not only be prohibitively impractical and expensive, but would also prove to be ineffective and unworkable.

Some cultural anthropologists have all but dichotomized various cultures as either guilt- (conscience-) or shame-regulated. They perceive the Japanese, for example, as shame-regulated. But when interpersonal behavior in the latter culture is actually observed, it is more often found to be responsive to the sanctions of guilt rather than of shame. Shame and guilt, furthermore, are by no means mutually preclusive; both normally occur when an individual perceives his conduct to be at variance with his internalized moral values of the culture. Shame is normally part of the guilt response to the perception of one's culpability, in addition to occurring independently of guilt. Lastly it seems quite plausible to interpret guilt-like behavior among the Japanese as indicative of genuine guilt since the capacity for developing such behavior is a genotypic potentiality of men in all cultures.

Social Class Factors

It has already been observed that differential social environment within a culture exerts a profound influence on various aspects of ego development. Hence, it would certainly be legitimate to inquire to what extent the development of conscience is influenced by the value systems of the social groups to which the individual belongs, or to which he relates himself positively or negatively. The values held by the family, by the dominant groups and institutions in the community, and by persons in positions of authority and high status constitute the "moral climate" in which a young person grows up. These groups and persons are in a position to punish undesirable conduct and reward desirable conduct, and their expectations have much to do with the standards of behavior developed by the individual.

Within a given social-class environment and peer group, not only are there distinctive educational and vocational aspirations and accepted forms of social participation for adolescents, but also characteristic moral values relating to sex, aggression, honesty, community responsibility, thrift, loyalty, and so forth. These value systems in the peer group parallel for the most part the value systems espoused by the adult members of the subculture despite the well-known refractoriness of adolescents to adult direction; the peer culture simply takes over the task of enforcing this conformity since adolescents can accept its authority without resentment.

This differentiation of moral value systems on the basis of social class does not mean that complete homogeneity prevails within a given class. Actually, considerable interaction and interchange occur, with the lines of influence generally proceeding in a downward direction. Where a single institution such as the high school becomes the common meeting ground of a number of subcultural groups, the moral standards of the resulting adolescent peer society reflect the morality of the middle class which controls it. Adolescents from other social class backgrounds

must either adapt to these standards or choose to remain on the periph-
ery of social acceptance.

In the light of these considerations, therefore, the proposition that a
given individual must *inevitably* assimilate the particular values of his
own social class is absurd, although it is true that this phenomenon is
facilitated by the presence of segregation and "disorganized areas" in large
urban centers. Equally implausible, on the other hand, is the notion advanced in some quarters that modern forms of communication have *completely* broken down class differences in moral beliefs and behavior.

A general problem transcending social-class differences is the impact
of culture on conscience development when serious discrepancies or inconsistencies prevail between the professed (official) moral ideology of
the culture and the ideology that is really believed and actually practiced.
This situation is illustrated in our culture by the formal endorsement of
humility, kindliness, helpfulness, and fair play and the simultaneous
overvaluation of aggressiveness, prestige, and success at any price. It is
symptomatic of both a rate of social and economic change that has by far
outstripped its ideological substrate and of widespread moral disintegration and confusion.

The gap between official and actual moral ideology is perhaps most
marked in lower-class children since their parents do not consistently enforce middle-class standards despite verbal affirmation of same. Furthermore, the teachings of middle-class parents are reinforced by other cultural
agencies such as school, church, and community organizations. The lower-
class child, on the other hand, experiences considerable conflict between
the ethical standards of his home and the moral expectations of his teachers
and Sunday school and club leaders but typically resolves it by participating in few activities outside the home, neighborhood, and his peer group.

What it means for a child or adolescent to grow up in a culture with such
a moral gap is something that still requires considerable investigation. We
can only predict that it will bring out the worst aspects of the rational-objective orientation in moral behavior, encouraging expediency, lack of principle, and cynical acceptance of moral depravity. We can expect children
to grow up unconcerned with human values and the welfare of others, indifferent to the existence of injustice, and sold on the attitude of getting the
most out of people and valuing them solely on the basis of their market
price. The character traits that will impress them most will be duplicity,
hypocrisy, insincerity, chicanery, and double-dealing.

Many children may conceivably fail to perceive that any problem of moral inconsistency exists; others may be acutely disillusioned, and still others may perceive the problem but fail to be disturbed by it. This type of moral climate is, in a sense, made to order for the ego needs of the nonsatellizer, except when he or she happens to have a strong rational conscience.

On the other hand, the satellizer who perceives what is going on is often unable to make the required adaptations without experiencing feelings of conflict, guilt, and resentment toward a culture that requires such moral compromises for the sake of survival and legitimate ego enhancement.

At the very best, this situation leads to ethical confusion and inconsistency and a potentially heavy burden of guilt. However, because of the prestige suggestion inherent in the operation of social norms, and because of extremely high tolerance for moral ambiguity, inconsistent values may be assimilated in such a way that their incompatibility is never perceived. It is presumed by the perceiver that inconsistency in cultural values is inconceivable; hence, an advance "set" exists to perceive such values as consistent regardless of their manifest content, and consequently, logic-tight compartments must be constructed. Even if perceived, awareness of moral inconsistency and culpability may be subsequently repressed or disowned.

Positive relationships have been reported between lower social-class status in children and both more absolutistic, rigid, and authoritarian conceptions of moral law and more primitive and retaliatory notions of discipline. Middle-class children react to their own transgressions with more self-criticism than do their lower-class counterparts. This situation is undoubtedly reflective, in part, of the authoritarian lower-class parent-child relationship and of inconsistent training in the "official" moral ideology; since the latter is accepted only halfheartedly and is inconsistently enforced, it must be adhered to rigidly if it is to be maintained at all. In middle-class families there appears to be greater homogeneity of values than in lower-class families.

Middle-class children are also consistently more honest and truthful, and parents also mainly use a verbal medium of discipline and explicit withdrawal of affection. Moreover, lower-class parents exercise less immediate control over their children's activities and seem to give their attention primarily to overt manifestations of transgression. The more direct kind of punishment utilized in lower-class families seems to sensitize children to the external consequences of transgression.

Middle-class children anticipate assuming responsibilities earlier than do lower-class children, but this may be more reflective of social stratification than of parental upbringing. The fact is that lower-class children do not and cannot feel as much of a sense of power in, and responsibility for, the institutions of government and economy as do middle-class children. This lack of participation generates less disposition to view these institutions from a generalized, flexible, and organized perspective based on various roles as vantage points; that is, law and government are perceived quite differently by children if they feel a sense of potential participation in the social order than if they do not.

Social-class differences with respect to certain aspects of moral development appear to have been diminishing over the past thirty years. In some cognitive aspects of conscience development, as a matter of fact, recently obtained differences are negligible. This phenomenon may reflect the diminution of class differences, over this period of time, in child-rearing practices.

The diminishing class differences may also reflect, partly, the negative effects of decreasing social involvement on the part of middle-class children in the new suburban "bedroom communities" with transient populations. These children are cut off from close interaction with adult social models and also receive less parental supervision. They are more likely to feel hostile to adults, to be more peer-oriented, and to be less integrated into society than children in older, more stable communities. These conditions are, thus, likely to promote juvenile delinquency such as is found under certain lower-socioeconomic conditions.

A moderately high positive relationship exists between social class and the character reputation of adolescents, which cannot be explained on the basis of prevailing stereotypes about social class. It seems more likely that the determining factor in this relationship is conformity to school requirements, which in turn implies acceptance of middle-class values. This interpretation is substantiated in part by the high relationship between school achievement and character reputation and the comparatively low relationship between school achievement and social-class membership.

Notes

1. According to Freudian doctrine, conscience is usually regarded as synonymous with the superego, and as the successor to the Oedipus Complex.

2. The reason for this cultural reluctance to perceive unethical tendencies in others is partly a historical reaction to the witch-hunting proclivities of previous generations, and partly an institutionalized defense against insecurity, that is, there is less reason to be fearful if people are generally perceived as more benevolent than they really are.

II

Clinical Applications

4

General Psychopathology

In this chapter I shall attempt a systematic application of the dynamics of ego development to the pathogenesis of the behavior disorders. What is needed now is a more formal classification of these disorders so that the relationships of the various diagnostic categories to their developmental matrices and to each other can be more readily appreciated.

The proposed system of classification is based on the assumption that developmental factors in ego formation represent the most salient and critical factors in the etiology of personality and behavioral psychopathology, and account most meaningfully for the differences in onset, symptomatology, and prognosis that hold for the recognized clinical entities. This by no means rules out the importance of other interpersonal, cultural, or situational factors, or of other aspects of personality development. By definition, however, classification in science aims at defining relationships between phenomenological entities in terms of the most prepotent factors responsible for their evolution and with the least possible degree of overlapping categories.

The Ego-Development Approach

The principal theoretical implication of naturalistic ego psychology for the psychopathology of the mental disorders is that both normal and aberrant personality, that is, largely ego, functioning, can be most cogently understood and explained in terms of an individual's ego structure and development at any given point in his or her life cycle. More specifically, because ego structure in large measure reflects how, and in what manner, he or she had traversed the two critical transitional phases of ego development, namely, the ego devaluation (satellization) and desatellization crises described above, it behooves the psychopathologist to pay scrupulous attention to patients' ego development. This is why detailed attention was devoted to the three principal stages of ego development, to their determinants and developmental outcomes, and to the implications of these outcomes both for current and later, normal and impaired, ego functioning and development, as well as for current and later vulnerability to particular kinds of mental disorder.

In other words, the hypothesized most significant and critical factors predisposing individuals to various mental disorders, in my view, are developmental defects (i.e., complete or partial deficiencies, failure, distortion) that arise at crucial transitional phases of ego development. This does not imply in the least that these above causal factors are simply determinative, but rather that they interact with genic, temperamental, and coping predispositions; with the individual's degree of exposure and resistance to stress; and with his adjustive and adaptive reactions to situational vicissitudes. Mental disorders, like all complex behavioral and social phenomena, are obviously a product of multiple causality. I choose to classify them in terms of their developmental history and outcomes largely because these factors, in my opinion, have the greatest discriminating power in delineating etiological, functional, and phenomenological similarities and differences among the various clinical psychiatric syndromes, as well as exhibit greater explanatory power than the causal factors implicated in other possible classificatory schemes.

The Major Differential Factor: Satellizer versus Nonsatellizer

Broadly speaking then with certain notable exceptions, most persons can be divided into two main groups in terms of ego development outcomes and susceptibility or vulnerability to the various mental disorders, namely, satellizers and nonsatellizers. This, of course, should hardly come as a surprise to anyone who is familiar with the tremendous ego changes that accompany satellization. If these changes characterize the personality functioning of the satellizer, then the absence of these same changes in a nonsatellizer should be equally conspicuous and determinative, making this dichotomous pair of contrasting opposites a natural basis for a psychopathological classification.

Because of the incomparably attractive features of satellization for the child's self-esteem, namely, guaranteed intrinsic feelings of adequacy and security related to his derived status as a satellizer, the great mental health hazard confronting satellizers is failure to undergo ego maturation or desatellization under those familial and/or cultural conditions fostering exaggerated satellization—that is, intensifying it unduly or overextending it in time. The principal disorders of ego maturation (desatellization) that emerge under these conditions are: (1) early, insidiously developing Process Schizophrenia in individuals with schizoid and introverted temperaments (hedonistic and narcissistic gratification in fantasy); and (2) Inadequate and Immature Personality Disorders—hedonistic and narcissistic gratification in reality (acting out of motivationally immature drives and impulses).

Corresponding to the major underlying ego development defects in satellizers (i.e., oversatellization; failure to desatellize or to undergo ego maturation) that gives rise to such psychopathology as Process Schizophrenia and Inadequate Personality Disorder are the following comparable indications of such general underlying psychopathology in nonsatellizers as lack of derived status, low intrinsic security and self-esteem, inordinate need for earned status and volitional independence, and unrealistically high and tenacious aspirations for achievement.

Some of the more specific mental disorders in nonsatellizers that follow from the latter predisposing factors include: ego hypertrophy or anxiety disorders[1] (contributing, for example, to the rejected nonsatellizer's impaired self-esteem, which is inherent in the childhood rejection scenario itself, is his long history of defeat of his unrealistically high and tenacious aspirations for achievement and for compensatory earned status); disorders that serve as defenses against anxiety or guilt, for example, phobias, delusions, hypochondriasis, obsessions, compulsions, dissociative disorders; and complications of anxiety, for example, Reactive Schizophrenia, agitated and retarded depression,[2] and Mania.

As stated above, nonsatellizers generally do not manifest failure in ego maturation at adolescence because they do not satellize to begin with and, thus, do not have to desatellize, and also because they have been striving continuously for high current academic and future vocational status throughout childhood and adolescence. However, teenagers, especially girls, who are paradoxically subjected by parents to increased (rather than reduced) restrictions at adolescence, often react vindictively against their parents by repudiating and sabotaging the goals of adult ego maturation. Thus, they unexpectedly develop a form of psychopathology that is phenotypically (clinically) indistinguishable from clinical Inadequate and

Immature Personality Disorder, although having a very atypical geno-typic (nonsatellizing) history in childhood.

The latter defense mechanisms referred to above may be conceptualized as follows: (1) *rationalization*—providing good or acceptable (but not always credible or plausible) reason(s) to justify or make tolerable unacceptable attitudes, motives, feelings, or behavior; (2) *minimization*—an attempt to justify, or make more acceptable intrinsically unacceptable behavior by understating its consequences, frequency, severity, significance, and so forth ; (3) *displacement*—transferring the source or target of a negative emotion, such as fear or hostility, from its original source or target to a less disturbing and more acceptable substitute; (4) *reaction formation*—the development of conscious, socially acceptable activity that is diametrically opposite to its repressed counterpart that is inaccessible to awareness; (5) *dissociation*—the splitting off (segregation) from consciousness of certain memories or mental sequences from the main body of consciousness which then function independently and are inaccessible to the latter, and vice versa; (6) *projection*—a defense mechanism in which anxiety, feelings of guilt or inadequacy, and unacceptable ideas or motives are disowned by attributing them to others.

The following definitions apply to specific mental disorders that also defend against anxiety or guilt: *Phobia*—displacement of the source of fear or anxiety from an unidentifiable or irremediable object or situation to a more identifiable and tangible situation that can be more readily avoided; (2) *Hypochondriasis*—a chronic condition in which one is morbidly preoccupied with one's own physical or mental health and believes that one is suffering from a grave bodily disease, but without demonstrable organic or pathophysiological findings; (3) *Conversion Hysteria*—a neurotic condition in which unconscious conflict, or the psychosocial threat ordinarily causing anxiety, induces gross functional deficits in the special senses or in the voluntary musculature (i.e., paralysis); (4) *obsession*—an intrusive, unwanted idea or emotion that tends to persist and monopolize the center stage of consciousness, thus preventing the entrance of other threatening ideas or emotions; (5) *compulsion*—an unwanted, insistent, repetitive, intrusive, irresistible impulse to do something which is against the will or moral norms of the individual, and which is also socially unacceptable—failure to perform the act in question gives rise to overt anxiety; and (6) *Mania*—an affective state of elation, euphoria, and unwarranted feelings of extreme well-being, characterized also by expansiveness, grandiosity, pressure of speech, loquacity, flight of ideas, hyperactivity, and diminished need for sleep.

In both Process Schizophrenia and Inadequate and Immature Personality Disorders, generally occurring in satellizers, it will be recalled that ego devaluation, as well as preliminary (childhood) maturation and attenuation of infantile ego attributes, take place normally. That is, these children are generally accepted and intrinsically valued by parents (although some are also treated in an overpermissive, overprotected, overdominated, or underdominated manner) and hence undergo normal early satellization. Preliminary increments in executive independence, sense of responsibility, and frustration tolerance occur normally during childhood and are implicitly internalized on the basis of personal loyalty. But presumably because of genic predispositions, various temperamental qualities, and, particularly, because of certain pervasive parent attitudes (e.g., overprotection, overindulgence, overpermissiveness, underdomination, or overdomination), normal ego maturation (desatellization) fails to take place. Introverted and schizoid children with this type of personality structure are, thus, extremely vulnerable to *Process* Schizophrenia, whereas extroverted children tend to become Inadequate and Immature personalities strongly predisposed toward seeking drug-induced euphoria.

The underlying developmental history and psychopathology in Infantile Autism and childhood Schizophrenia, on the other hand, are markedly different despite basic similarities in parent child-rearing attitudes and in gross clinical appearance to Process Schizophrenia. Unlike Process Schizophrenia and Inadequate and Immature Personality Disorder, however, ego devaluation and satellization do not occur in Infantile Autism probably because of a potent, genically determined incapacity for relating emotionally to others—not because of rejection or extrinsic valuation by parents. In these latter disorders the basic psychopathology is not failure to desatellize, since this eventuality pertains to a future developmental task that will not be encountered yet for several years, but rather the failure to satellize in the first place, presumably because of a relatively rarely occurring difficulty in (or incapacity for) relating emotionally to others, or in exhibiting normal attachment behavior. This can be best explained on the basis of prepotent genic predispositions, coupled both with secondary disturbance of communication skills and with bizarre behavior reflective of the absence of normal manifestations of attachment and of corresponding patterns of communication.

Very similar underlying psychopathology is typically found in under-socialized Conduct Disorder (especially in the aggressive subgroup) and in Antisocial Personality Disorder. In these latter disorders, for the most part, the principal locus of the developmental deficit lies in the absence of internalized moral values and/or of moral obligations to conform their conduct to such values by exercising appropriate behavioral restraints.

Satellizing individuals who fail to undergo normal personality maturation in adolescence, however, are typically protected against Neurotic Anxiety and hence against its defenses and complications as well, because of their strong intrinsic feelings of adequacy and security, which is a product of the derived status they enjoy. Thus, they tend to feel adequate simply because they have had the experience of being accepted and intrinsically valued for themselves, irrespective of their prior or current level or capacity for achievement. Paradoxically, their self-esteem is also unnaturally high because of a poorly developed self-critical faculty. Because of this severe maturational defect or failure, however, they become functionally inadequate adults, incapable of acquiring both adult motivational and volitional status, as well as the personality traits necessary for their implementation.

Exceptions to the Satellizer-Nonsatellizer Dichotomy

The chief exceptions to this rule linking the genesis of Neurotic Anxiety to nonsatellization are: (1) high susceptibility to Separation Anxiety of Childhood and to Neurotic Anxiety in grossly overprotected and over-dependent satellizing children; and (2) vulnerability of satellizing children to anxiety disorders and depression following loss of a parent or parents because of death or divorce.

Contrariwise, failure to undergo ego maturation is quite rare in nonsatellizing children inasmuch as satellization does not occur in the first place. In a very real sense the goals of desatellization and ego maturation can, therefore, be said to be accomplished in advance, since there is obviously no need for a nonsatellizer to desatellize.

The reverse of this latter situation, as indicated above—later reactive maturational failure in nonsatellizers, resulting in motivational immaturity and inadequacy with respect to both ego-status and ego-maturity goals—occurs relatively frequently in adolescents following the paradoxical parental imposition of more restrictive discipline to which the latter react with both passive and active sabotage of these goals.

These latter three conditions, therefore, constitute the principal exceptions to the dichotomy of satellizers and nonsatellizers with respect to the categories of mental disorder associated respectively with each member of the dichotomy.

Determinants of Mental Disorder[3]

At this point it would be helpful to relate the developmental approach adopted in this book to the more general context of psychopathological determinants implicated in mental disorder. If we are to adhere to the general proposition that any complex psychopathological mental and/or behavioral outcome must be considered a summated resultant of various influences impinging upon an individual's psychological field, what are the relevant variables that should be considered in assessing the possibility that he may or may not develop a behavior disorder or a particular type of behavior disorder?

The following is a list of the principal factors that should be taken into account: (1) genetic predisposition as determined by a single dominant gene, two recessive genes, or polygenes; (2) inadequacy of constitutional defense factors (based on multifactorial genetic patterns) that do not provide sufficient resistance to mental disease; (3) the objective magnitude of the adjustive stress or deprivation confronting the individual; (4) predispositions arising from aberrant ego development, for example, lack of ego devaluation or maturation; (5) frustration tolerance, that is, the degree of frustration an individual can withstand before succumbing to either disruption of performance ability, loss of self-esteem, or lowering of aspirational level; (6) various subjective factors that determine to what extent deprivation will be interpreted, or reacted to, as frustration, that is, general level of prestige aspiration, specific ego involvement in a given activity, capacity for selective ego disinvolvement; (7) the self-critical faculty, that is, the ability or tendency to evaluate oneself more or less severely; (8) introversion-extroversion; (9) previous mode of adjustment to stress, that is, canalized types of adjustive mechanisms employed, and at what level of integration; (10) accessibility of motivations, attitudes, and emotions to consciousness, degree of insight into adjustive techniques; (11) level of energy or stamina; (12) complexity of personality organization; (13) level of neurophysiological irritability as influenced by fatigue, emotion, sleep deprivation, hormonal balance, and so forth; (14) level of resistance to stress situations in terms of reacting with somatic dysfunction (adrenocortical sufficiency); (15) tolerance for anxiety, guilt, ambiguity, and inconsistency; and (16) level of intelligence and problem-solving ability.

One reason why ego development is the central organizing factor in the etiology of behavior disorder (as has been shown in the preceding chapters) is because it crucially affects so many of the other important etiological factors, for example, level of prestige aspiration, self-critical faculty, introversion-extroversion, frustration tolerance, tolerance for anxiety and guilt, and so forth.

Experimental Psychopathology in Animals

Whether behavior disorder is a peculiar product of man's superior mental processes and the complexity of his cultural organization, or is a significantly different and more fundamental psychological pattern of response to frustration, adjustive stress, and conflict that is also found among most of the higher vertebrate species is a question that can only be answered by experimental animal psychopathology and comparative psychology. The conclusion to which I am led by the evidence presented below is that behavior disorder in man is continuous in kind with the disturbances manifested by lower animals, differing mainly in complexity, abstractness, degree of verbal symbolism, richness of subjective components, and importance of social determinism and ego relatedness.

As in man, *primary* behavior disorders in animals are also caused by psychosocial factors (e.g., excessive frustration, adjustive stress, and psychological conflict) in which neurobiological variables may play a mediating role, whereas *secondary* behavior disorders, as in man, reflect impairment of the neural substrate itself.

Pooling the results of these various "animal neuroses" experiments, we find the following general pattern emerging as characteristic of the resulting altered state of behavioral reactivity: First, in relation to the problem-solving situation itself, the animal reacts to a less intense and less specific stimulus with greater intensity and less specificity of behavior. There is a loss of differentiated behavior and a tendency toward rigid and "compulsive" perseveration of an unadaptive and even punished response. He cannot learn new responses even when the situation ceases being insoluble. At other times, complete blocking of response occurs, or regression to a more primitive type of solution.

Second, various general disturbances of behavior occur in some of the species and individuals studied: restlessness and excitement; tremors, quivering, and convulsive-like seizures; physiological signs of fear: various phobic manifestations; hypersensitivity to stimuli; exaggerated startle responses; cataleptic immobility and aimless hyperactivity; repetition of compulsive rituals and stereotyped behavior; extreme retardation of movement; refusal to take food; carelessness in disposition of feces; aggressive attacks on other animals; and substitutive bids for affection.

It is evident that this inventory of responses characterizing the neurotic altered state of behavioral reactivity is descriptive of a state of panic and disorganization, that is, the "catastrophic reaction." Anxiety in this latter state is merely the animal's subjective awareness of being immersed in the catastrophic situation. It is also evident that all behavior is not motivated and that all behavior in response to frustration is neither adjustive nor adaptive.

What relevance does the evidence concerning "experimental neurosis" in animals have for behavior disorders in human beings? How does it tie in with our theory of aberrant ego development as the principal variable in the etiology of such disorders? In the first place, it establishes behavior disorder as a fundamental psychobiological response pattern of higher animals to adjustive stress, a pattern that can be designated as a state of altered behavioral reactivity. Continuity prevails not only with respect to the causes of this altered behavioral condition, but also with respect to its component responses. These responses are reflective of both behavioral disorganization, which is maladaptive and maladjustive, and behavior that is compensatory and directed toward need reduction. But whereas frustration in animals must be related essentially to the objective magnitude of the threat, in humans subjective factors derived from ego development are more crucial, namely, magnitude and tenacity of aspirational level, frustration tolerance, the availability of intrinsic feelings of security and adequacy, and self-critical faculty; and in terms of response characteristics, human reactions are more verbal, symbolic, and ideational rather than occurring mostly on a motor and emotional plane.

Contrast to Human Psychopathology

In contrast to the foregoing description of experimental behavior disorder in animals, in which self-concepts play a relatively negligible role, the ego is of such crucial importance in human psychopathology because it is the central organizing value in personality structure. Our relationship to the environment is ordered on a hierarchical gradient of ego involvement. Most motivations bear some relationships to ego needs, for example, security, adequacy, prestige, status, power. What we wish to derive from life in terms of work, interpersonal relationships, love, status, and so forth, usually bears some relation to our self-concept, that is, the magnitude of our ego aspirations, how compelling the need for ego enhancement is, and how important we think we are or ought to become. The ego is the one value in personality that people are most concerned about. Whatever else we may love, it is evident that we love our ego best of all. It elicits greater efforts toward defense and enhancement than any other value.

The causes of frustration and conflict in human beings must also be largely formulated in terms of ego needs. When these are thwarted by delay, denial, or conflict, when ego status is debased or threatened, frustration ensues. More important than actual deprivation in determining the degree of frustration experienced, however, is the individual's level of prestige aspiration, his specific ego-involvement in a given task, and his frustration tolerance and self-critical faculty. All of these factors are greatly influenced by the course of ego development, which, in addition, helps determine the source from whence status is sought, the degree of volitional and executive dependence desired, the need for hedonistic gratification, the type and degree of security and adequacy feelings possessed, the sense of moral obligation adhered to, as well as tendencies toward introversion-extroversion and egocentrism. In short, ego development forms the core of personality development; hence, it would not be at all surprising if the major predispositions toward acquiring behavior disorder were to be found in aberrant varieties of ego development.

Responses to frustration can likewise be more meaningfully categorized as forms of defense, escape, and damage of self. Defense mechanisms are mainly compensatory attempts to enhance self, to make the ego appear powerful, blameless, and more worthwhile—through substitutive or fantasy achievements, rationalization, disowning weaknesses and perceiving them in others (projection), burying ideas that are unfavorable to self (repression), distorting reality, providing excuses for failure in illness, and so forth. Escape mechanisms, on the other hand, allow for withdrawal of self beyond the reach of environmental threats, for example, insulation, negativism, and other threats. Various forms of ego damage will be described later. They include loss of self-esteem, anxiety, agitation, depersonalization, and depression.

The "Unconscious" as a Source of Psychopathology

In psychoanalytic theory, "the unconscious" forms the cornerstone of psychopathology. It is the domain of instinctual urges and the locus of repressed libidinal impulses referable to earlier alleged stages of psychosexual development which for some reason (e.g., under- or over-gratification) had become fixated at a primitive level of evolution. It is also the region to which unacceptable feelings, ideas, and regressive desires are banished if they somehow manage to enter the "sacred" precincts of consciousness. Through the surreptitious influence exerted by unconscious motivation, symptoms are allegedly formed which symbolically fulfill the goals of their hidden progenitors. In the absence of the unconscious, behavior disorder is unthinkable in the psychoanalytic sense of the term.

My objections to this concept of the unconscious are threefold: (1) I have already rejected the dichotomous notion that all acceptable and self-enhancing motives prevail at the conscious level while their opposite counterparts influence behavior solely from an unconscious base of operations; (2) psychoanalytic theories of the unconscious are topographical rather than functional, implying an all-or-none differentiation between the conscious and the unconscious depending on regional location—it does less violence to modern concepts of psychological functioning to conceive of varying degrees in the accessibility of a person's both discrete and related ideas and behavior to his own analysis; and (3) I can agree that unconscious motivation gives rise to symbolic symptom-formation, and that repression compounds the seriousness and intensity of guilt and anxiety by impeding integrative and constructive solutions. But it must be reiterated that these consequences of repression are not mainly responsible for the evolution of mental disorders but merely have the status of complications.

In ascending order of importance we may differentiate between four different varieties of inaccessibility: (1) perceptions or motives that are attended to on a subthreshold level of awareness because of their habitual, autonomous, or unobtrusive nature; (2) experiences occurring in a state of panic or behavioral disorganization with consequent impairment of perceptual and memory functions; (3) emotional and visceral feelings or attitudes that cannot be formulated in verbal terms, and hence are recalled or reidentified with great difficulty; and (4) material that is actively repressed as a form of adjustment. In repression, either (a) motives, attitudes, or feelings are repressed; (b) a response to an otherwise adequate stimulus is inhibited; or (c) neither motive nor response is inhibited, but rather the perception of a connection between them. Repression as an adjustive mechanism is resorted to in order to avoid insecurity, guilt, or punishment.

Another psychoanalytic concept lacking in clarity and precision but very important for general psychopathology is the concept of *regression*. Psychoanalytically, the depth of regression with respect to psychosexual development is supposed to account for the degree of behavioral disorganization, for example, the etiological distinction between neurosis and psychosis. Unfortunately, however, this concept does not differentiate between genuine retrogression (true regression) and mere lack of maturation. In addition, it conceives of regression only in a psychosexual sense rather than in terms of ego development. Furthermore, differences in type and degree of regression are not related to a developmental history of satellization or nonsatellization. Most apparent regression in satellizers represents maturational failure, whereas in nonsatellizers, who rarely fail to undergo maturation, regressive behavior is more indicative of genuine retrogression. Depth of regression is also greater in nonsatellizers since the developmental failure to which it relates occurs at an earlier stage of ego development, that is, the ego devaluation crisis as opposed to the ego maturation crisis.

Classification of Mental Disorders

No matter how great an improvement DSM III and IV may be over their predecessors, they are still basically descriptive classifications comparable in method and approach to the scheme of classifying medical disorders in the pre-Pasteur and pre-Koch portion of the nineteenth century, that is, identifying clusters of signs and symptoms that co-occur, follow a common course, and have a similar onset, epidemiology, outcome, prevalence, and prognosis. A good descriptive classification is, naturally, more useful than a poor one and, of course, better than nothing at all. It does bring *some* order out of chaos; but it gives us very little insight into the etiology or psychopathology of a given disorder and, thus, of course, little opportunity of understanding the etiological and psychopathological relationships between the various disorders.

The Role of Classification in Mental Disorders

Classification is not simply a matter of categorizing diseases into clinically distinct and descriptively distinguishable entities for purposes of keeping hospital records and assigning convenient labels to patients. Rather, it both reflects, on the one hand, the scientific maturity of a clinical field of knowledge, and the validity of that knowledge, as well as its relation to the "real world," and, on the other hand, is a powerful conceptual tool in the diagnosis and treatment of patients, as well as of great heuristic value in the discovery of new clinical knowledge. A good classification is the most effective means of making valid and precise diagnoses and of formulating appropriate treatment plans. Thus, every time I hear self-described "true clinician" types of colleagues proudly asserting, "It doesn't make a particle of difference how we *label* this patient as long as we *understand* the underlying psychodynamics (or neurobiology) of his condition," I cringe, because it really does make *all* the difference in the world. They have turned the reality of the situation upside down, for until we arrive at an appropriate diagnosis (rather than merely a label) we really do *not understand* the psychodynamics of *any* case.

Hence, it is not a trivial matter to determine which comes first, anxiety or depression, or which is masking which. In my opinion, it is one of the central issues in psychopathology today. For depending on the resolution of this and similar problems we may finally be able, for example, to solve the riddle of the relationship between the neuroses and the psychoses and to formulate a more coherent and heuristic classification that defines a given mental disorder and its relationship to other disorders in terms of its etiological and psychopathological "genotype" instead of in terms of its "phenotypic expression." As is well known, a given genotype, depending on its environment, may result in many different phenotypic manifestations (signs and symptoms); and, conversely, many different phenotypic expressions may similarly express the same genotypic core of etiology and psychopathology.

Classification, therefore, is as necessary in psychiatry as in all scientific disciplines to make possible generalization, concept formation, and

investigation of relationships between important causal factors impinging upon the phenomena encompassed within the discipline. Without classification a separate equation would have to be written for every individual
reaction, since identity never prevails phenomenologically. General laws
could never be formulated, and scientific anarchy would prevail. Classification does not presume identity, but similarity between events subsumed
under a given category. The use of a given diagnostic entity in this sense
does not in the least interfere with the further description of the unique
personal evolution of a case within a more general category. Hence, it is
indulging in sophistry to urge the abolition of classification in favor of
"just understanding the mechanisms underlying each case without wor-
rying about diagnostic labels."

The claim that outmoded classification in psychiatry is retarding the
progress of the science also confuses the issue. Generally speaking, classification mirrors the state of clarity prevailing as regards the various concepts and their interrelationships within a given discipline. Hence, an
inadequate classification is less the cause of theoretical confusion than a
reflection of it. If we still adhere to the Kraepelinian descriptive nomenclature, it means that our so-called dynamic systems of psychopathology
are lacking in sufficient clarity and self-evident plausibility to command
widespread adoption for clinical or research purposes.

Primary and Secondary Mental Disorders

It should be frankly stated at the outset that the author categorically
rejects all biological viewpoints in psychiatry, be they neurotransmitter,
neuroendocrinological, or others that are scientifically reductionistic in
orientation, or that advance and support the hypothesis that mental disorder can be reduced to dysfunction of the neural or neuroendocrinological
substrate of consciousness and behavior. Such reductionism, in my view,
is scientifically and philosophically insupportable because it ignores the
fact that the higher mental processes, as well as personality itself and the
organization and control of complex primate behavior, are psychological
emergents of biological evolution that exist at a phenomenological level
of complexity superseding the operation of their biological substrate.

Hence, although this substrate probably plays a *mediating* role between
antecedent psychological determinants of mental disorder and the consequent signs and symptoms thereof, its loss of integrity (anatomical or physi-

ological) cannot possibly explain *primary* disorders of personality and psychological functioning, as distinct from *secondary* disorders reflective of impairment of the substrate itself (e.g., inflammation, infection, neoplasm, allergy, degeneration, poisoning, and homeostatic [electrolyte, hormone, vitamin, enzyme, neurotransmitter, endomorphin] imbalance).

A genuinely psychogenic approach to classifying mental disorders, in other words, attempts primarily to identify causes of such disorders (and the relationships among them) that exist and operate at a psychological level, that is, that inhere in the nature, organization, development, and regulation of both normal and aberrant *psychological* processes and in their intrapsychic, situational, familial, social, and cultural determinants.

Adherents of such a psychogenic approach readily concede, of course, both: (1) that the conversion of psychogenic determinants of mental disorder into actual psychological (and sometimes somatic) signs and symptoms of psychiatric illness may be *mediated* by biological changes in the neural substrate of psychological functioning; and (2) that impairment of the anatomical or physiological integrity of this substrate by purely biological and physical factors may *independently* disrupt particular aspects of psychological functioning in accordance with the psychophysiological and psychoanatomical correlations prevailing in the area of involved substrate, and, thus, give rise to signs and symptoms of secondary mental disorder in the absence of adequate psychogenic causes. These latter signs and symptoms should, therefore, really be considered psychiatric reflections of neurological disease.

The classification of mental disorders delineated in table 4.1 reflects the psychopathology and psychopathological relationships proceeding from predispositions to mental disorder that follow from difficulties, distortions, or failure to resolve satisfactorily maturational or transitional crises in ego development, as described in chapters 1–3 (ego development) and (general psychopathology) in relation to ego development.

It should be noted that, since this is not a textbook or encyclopedia of mental disorders, coverage of the specific mental disorders and clinical syndromes in Part II of this book is by no means exhaustive: only the major and least equivocal of the clinical conditions, and especially those distortions that are particularly relevant for, or illustrative of, ego-development considerations, have been chosen for inclusion in this clinical section.

By a "defense against" a distressful symptom, mental or emotional state, or disorder is meant a cognitive, affective, or behavioral content that dis-

TABLE 4.1
Classification of Mental Disorders from the Standpoint of Ego Development

I.   Disorders Reflective of Seriously (Catastrophically) Impaired Self-Esteem
  A.   Anxiety Neurosis
  B.   Panic Disorder (with and without Agoraphobia)
  C.   Separation Anxiety Disorder
  D.   Post-Traumatic Stress Disorder

II. Complications of Anxiety States (i.e., of Collapsed Self-Esteem)
  A.   Psychotic Depression
  B.   Dysthymic Disorder
  C.   Cyclothymic Disorder
  D.   Psychotic Mania

IIA. Other Complications of Anxiety (i.e., of Impaired Self-Esteem
  E.   Reactive Schizophrenia
  F.   Schizo-affective Disorder
  G.   Delusional Disorder

III. Personality Disorders Due to Maturational Failure in Desatellization (mostly in satellizers)
  A.   Inadequate and Immature Personality Disorder (mostly in extroverts; hedonistic gratification in reality)
  B.   Drug Addiction: Same as above
  C.   "Process Schizophrenia (mostly in introverts; hedonistic gratification in fantasy)

IV. Reactive Counteraggressive Personality Disorder (in nonsatellizers)
  A.   Aggressive Antisocial Personality Disorder
  B.   Conduct Disorder and Juvenile Delinquency due to Unstable or Absent Conscience Formation
  C.   Substance Abuse

V.   Disorders Serving as Defensive Reactions Against Anxiety
  A.   Obsessive-Compulsive Disorder
  B.   Specific Phobias
  C.   Social Phobias
  D.   Somatization Disorder
  E.   Hypochondriasis
  F.   Conversion Disorders
  G.   Hypomania
  H.   Dissociative Amnesia
  I.   Dissociative Fugue
  J.   Dissociative Identity Disorder
  K.   Depersonalization Disorder
  L.   Brief Miscellaneous Defenses

VI. Malingering

counts, reduces, counteracts, compensates for, or minimizes the impact of the underlying disorder on the patient's feelings, awareness, cognition, or personality. In some instances, of course, the "defense" itself becomes a disorder in its own right, especially if it's highly stable, exaggerated, organized, or systematized. Because of the great influence of Darwinian theories of biological evolution and of teleological thinking on both medical and behavioral pathology, however, there is a pervasive tendency in our culture to interpret all symptoms (mental as well as physical) as compensatory and adaptive/adjustive in nature, even when they are simply dysfunctional and reflective of the underlying psychopathology. In this classification, therefore, only those conditions subsumed directly under "Defenses against Anxiety" are considered to have compensatory/adjustive properties; anxiety itself and the "complications of anxiety" do not have these properties.

Table 4.1 presents a classification of the specific mental disorders that will be considered in the following clinical section of this book, of their placement in more inclusive psychopathological categories, and the general conceptual relationships between the larger categories themselves (discussed in this chapter) in relation to ego development (chapters 1-3).

Notes

1. Neurotic Anxiety is defined in this volume as an anticipated fear reaction to a future psychosocial threat to an individual's self-esteem because of the very severe existing impairment of this self-esteem, as a result of which he lacks confidence in his ability to cope with any new and unfamiliar threatening adjustive situation and therefore anticipates further loss of self-esteem from the anticipated threat.
2. In this volume, depression is regarded as a mood of extreme sadness and dejection, that is, an intense but proportionate emotional response to a catastrophic diminution (or collapse) of the patient's self-esteem, which is objectively and unrealistically disproportionate to the precipitating instigating threat. The collapsed self-esteem, therefore, rather than the proportionate (normal) affective response to same, is considered to be the basic psychopathology of depressive disorder.
3. In the second or clinical half of this book, each of the major specific mental disorders will be discussed fully in adequate detail. In this section, reference is made to different symptoms or aspects of a particular disorder for illustrative purposes only.

5

Anxiety States

Definition, Nature, and Criteria of Neurotic Anxiety[1]

Anxiety provides the crucial connecting link between the two major strands of this book that have been pursued thus far: the nature and sequences of ego development, on the one hand, and the relationship between aberrant ego development and the psychopathological predispositions that both follow from them and may also give rise to mental disorder, on the other hand. In anxiety states there is at the same time both: (1) a product of disordered ego development, lack of ego devaluation and of satellization, with many characteristic signs of ego damage that constitute the basic mental disorder of generic Anxiety Neurosis (Generalized Anxiety); and (2) the various defenses against and complications of the underlying generic anxiety, many of which are mental disorders in their own right.

Neurotic Anxiety is defined as a form of developmental anxiety (occurring usually in a nonsatellizing individual with a history of failure in ego devaluation) in which the essential source of the threat to self-esteem arises from a severely impaired sense of adequacy. It manifests itself as a tendency to overreact with fear to any stimulus that threatens to impair self-esteem further. Such stimuli generally consist of a limited group of adjustive situations having special reference to prestige areas in which there is selective ego involvement or painful memories of an especially dismal or humiliating nature.

This definition makes explicit both the predisposing and the precipitating causes of Neurotic Anxiety. This condition could not generally occur in the absence of the particular disturbed parent-child relationship which leads to a failure in ego devaluation with its associated nonsatellization, failure to acquire intrinsic security and adequacy, and retention of hypertrophic ego aspirations. In the first place, an individual possessing intrinsic security and adequacy could never suffer a sufficiently severe and central blow to self-esteem that would eventuate in Neurotic Anxiety, since such environmental debacles could result only in deflating consequences confined to the peripheral reaches of self-esteem. Secondly, in the case of rejected children, the severe impairment of self-esteem inheres in the catastrophic-like act of rejection itself. And lastly, if the catastrophic event must occur later, as in extrinsically valued individuals, it is rendered almost inevitable by virtue of the individual's vulnerability to core involvement of his impaired self-esteem in responding to novel adjustive threats (in the absence of intrinsic adequacy) and the large-scale frustration of his goal structure because of his unrealistically inflated ego aspirations.

Hence, the very occurrence of Neurotic Anxiety becomes both a prerequisite for its further existence, and a discouraging prognostic indicator that the underlying pathological condition will be indefinitely perpetuated as a chronic disorder punctuated perhaps by sporadic acute exacerbations. It is the writer's firm belief, therefore, that the predisposing and precipitating factors mentioned above constitute the sole necessary causal ingredients required for initiating the underlying mechanism of Neurotic Anxiety. The factors of repression, hostility, and conflict, which figure so prominently in other theories, can either complicate and intensify existing Neurotic Anxiety or can occur independently in the form of symptomatic anxiety. The only other psychopathological channel that could conceivably lead to Neurotic Anxiety is the occurrence in mild satellizers of overdependent traits due to parental overprotection, of inordinate temperamental needs for volitional independence, or of a particularly traumatic blow to self-esteem that has permanent implications (e.g., death of a parent, a disabling or disfiguring disease). But even in such cases, it is doubtful whether the anxiety is as intense or as irreversible as in the more usual sequence of causative events.

Etiologically speaking, Neurotic Anxiety is the product of several different potent sources of damage to the rejected individual's self-esteem, each of which must be accounted a severe narcissistic blow to his self-esteem. First is the realization that he is not accepted and intrinsically valued by his parents and that the latter consider him unworthy of acceptance. This usually constitutes the precipitating catastrophic-like trauma to self-esteem creating the reaction sensitivity to Neurotic Anxiety. Second is the failure of the omnipotent infantile ego to be devalued because satellization doesn't take place, with resulting ego hypertrophy reflecting (1) residual volitional omnipotence and independence from the infantile ego structure, and (2) unrealistically and tenaciously high aspirations for achievement and other forms of earned status to compensate for the derived status and the intrinsic feelings of security and adequacy which he did not obtain from his relationship with his parents because of his failure to satellize in relation to them.

Last, due to this lack of continuing satellizing experience in childhood, the Anxiety Neurotic fails to develop a residual inner core of self-worth that could have protected him forever afterwards, at least in part, from any of life's vicissitudes threatening his self-esteem.

The main reason in anxiety disorders for overreacting with fear to an ostensibly inadequate threat (judged in terms of its objective hazardousness to persons not suffering from Neurotic Anxiety) is an inner feeling of inadequacy that reflects impaired self-esteem. In Neurotic Anxiety the principal perceived threat eliciting the anticipatory fear response comes from within, that is, from the individual's conscious or subliminal awareness that his vulnerability to the threat of a novel adjustive situation inheres in his own severely impaired self-esteem, as a result of which he lacks self-confidence in his ability to improvise an adequate response to a novel problem-solving or adjustive situation. This is roughly comparable to the situation of a patient with decompensated cardiac damage where the threat of acute congestive heart failure lies less in external demands for greatly increased cardiac output (e.g., exercise, emotional agitation) than in the existing degree of cardiac impairment itself which precludes any compensatory output whatsoever.

Neurotic Anxiety: Why in Nonsatellizers?

The rejected nonsatellizer, generally experiencing and being cognizant of his rejection as a toddler, develops his Anxiety Neurosis at the same time as his rejection, because it constitutes the catastrophic-like blow to his self-esteem (i.e., the undeniable narcissistic injury to it inherent in the act itself) that is necessary to give rise to this anticipatory fear response on a permanent, irreversible basis. This latter fear (anxiety) response is evoked whenever he is confronted by a novel and threatening adjustive situation that he perceives as potentially capable of impairing further his already impaired self-esteem.

This same situation, of course, would not be perceived as threatening and would not be evocative of anticipatory fear of further injury to his self-esteem (anxiety) unless he lacked confidence in his ability to handle it because of existing impairment of his self-esteem and consequent awareness of this subjective vulnerability to the appearance of threat. In other words, what constitutes a definite threat to him, capable of precipitating anxiety responses, is only so subjectively because of his prior history of experiencing catastrophic-like impairment of his self-esteem followed by more chronic experience of impairment. Objectively speaking, it does not pose sufficient hazard to a non-Anxiety Neurotic to evoke any fresh manifestation of anxiety.

Catastrophic-like impairment of the overvalued nonsatellizer's self-esteem, however, does not usually occur until late adolescence because he is largely protected at home by his parents from failure and frustration until then; he lives at home in an atmosphere of imperiousness and adulation where he reigns as a semi-absolute monarch. The extrinsically valuing parents deliberately seek to maintain and foster as long as possible the fiction of his infantile ego omnipotence as portentous of future eminence and hence as a prime source of vicarious earned status (reflected glory) for themselves in the future.

In a sizable number of such overvalued cases the anxiety remains latent until the catastrophic blow that reveals the emptiness of their baseless and unrealistic achievement aspirations is made manifest and can no longer be hidden. After they recover to some extent and become more stable, however, they typically become obnoxiously aggressive, ruthless, self-centered, rigid, humorless, and determined to achieve success at any price—which they seldom do achieve. Later, after experiencing considerable frustration, a note of bitterness and cynicism creeps in. It is at this stage that they are ready to seek compensation through the exploits of their own children, thus perpetuating the same vicious cycle of overvaluation of which they themselves were victims.

Dimensions and Classification of Fear States

Fear, as a generic term for a general class of emotions, is a differentiated emotional experience that betokens awareness of threat to some aspect of the organism's existence, integrity, safety, or well-being. Involved is not only a subjective content encompassing the source of the danger, its object and possible consequences, but also a specific train of visceral and somatic reactions set in motion by this special cortical experience through the excitation of intermediate and lower brain centers. The experience of fear is then completed and given further identifying characteristics when the sensation of these visceral and somatic reactions reaches consciousness via sympathetic afferent and proprioceptive fibers originating in the effector organs involved.

This then is the definition of fear as a generic term, as a general category of experience sharing certain conditions and properties in common, whether we speak of fear in the specific sense, phobia, insecurity, or anxiety. It is here, however, that commonality ends and differentiation begins as we seek to identify criteria that set apart these component derivatives of generic fear from one another.

First of all there is a temporal distinction to be made. Every person lives in the past, present, and future. That which is presently happening, or has already happened and is being reenacted in memory, is characterized by the mark of reality. It is logically and experientially distinguishable from the hypothetical quality that characterizes anticipated experience. Hence, we must differentiate between fear as a current experience (or as a current reenactment of an old experience) and fear that is experienced in contemplation of the future. Following historical usage, it will be best to refer to the former as fear in the specific sense, and to the latter as insecurity. Where the object of the threat eliciting a fear state (in the generic sense) is self-esteem, we can use the terms *anxiety-fear* and *anxiety* respectively to cover the past-present and future time relations. Fear and anxiety-fear, therefore, refer to current fear states, whereas insecurity and anxiety refer to anticipated fear.

In the latter situation, however, where fear is projected into the future, it is apparent that more is involved than just an emotional content. On the eve of an impending battle, a soldier may experience insecurity, that is, an actual emotional content of fear as he anticipates the events of the morrow and contemplates the possibilities of injury or death. On the other hand, his insecurity may *not* be manifested as an emotional content evoked by a hypothetical anticipated experience pre-lived in advance of its actual occurrence, but rather as an advance "set" or exaggerated tendency to react with fear upon actual confrontation with the dreaded class of stimuli constituting the threat. In this case there is no fear content in advance of the actual event but only a sensitization to react with fear at the

TABLE 5.1
Classification of Fear States

Temporal Dimension	What Is Threatened	
	Self-Esteem	*Biological and Physical Integrity*
Present or Past	Anxiety fear	Fear
Future	Anxiety	Insecurity

appropriate moment or a differential lowering of the fear threshold to a specific category of future threatening events.

What Is Being Threatened

In the definition of generic fear, it was implied that the object against which the threat is directed must of necessity represent something that is of vital value to the organism. Fear, in other words, is no laughing matter. It is not invoked in situations of trifling import. Life, wholeness of limb, health, reputation, and freedom to pursue central goals, for example, must be at stake before an individual will react with fear to a threatening situation.

Among all those values that are subject to attack, one stands out as possessing unique and central significance, namely, self-esteem, or the individual's feeling of adequacy and competence as a person in relation to his environment. The goal of much everyday activity, as well as the motivation for most adjustive mechanisms, has the enhancement or defense of self-esteem as its chief object. Hence, it seems legitimate to regard threats directed against self-esteem as eliciting a special variety of fear state, which may be termed *anxiety-fear* when appearing as a current emotion, and *anxiety* when projected into the future.

A parallel set of values (and corresponding fear states, i.e., fear and anxiety fear) that can be counterpoised against self-esteem in a dichotomous classification of fear states, and is obviously a conspicuous object of threat in the minds of most persons who feel themselves, or aspects of themselves, threatened or under attack, centers around life and bodily health, physical well-being, biological integrity, safety, and security.

Source of the Threat

In addition to asking the question, "What is being threatened?" one may further delineate the characteristics of a given fear state by posing the query, "Who or what is threatening?" A description then of the various qualities characterizing the source of the threat adds further data on the nature of the fear state being experienced. Among the chief distinctions that can be drawn from this inquiry are those between fear (or anxiety) and phobia, and between normal and Neurotic Anxiety. The main dimensional criteria that describe and define the characteristics of the person or object that is doing the threatening are: (1) identifiability, (2) accessibility, and (3) displacement.

Identifiability

Threats obviously differ in their degree of identifiability. An identifiable threat is one which is relatively specific, unitary, and clear-cut in its implications. An unidentifiable threat, on the other hand, tends to be vague, ambiguous, generalized, and fraught with multiple implications, some of which may be contradictory. It can be readily appreciated, therefore, that unidentifiable threats produce more intense fear states and give rise to defensive behavior that is less specifically adaptive. What cannot be identified cannot be avoided; nor can specific preparatory steps be taken to contend with the threat. The organism can only place itself in a state of general alertness or mobilization, and take its chances when the dreaded situation appears on the scene. Furthermore, unidentifiable threats are less subject to experimental extinction, since it is less likely that they are, and can be, linked with innocuous consequences contiguous in time.

Accessibility

How accessible an individual's awareness is regarding the source of the threat confronting him is obviously an important dimension of his fear experience. Historically, Freud's revised theory of the relationship between anxiety and repression postulated that the individual's aggressive, hostile, and libidinal impulses instigated anxiety by potentially exposing him to danger (social reprisals), and that the anxiety's chief function then was to serve as a cue or signal to him to repress these dangerous impulses and thereby to circumvent the source of the danger.

As pointed out above, repression is usually a maladaptive defense against anxiety. It does not enable the individual to deal constructively with threatening situations, since the implications of threats cannot be examined openly or critically. Despite the repression, anxiety continues to be generated; and since its cause cannot be coped with consciously, "unconscious" defenses (often of a psychosomatic nature) are elaborated. This fact explains the inverse relationship invariably found between the degree of conscious anxiety and the presence of psychosomatic symptoms. Repression, in addition, tends to become a habitual defensive mechanism which is indiscriminately overgeneralized to many inapplicable situations, leading to a generally inhibited individual devoid of spontaneous affective impulses.

There are also several other theoretical difficulties of a conceptual nature with repression. First it is indeterminable to what extent repressed ideas, impulses, and motives are active and viable (although inaccessible) and, thus, capable of still influencing a person's thinking, feeling, and behavior. How do we know, for example, that an alleged repressed idea has not been selectively and irretrievably forgotten (rather than just repressed) and, thus, rendered harmless without repression. Second, as was emphasized in the discussion of conscience, there has been a pervasive tendency in our culture to underestimate the amount of conscious guilt, shame, and so forth, that most individuals can tolerate with equanimity and without the need for denial, repression, rationalization, displacement, and other adjustive but unadaptive responses. This suggests that the frequency and psychological significance of repression in the expression and control of anxiety has been greatly exaggerated.

Last, repression is not an all-or-none phenomenon. Its effectiveness in suppressing conscious accessibility to, or awareness of, the interdicted ideas, motives, and impulses in question varies tremendously from one individual to another, and similarly for different ideas within a person.

Displacement

Another dimension relating to the source of the threat, and not unconnected with the problems of identifiability and accessibility, is the question of whether the individual experiencing fear or anxiety perceives the actual threat or projects his perception of the offending stimulus onto an intrinsically unrelated cause. Unlike inaccessibility, however, displacement has very definite adjustive value, at least of a palliative nature, if not inherently constructive in terms of eliminating the cause of anxiety. It enables him to deny the real source of the threat and to substitute in its stead something that is less formidable and more easily manageable. Consequently, the displacement is always in the direction of greater specificity, concreteness, and identifiability, since these factors make either complete avoidance or planned defense more feasible. In short, the description of displacement just given defines the term *phobia,* which is simply a form of fear or anxiety in which the source of the threat is displaced onto a more identifiable object.

"Free-Floating Anxiety"

In contrasting anxiety to fears and phobias, it has been customary in the past to refer to it as "free-floating" or "objectless." The writer contends, however, that these qualities are more apparent than real, and that the entire notion of an affect that is unrelated to a stimulating object is a psychological absurdity. A person who is afraid must be afraid of something. A person who is angry must be angry at something. A person who is in love must be in love with somebody. That loose, undifferentiated pools of unattached affect (aggression, anxiety, or affection) float around and are at liberty to attach themselves at various times to specific objects is a relic of Hippocratian psychology in which various affects were identified with finite quantities of various body fluids that could be poured as it were out of a central reservoir into specific vessels. The modern concept of emotion, on the other hand, is that of a capacity to react in a particular intense way in response to an adequate stimulus, a capacity that has no corporeal content apart from its phenomenological existence during such time as it is elicited by appropriate situations.

There are several plausible reasons, however, which may help account for the apparent "free-floating" quality of anxiety. The relative unidentifiability and inaccessibility of anxieties (which have not undergone displacement) as contrasted with fears are largely responsible for their objectless appearance. Threats which cannot be concretized or which are banished from consciousness cannot be easily perceived as the cause of a diffuse and apparently all-pervasive affect, especially when the source of the threat is internal. But because a threat cannot be identified or made accessible to consciousness is obviously no proof that a causal relationship does not exist between it and a given affect of anxiety.

Objective Magnitude of a Threat

Whenever a fear response is elicited which is proportionate to the objective degree of danger inherent in the threat, there is good reason to believe that we are dealing with *normal* fear or anxiety. Situations productive of normal fear or anxiety are common enough in anyone's experience, since life is full of hazards and unpredictable contingencies; and to respond to such situations with fear is to behave normally enough. Fear of this kind probably serves a useful adaptive purpose since it alerts the organism to danger and mobilizes its defensive faculties. It is purely situational in nature, since it can be relieved by removal of the inciting situation. Following the initial shock of confrontation, the organism is generally able to recover, avoid panic, and set about constructively to cope with and contain the threat. However, it is conceivable that threats of near-catastrophic, objective magnitude to self-esteem can induce overwhelming anxiety tantamount to panic, which, not being disproportionate to the danger involved, must still be considered as normal anxiety. The same result could also be produced by an objective incapacity on the part of the individual which renders him relatively helpless to deal with minor environmental hazards.

Since the distinction between normal and Neurotic Anxiety hinges mainly upon the disproportionateness of the response, the latter should be suspected in all cases where the symptoms are severe enough to result in panic, paralysis, or progressive disorganization of behavior. And if further search fails to uncover an objective threat of sufficient magnitude to account for the intensity of affect instigated, clinical investigation aimed at discovering subjective sources of anxiety is certainly warranted.

Subjective capacity for meeting the threat. If we turn now to instances where the *same degree* of anxiety appears in the absence of what seems to be an adequate external threat, we cross the boundary into Neurotic Anxiety. However, by adhering to our original conception of fear states as responses made to *serious* threats to an organism's integrity or well-being, we are compelled to look for an adequate excitant that is subjective in nature. Then, if we find that an individual's self-esteem is impaired to the point where he no longer has confidence in his ability to cope with problems of adjustment, the degree of anxiety manifested no longer appears disproportionate despite the relative insignificance of the environmental threat which is perceived as the precipitating cause of the affect. In contrast to normal anxiety, where the occasion (i.e., the situation which cues off the anxiety) and the cause of the affect are nearly identical, the occasion of Neurotic Anxiety is merely the stimulus that creates the necessity for adjustment; and the cause of the latter is the impaired self-esteem that makes the individual feel inadequate to cope with the adjustive problem, and hence fearful of the further ego-deflating impact of this failure on his already battered self-esteem. Since the main source of the threat is internal, and in addition is frequently unidentifiable and inaccessible, it is not surprising that such anxiety may often give the impression of being "free-floating."

Relationship between Intrinsic and Extrinsic Systems of Security and Adequacy

When the adolescent finally begins to derive the greater portion of his security and adequacy feelings from extrinsic sources, what is the fate of their intrinsic counterparts which for so many years occupied such a central position in his ego organization? Two suggestions have already been offered in answer to this question: (a) the hypothesis that satellization leaves a permanent residue in personality structure; and (b) the reference to extrinsic status as the major *current* source of adequacy feelings in adult life.

These statements imply that as a consequence of experiencing feelings of intrinsic security and adequacy over a prolonged period of time, a permanent change occurs in the way in which an individual (i.e., adult satellizer) tends to value himself and to estimate the extent of the jeopardy menacing his future safety. Hence, a certain residual or underlying *quality* of security and adequacy feelings carry over into the future despite the absence of adequate current experience that could give rise to same. (Actually, of course, the adult who satellized as a child also continues to form many satellizing-like relationships as an adult; and generally speaking, he tends to be loved and accepted for himself by his family and by several close associates.)

It would appear, therefore, that feelings of intrinsic security and adequacy constitute a fairly stable, ongoing cluster of attitudes related to self which persist into adult life and interact with current variables that influence extrinsic security and adequacy as well as their correlates. In an individual endowed with residual feelings of intrinsic security and adequacy, his intrinsic feelings tend to remain fairly constant regardless of the environmental vicissitudes met with in later life. Even in the face of prolonged and consistent reverses in those areas of activity reflecting adversely on extrinsic security and adequacy, he stands a good chance of remaining basically secure and adequate. Applying this principle specifically, the amount of intrinsic security possessed by an individual predetermines to a large extent his capacity to benefit from extrinsic security.

Security and adequacy feelings are related insofar as severe impairment of self-esteem (i.e., impaired feelings of adequacy) causes sufficient disorganization and disruption of adjustive behavior and of coping and problem-solving skills to threaten the individual's security, safety, physical well-being, and biological integrity as well; and if self-esteem is impaired to catastrophic proportions, such complications of anxiety as Psychotic Depression and Reactive Schizophrenia may possibly ensue.

Ego Damage, Defense, and Escape in Anxiety Responses

As a central value in personality organization, the enhancement and defense of which is one of the most powerful drives motivating human behavior, it is only to be expected that threats directed against self-esteem would provoke a wide variety of responses. These responses may be divided into three general categories: defense, escape, and ego damage. Defense efforts include reactive attempts to enhance threatened self-esteem, to make the self appear strong, competent, and masterful, to excuse, explain, and rationalize failure. Escape mechanisms provide opportunities for withdrawing the self beyond the reach of possible threats. Ego damage, on the other hand, includes current and residual reactions to threats against self-esteem, which in and of themselves have no adjustive value, but are merely reflective of the disruptive and disorganizing effects which such threats have wrought on personality structure.

Depending on its intensity and relation to actual impairment of self-esteem, anxiety itself may be considered either a defense reaction or a manifestation of ego damage. When a threat to adequacy becomes sufficiently serious to challenge the safety of an individual, it elicits the affect of anxiety. Moderate amounts of this affect in a reasonably secure and adequate person have adjustive value in that they facilitate the mobilization of the individual's adaptive efforts. However, if anxiety reaches the proportions of panic, behavior becomes hopelessly disorganized and maladaptive.

If the threat is pushed still farther it may very well gain its goal, that is, an actual impairment of self-esteem may result. This may be the outcome of a humiliating defeat, a loss in biosocial status, or extreme frustration in an ego-involved area. It is clear, however, that this impairment and the accompanying anxiety can only be considered as evidence of ego damage that serves no adjustive function per se, although in creating a need for anxiety reduction, it gives rise to many defense and escape mechanisms. Again, in persons who are intrinsically secure and adequate, such damage is peripheral and transitory. But in the case of Neurotic Anxiety, impaired self-esteem is a permanent and relatively irreversible form of ego damage, in much the same sense as the replacement of functional cardiac muscle by fibrous tissue in coronary artery disease of the heart.

This latter residual damage is severe enough to constitute the main source of threat in Neurotic Anxiety, since in the absence of sufficient confidence in one's ability to cope with novel adjustive problems, almost any insignificant environmental threat to self-esteem appears extremely menacing. Returning to our analogy of the heart, we could say that in persons with normal hearts, the source of the threat of cardiac failure lies in excessive environmental demands, for example, sustained overwork, insufficient rest. However, when the heart is severely damaged, its adaptive powers to stress are seriously impaired, and any additional burden, no matter how trivial, is dangerous. And just as the main source of the threat of heart failure in organic heart cases lies *within* the damaged heart muscle itself, the main source of the threat of impaired self-esteem in Anxiety Neurosis lies *within* the individual's impaired self-esteem. The threat of failure induces impairment because life has been structured in terms of self-enhancement, and because the struggle to earn a favorable view of the self has been unremitting.

If ego damage does not go beyond the stage of anxiety, however, the individual may be considered fortunate indeed. In fact, the psychopathologist working in a hospital for mental disorders rarely finds indications of only pure, uncomplicated anxiety; and when he does, he regards them as excellent prognostic indicators. Anxiety is a sign that vigorous striving for adult adjustment in a reality setting is still in progress. Besides indicating that the patient is not yet utilizing some of the more objectionable defenses, it conveys the more important assurance that he has not yet availed himself of the relief from anxiety which can be obtained from succumbing to further ego damage. This relief is available when the individual finally decides that he needs it badly enough to relinquish the self-esteem he has been defending at such cost. It can be gained either by accepting defeat and ceasing to strive (Reactive Depression), or by ceasing to strive for adult goals on a reality level (Reactive Schizophrenia). Both alternatives result in extensive ego damage and personality disorganization.

Agitation is an intermediate stage between anxiety and its two psychotic complications, more usually depression rather than Reactive Schizophrenia. It is indicative of the fact that anxiety bordering on panic has become so severe and continuous that even the everyday routines of living can no longer be managed successfully. All of the individual's organized defenses have broken down, and disorganization is rampant. When anxiety reaches this point, the pressure for yielding to one of the two psychotic solutions promising relief from this agony becomes almost unbearable.

Teleological reasoning, however, is so ingrained in the biological and social sciences that it is very difficult for a psychopathologist to concede that a given behavioral symptom of reaction to stress could be anything but adjustive and compensatory. Even organic pathologists lapse into the same error in interpreting physical symptoms as compensatory responses of organs to physiological stress. Although many psychopathologists are now willing to recognize Neurotic Anxiety as a reflection of ego damage rather than as a compensatory form of defense, the influence of the teleological approach is still discernible in present-day theorizing about the nature of anxiety.

Anxiety in Rejected and Overvalued Individuals

One of the most striking differences between rejected and overvalued children in their anxiety manifestations is the latency of the condition in the case of the latter. This is due to the postponement of the catastrophic blow to self-esteem, an event which in rejected children occurs at the close of infancy. Related to this difference is the fact that the overvalued child enjoys a superfluity of extrinsic adequacy at home, while the rejected child is enveloped in a stern, hostile environment which persistently emphasizes his worthlessness, thereby continually widening the gap between his aspirations and reality. The rejected child, therefore, carries within him a greater burden of repressed hostility, bitterness, and resentment. It is no wonder then that much of his motivation has a negative quality, being inspired by considerations of revenge and an "I'll show them" attitude.

The blow that results in catastrophic-like impairment of self-esteem is also much more devastating in the case of the rejected child because it occurs at a time when ego defenses are weaker, and because the ego has not as yet had any opportunity to be fortified by experiences productive of extrinsic adequacy; nor, in view of the child's complete dependence on his parents at this stage of his development, is there any possibility of obtaining other sources of extrinsic status. His self-esteem, therefore, is more completely shattered, and hence less able to be benefited by gains in extrinsic adequacy. Regardless of the objective magnitude of his success, he can never quite take himself or his accomplishments very seriously; for indelibly engraved in the innermost reaches of his self-esteem is the unshakable conviction that he is the worthless, despicable little creature whom even his own parents could not accept.

In contrast, the overvalued individual in periods of remission from acute attacks of anxiety is buoyant, exuberant, self-confident, and full of self-assurance. He does not suffer at all from inability to take himself or his success seriously. But this expansiveness which he manifests in "good times" makes him less able to weather subsequent acute attacks of anxiety than the rejected individual, the very relative invariability of whose depressed self-esteem protects him somewhat from the impact of violent and abrupt fluctuations in fortune.

In terms of the possibilities for improvement that depend on more than superficial situational factors, the rejected individual also shows to advantage. He still enjoys the option of establishing satellizing-like relationships with others, and is generally more capable of being loved for himself. The resulting feelings of intrinsic security and adequacy which he gains from such experiences not only reduce his current load of anxiety, but also make it possible for him to lower his level of aspiration. The overvalued individual, on the other hand, finds satellization too degrading, and is usually too obnoxiously self-centered to inspire genuine feelings of love for himself in other persons.

Because of his extended training in the ways of infantile omnipotence, the overvalued child is also more reluctant to surrender the prerogative of executive dependence. However, when he realizes the expediency of acquiring executive independence, he is not hampered to the same degree as the rejected child by overt anxiety in the learning of new motor, social, and intellectual skills. Nevertheless in periods of acute anxiety in later life, he is more apt to regress to the position of demanding assistance from others.

We have also seen that the rejected individual, trained in the habit of repressing self-assertive and aggressive feelings, develops introverted and withdrawing tendencies, tends to avoid situations involving conflict, and intellectualizes his aggression. As a result he fails to master effective social techniques of expressing aggression, a circumstance that makes him vulnerable to exploitation by others and generates more hostility that requires repression. This seething internal reservoir of repressed hostility in turn intensifies existing anxiety. The overvalued individual, on the other hand, has had abundant experience of giving vent to hostile feelings. His problem is to learn how to make his aggressive tactics seem less offensive and ruthless than they really are.

Other Varieties of Anxiety

The term "Neurotic Anxiety" has been identified above with the principal type of anxiety induced by a subjective threat. This is the traditional Anxiety Neurosis, the origin of which has been related to a primary defect in ego devaluation and to a failure to satellize that results eventually in catastrophic impairment of self-esteem. It is this damage to self-esteem which then constitutes the subjective threat. Apart from *situational* (normal) anxiety, however, there are still two types of anxiety induced by *subjective* threats that have yet to be considered. When the source of the threat is related to normal developmental pressures found in transitional (crisis) periods of ego development it may be termed *transitional*. And last, there is *symptomatic* anxiety that is associated neither with normal developmental pressures nor with residual developmental defects but with other psychopathological mechanisms, namely, conflict and guilt, which expose the individual to the danger of aggression and retaliation, if acted upon (in the case of hostility and conflict), and of impaired self-esteem in the case of guilt. Thus, as discussed above, in response to the threat generated by these three cognitive-emotional complexes, the individual supposedly tends to experience anxiety, which, in turn, acts as a signal for their repression—as a means of defusing ideational and emotional material in his memory store that exposes him to danger and impaired self-esteem.

Situational Anxiety

Situational anxiety is the normal type of anxiety that arises in relation to objective threats to an individual's self-esteem. It is a self-protective reaction that is limited to the duration of the situation that elicits it, and is proportionate to the objective magnitude of the threat involved. Three types of situational anxiety are considered here: (1) that which is derived from the cultural situation; (2) that which follows from special individual incapacities; and (3) that which inheres in all constructive, problem-solving activity.

Cultural Factors

Cultural factors produce or alleviate anxiety in many different ways. In the first place, just as a child may be intrinsically valued for himself by his parents, an adult may be more or less valued for himself by his culture. The intrinsic worth of a human being can be extremely high, as in the Arapesh culture, or it can be almost nil, as in our society, where a man's value is largely a reflection of the price he fetches in the marketplace. This distinction by Fromm is an exceedingly valuable one, but makes a serious error in assuming that the self-esteem of all men will be similarly affected by its dependence on its market value. Actually, the impact of this situation on the individual's self-esteem will be peripheral in the case of satellizers and central in the case of nonsatellizers.

Nevertheless, if we bear the latter difference in mind, it would be legitimate to say that the level of extrinsic status toward which a person feels impelled to strive is inversely related to the intrinsic cultural valuation of man (or directly related to the emphasis placed upon his market value). In our society, maximum value is placed upon the goals of social prestige and hierarchical status; and it is in the struggle for these goals that an individual either attains or fails to attain extrinsic adequacy. The more violent the competition for these individual goals, the greater the amount of intracultural hostility that is generated, the less ego support an individual can derive from group relatedness, and the greater his psychological isolation.

Another cultural factor influencing the level of situational anxiety has to do with the *availability* of the extrinsic status for which a particular culture motivates its members to strive. If, for example, as in our culture, adolescents and adults are drawn into a mad race for competitive status, and the possibility of many individuals acquiring such status is greatly limited, it stands to reason that situational anxiety will be relatively intense and widespread. This is especially true in periods of economic depression when youth spend many years of apprenticeship, education, training, and self-subordination only to find unemployment at the end of the arduous and anxiety-laden trail. But even in normal times, adolescents must tolerate prolonged status deprivation; and the bitter pill is not made any easier to swallow when it is compounded by an apparent capriciousness in the cultural distribution of rewards. The theory that success is the inevitable reward for conscientious work, self-denial, and superior ability bogs down as adolescents begin to see rewards monopolized by individuals whose sole entitlement to same springs from wealth, inherited position, family connections, or a highly developed capacity for double dealing and sycophancy.

In addition to the situational anxiety that can be attributed to general status deprivation, economic depression, and differences in the accessibility of cultural rewards on the basis of social class membership, special groups of adolescents and adults in our culture experience further cause for anxiety in social and economic discrimination related to their sex, race, religion, or ethnic and national origin. Furthermore, situational anxiety tends to be accentuated during periods of rapid social change, war, international tension, political upheaval, and deterioration of public and private morality.

It not infrequently happens that when situational anxiety is prolonged and intense, it also acquires some subjective components. The chronic threat to self-esteem finally leads to an actual impairment of the sense of adequacy that is peripheral in the case of satellizers and central in the case of nonsatellizers. This in turn becomes a further source of threat, especially when the individual unwarrantedly attributes the failure he experiences on the basis of cultural factors to his own ineptitude.

These feelings of inadequacy must be differentiated from the anxiety that is derived from objective organic or intellectual deficiencies which constitute a threat to self-esteem insofar as they expose the individual to ridicule and ostracism, or predispose him to failure in various adjustive situations. We have seen, however, that adolescents often tend to exaggerate the importance of such defects; and as a result of this overvaluation, the greater part of the source of threat may become subjective rather than objective. Except in cases of permanent crippling or disfigurement, however, organic defects are seldom severe enough to produce Neurotic Anxiety.

"Constructive" Anxiety

Many writers on the subject of anxiety point out that anxiety inheres inevitably in all constructive activity leading toward self-actualization. The development of any individual's potential capacities depends on his willingness to experience frustration, solve new problems, risk the possibility of failure, face unpleasant, threatening situations, and to abandon established positions of security for exploration of uncharted fields. This means that individual as well as group progress can only take place if there is a positive disposition to accept and "move through" the burden of anxiety inherent in each new learning situation.

Anxiety and Motivation

Anxiety reduction can be a potent motivating factor in learning. Although in laboratory experiments with humans, punishment has not proven to be a very effective incentive for learning, the weight of the evidence shows that it is more efficacious than a neutral motivational environment. Further, the relative efficacy of reward and punishment, as determined for a short-term laboratory task, might easily be reversed were we to consider the real-life situation over an extended period of time.

In our particular culture at any rate it is quite evident that, whether desirable or not, anxiety is one of the most common motivating devices employed by parents, teachers, employers, and others. It is undoubtedly true that positive motivations such as job satisfaction, joy in craftsmanship and creative effort, and desire to be socially useful are much more wholesome than anxiety reduction, but few motivations *today* are still as compelling as the fear of losing one's job. The source of anxiety motivation lies not only in various natural contingencies (e.g., sickness, death, starvation) that threaten existence, but also in a series of cultural derivatives arising from fear of physical punishment, guilt, disapproval, social reprisal, ostracism, and loss of status. "Socially adaptive" anxiety, for example, helps provide the adolescent with motivation to attain the general developmental goals appropriate for his age group and the more specific goals appropriate for his social class membership; it is powered by the threat of failure to acquire the status prerogatives associated with successful maturation.

However, to acknowledge the potency of anxiety motivation is not to assert that it is the only or the chief source of motivation. This would be committing the same error as Freud, who failed to see any motivation arising except in a negative fashion, that is, as the product of sublimation or reaction-formation. Motivation can be derived from many positive sources such as curiosity, interest, or ability. And even if the original source does happen to be related to anxiety reduction, it is possible that in the course of pursuing the activity that it inspires, other more positive motivations might develop, which in time may assume the more dominant emerging role.

It is in nonsatellizers, however, that anxiety reduction really occupies the central position in the motivational picture. There is a relentless drive for extrinsic adequacy and ego enhancement to fill the void of absent intrinsic self-esteem and to allay the anxiety that arises from its impairment. The tremendous amount of prestige motivation generated by hypertrophic and tenacious ego demands leads to greater accomplishment than could otherwise be expected from a given level of ability, despite the tendency toward disruption of performance efforts because of anxiety and overreaction to frustration. In nonsatellizers, goal frustration tolerance is extremely high, and performance as well as self-esteem frustration tolerance are relatively low; while in satellizers exactly the reverse situation prevails.

The more realistic and intelligent nonsatellizer spares himself continual frustration by refusing to expand his prestige motivation indiscriminately in all directions, including those areas in which his natural endowment is poor. By selectively disinvolving his ego from prestige aspirations in such activities and channeling his drive into areas where he is apt to face little competition, he manages to maintain extrinsic self-esteem at a higher level and anxiety at a lower level than the nonsatellizer who sees a threat to himself in anyone's accomplishments and feels obliged to compete with every individual who crosses his path.

The Self-Critical Faculty

Another important factor affecting the individual's extrinsic sense of adequacy, namely, the probability of his being frustrated, and the level of anxiety he accordingly manifests, is the state of his self-critical faculty. This refers to his tendency to evaluate with varying degrees of severity or lenience the acceptability of his behavior, the degree of status he has acquired, and the quality of his productions. It reflects in part the influence of maturational factors and various parental attitudes, and in part the level of his self-esteem and the critical standards that prevail in his environment. Although tending to remain fairly stable and consistent in line with long-range personality trends, it also retains a certain adaptive flexibility. In persons who are intrinsically secure and adequate, it tends to be more lenient and to fluctuate less than among nonsatellizers, in whom it is ordinarily not only more severe but also more variable.

We first meet the self-critical faculty (or the lack of it) in the presatellizing period when the infant is able to entertain grandiose conceptions of his volitional power *partly* because of his very limited capacity to perceive his actual status realistically. Afterwards, improvement in this ability becomes one of the precipitating causes of the crisis of ego devaluation. Nevertheless, self-critical ability is still rudimentary as evidenced by the child's tendency to overvalue the extent of his executive competency in the second stage of negativism. It is only when the self-critical faculty becomes a more important determinant of daily behavior (at approximately five years of age in Gesell's population) that this type of negativism really begins to subside and give way to a more consolidated and homogeneous form of satellization.

During the succeeding years, the further development of the self-critical faculty becomes a progressively more crucial aspect of personality maturation. This growth is facilitated by parental practices that require the child to take responsibility for the consequences of his inappropriate behavior or inadequate performances. Undue laxity in excusing misbehavior or in evaluating inferior performance favors the emergence of an impaired self-critical faculty. The acquisition of greater volitional independence on an adult and realistic level presupposes the ability to recognize imperfections in performance; otherwise the individual feels completely satisfied with a highly inferior product, aspires to nothing better, and initiates no efforts looking toward improvement.

The nonsatellizer's impaired self-esteem and lack of intrinsic self-acceptance also tend to make him adopt a harsh view toward himself. The same is true of the underappreciated child who assimilates his parent's tendency to regard his achievements with lack of enthusiasm.

Evidence has already been cited which indicates that self-estimate tends to be disturbed in the poorly adjusted individual and after experiences of frustration. It is also less accurate with respect to abilities that are rated low by other persons and in areas marked by conflict or insecurity. The precise interpretation of an overly severe self-critical faculty, however, offers many difficulties, since in various cases it can be indicative of a disturbed parent-child relationship, situational tensions, excessive ego demands, perfectionism, vanity, or impaired self-esteem.

The experience of several decades in the pharmacological, psycho-surgical, and electro-conduction treatment of psychopathological conditions in which the self-critical faculty is exaggeratedly severe, that is, anxiety, agitation, and depression, has provided us with considerable information about the neuroanatomical substrate of the self-critical faculty.[2] The most drastic of these measures, prefrontal leucotomy, which often relieves anxiety, depression, and agitation after other less radical forms of intervention fail, seems to exert an almost specific inhibitory effect on the self-critical faculty by interrupting thalamo-cortical fibers that connect the orbital quadrant of the thalamus to the frontal cortex. Electro-conduction therapy, which has a similar but more diffuse effect, results in probably reversible cortical damage; however, the exact locus of this damage has not yet been definitely ascertained.

Neurophysiological evidence from animal experimentation also suggests that the pharmacological locus of the euphorogenous action of narcotic drugs is the thalamo-cortical tract. The adjustive value of narcotic drug addiction probably depends at least in part on the inhibition of the self-critical faculty, which permits the addict with Inadequate and Immature Personality Disorder to retain extrinsic feelings of adequacy despite his manifest incompetency.

The above-cited evidence has been adduced to show that it is possible to change the psychological expression of the self-critical faculty by bringing physical influences to bear on its anatomical substrate. It is realized, however, that such change is normally effected on a psychological plane alone—in the course of ego defense measures or as the outcome of ego damage. Psychologically (defensively), adequacy feelings can be enhanced by inhibiting the self-critical faculty as in manic states, Inadequate Personality Disorder, and certain forms of moral delinquency. Exaggeration of the self-critical faculty, on the other hand, is usually a manifestation of ego damage, for example, anxiety, agitation, and depression. Under certain conditions (to be described below), however, it may serve a defensive function, as, for example, in compulsive perfectionism and in the "self-frustration" mechanism.

Depersonalization

Depersonalization has been generally viewed as a breakdown product of personal identity or awareness of self that occurs under conditions of catastrophic stress and frequently in states of acute anxiety. Eventually this condition develops into a disintegration of self-awareness and of the relationship between self and the outside world, making the individual unable both to evaluate his environment realistically and to identify the source of the threat precipitating his anxiety.

This type of depersonalization is definitely indicative of acute panic; its symptoms suggest that either severe ego damage has already taken place or that they are expressive of a desperate defense maneuver. Initially, at least, prior to depersonalization, an accentuation of self-awareness occurs in states of acute anxiety, leading to a transient consolidation of self-awareness prior to its eventual disintegration.

To understand depersonalization, therefore, it is necessary to distinguish between two types: (1) one type that primarily serves as an adjustive or defense mechanism by dissociating personal identity from humiliating and unacceptable experiences happening to self; and (2) another very different type that serves as a symptom of ego damage in which marked changes in personality occur, that is, the individual becomes depersonalized in the sense of acquiring a new and different personal identity, but accepts this new identity (with all of its regressive and unacceptable features) as his "real" self. Adjustive depersonalization also occurs in certain cases of acute anxiety (after accentuation of self-awareness): under conditions of involuntary or ambivalent participation in degrading experiences, and in amnesias, fugues, and in cases of "multiple personality." The "ego damage" type is illustrated by the depersonalization occurring in chronic cases of Reactive Schizophrenia when the regressive picture of self is accepted as real. "Adjustive" depersonalization, therefore, is a hopeful prognostic sign in early cases of Reactive Schizophrenia. Although there is some adjustive value (escape) in the extreme personality regression and the complete withdrawal from reality found in this psychopathological entity, such a fabulous price is paid in terms of personality disorganization that it would seem more appropriate to regard it as a form of ego damage complicating Neurotic Anxiety.

Prognosis of Anxiety

The development and nature of Neurotic Anxiety is such that predictions regarding its prognosis must be made separately for young children, on the one hand, and for all other age-groups, on the other. Only in terms of the former is the question of reversibility (cure) relevant. The very best the latter can look forward to is palliation. With respect to the possibility of reversibility, the issue in essence is whether or not and under what conditions the effects of parental rejection or overvaluation can be reversed.

Since the child is almost always reluctant to accept the verdict of rejection, and is more than receptive to any change for the better in his parents' attitudes, it is the variables affecting the probability of such change that are crucial in determining the prognosis of childhood anxiety caused by rejection. This brings us to the distinction already made between (1) benign parental rejection, which is not strongly predetermined by personality factors in the parent and hence fluctuates greatly with situational conditions, and (2) malignant rejection, which exhibits greater constancy of expression because of prepotent personality predispositions in the parent. The hypothesis has already been offered that the benign type of rejection is manifested most frequently by parents who were themselves rejected as children, while the malignant type is manifested most commonly by parents who were themselves exposed to overvaluation by their parents.

Parents who were rejected themselves tend more to retain a capacity for relating themselves to others (especially their own children), which can be fulfilled under favorable conditions, that is, minimal anxiety, whereas overvalued parents tend to acquire this capacity seldom if ever. The rejected parent is also influenced more by moral considerations, is more sensitive to public opinion, and tends to be less self-indulgent. Hence, the possibility of sufficient change occurring in the latter's attitudes to enable the child to satellize, acquire some intrinsic security and adequacy, and be largely purged of Neurotic Anxiety, is good providing that it does not come too late; in this writer's experience, almost complete elimination of anxiety has been accomplished with child patients until the age of seven. In cases of malignant rejection, however, the writer has never succeeded in effecting comparable results except in instances where a substitute parent (usually an interested relative) could be provided; it is futile for the therapist himself to attempt this role since he cannot provide sufficient sustained ego support to induce satellization.

The therapist's task of changing parent attitudes is lightened considerably if the parent is intelligent, has insight into the meanings of his attitudes and their effects upon the child, feels guilty about them, and is sincerely desirous of improving the parent-child relationship. Even more important, however, are those situational factors that regulate the current level of parental anxiety. A harassed, panic-stricken, and self-preoccupied parent cannot benefit sufficiently from therapy to change the quality of the parent-child relationship. The relevant situational factors, in turn, are largely dependent upon other personality traits of the parent, such as ability, capacity for disguising anxiety, and so forth.

Parental overvaluation—including the variety practiced by parents who had been rejected themselves (as well as those who were overvalued)—is a much more difficult attitude to change. In the first place, it has more adjustive value for the parent and tends to become a fixed, canalized defense against his anxiety. Second, overvalued children do not generally exhibit overt anxiety and are, thus, less likely to be brought to the attention of a therapist. Third, the overvalued child finds his grandiose ego aspirations quite tenable in his special environment and is not disposed to satellize.

Prognosis for Palliation of Anxiety

If cure cannot be effected in early childhood, the therapist can still attempt palliation. The value of such a goal should not be deprecated since success often means the difference between psychological invalidism, on the one hand, and sufficient freedom from anxiety to do creative work and experience some personal happiness, on the other. The important errors to guard against are unrealistic expectations of cure in adult cases of Neurotic Anxiety, and failure to take sufficient cognizance of the important role of situational factors.

The first error is quite universal among psychotherapists, and the second error is committed in different ways by psychoanalytic and nondirective therapists. The former tend to ignore the patient's current adjustive situation until insight is secured, and then attempt to have him apply this insight toward the solution of his everyday problems. But all along, an unfavorable environmental situation is operating to increase anxiety and prevent the patient from acquiring and utilizing the potential benefits of insight. If at the end of a two-year period of therapy, a young adult patient, for example, is still economically and volitionally dependent on his parents, has no way of earning a living, and has not even made a start in the direction of formulating his vocational goals, he is psychologically in a worse position than he was before beginning therapy.

The formation of satellizing-like relationships with an appropriately caring and benign spouse, employer, supervisor, or mentor can provide a modicum of derived status to the Anxiety Neurotic and thereby reduce his level of anxiety and insecurity, stabilize his condition, and prevent the occurrence of such complications as depression and Reactive Schizophrenia. It should, therefore, be encouraged and facilitated by the psychotherapist.

The following important good prognostic signs should be looked for by the psychotherapist: (1) a history of parental rejection rather than overvaluation; (2) the absence of psychosomatic symptoms and the presence of high tolerance for conscious anxiety; (3) the absence of fixed defensive techniques such as phobia, hysteria, compulsions, and so forth; (4) lack of excessive repressed hostility and resentment; (5) realistic ego-disinvolvement without undue constriction of the individual's psychological world; (6) insight into the nature of the threat and the meaning of symptoms, as well as ability to recognize the special factors that precipitate bouts of anxiety; (7) an attitude of "learning to live with" unavoidable anxiety, avoiding insoluble situations, and making advance preparations (within reason) for threatening situations that are manageable; (8) hopeful situational factors such as secure employment, opportunity for creative expression, and wholesome interpersonal relationships; and (9) the possession of other personality traits and abilities that help an individual create a secure environment for himself.

Unfavorable prognostic indicators include agitation and depersonalization. The most fateful of all unfavorable prognostic signs is evidence that the patient is ceasing to strive or is striving for regressive goals in an unrealistic setting, which is suggestive of Psychotic Depression and Reactive Schizophrenia, respectively.

Although psychopharmacological therapy is beyond the scope of this book, it should be mentioned parenthetically that modern treatment of acute anxiety neurosis is unthinkable without the anti-anxiety benzodiazepines (e.g., Alprazolam), which can usually stabilize the anxiety condition at a low, tolerable, and nondisabling level.

Clinical Anxiety Syndromes

Anxiety Neurosis

This is the original term for the condition more commonly called now "Generalized Anxiety Disorder" (also inclusive of Overanxious Disorder of Childhood). The original term was retained in this volume because it was considered to be more distinctive and discriminative of the disorder and also more expressive of its intense and aberrant nature that can be characterized most aptly as indicative of apprehensive expectation.

Typically, in Anxiety Neurosis, consciousness is dominated by persistent subjective anxiety and by excessive worries (often unrealistic) that are pervasive, distressing, long-lasting, and more or less uncontrollable. Accompanying physical symptoms include sleep disturbance (both falling and staying asleep), muscle tensions, irritability, restlessness, and fatigability. Many patients also complain about difficulty in concentrating or about their "minds going blank" at the most inopportune times. The cumulative load of anxiety and worry in this condition eventually results in significant emotional distress and in impairment of occupational and social functioning; untreated cases may be totally disabled vocationally.

As one might easily anticipate, the symptoms of Anxiety Neurosis are exacerbated by an increase in environmental stress. Most cases begin in childhood or adolescence and are the outcome of a profound disturbance of the parent-child relationship (rejection or extrinsic valuation), ending in nonsatellization. A much smaller percentage of the cases, occurring in satellizers, may be attributable to temperamental characteristics of the child that make satellization more difficult, for example, inordinate needs for volitional independence. Less rarely, in satellizers, the onset is related to parental overprotection, with resultant overdependency (over-satellization), or to abrupt separation from a parent because of death or divorce. A still rarer onset, occurring during the young adult years, typically follows a long, chronic period of humiliating and oppressive abuse by another (usually related) person(s) or spouse. Although the symptoms of Anxiety Neurosis may usually be controlled and rendered nondisabling and nondistressful, complete cure cannot be expected at this time; at least

I have never witnessed it myself, except, of course, in young children no older than 7. In older individuals there is good reason to believe that the underlying psychopathological changes are irreversible.

Panic Disorder without Agoraphobia

In contrast to Anxiety Neurosis, which is a diffuse condition, present in moderate or severely acute form most of the day and for most of its component activities and happenings, Panic Disorder consists of recurrent, unexpected, discrete, and self-limited panic attacks followed by persistent worry about having another panic attack and also about its implications (for organic disease) and consequences. The attack of many patients may follow exposure to an evocative situation but not invariably or usually so.

Also in contrast to Anxiety Neurosis, the symptoms of which are more or less constant and last all day and everyday at a more or less uniform level of intensity (barring sudden stress), panic attacks are paroxysmal and much more acute in nature, as well as self-limited in duration; between attacks there are usually no symptoms. Subjectively, an attack involves a discrete period of extremely heightened fear marked by an intuition of impending danger and doom. Accompanying somatic symptoms may include sweating, tremors, labored breathing, chest pain, choking sensations, nausea, abdominal distress, dizziness or lightheadedness, depersonalization, derealization, fear of losing control or "going crazy," numbness and tingling of the extremities, fear of dying, and chills or hot flashes.

If agoraphobia accompanies panic disorder, all or some of the following additional symptoms may be present: fear of leaving home alone or going beyond a certain very limited distance from home; mingling in a crowd; standing in a line or on a bridge; and traveling on a train, bus, or automobile. Underlying these symptoms is fear of being in places from which escape is difficult or embarrassing or in which help is typically unavailable in the event of having a panic attack.

The childhood background profiles of my panic disorder patients (with and without agoraphobia) were basically similar in terms of parent-child relationships to those of my much more numerous patients with Anxiety Neurosis: predominantly a history of rejection or overvaluation; a few cases of temperamental disinclination to satellize; an occasional case of overprotection with resultant overdependency; and a small handful of patients who as children had lost a parent through death or divorce. What they all had in common with each other, and with the Anxiety Neurotic patients, was a condition of ego hypertrophy, that is, lack of derived status and of intrinsic security and adequacy; catastrophic impairment of self-esteem; and unrealistically high and tenacious aspirations for achievement and earned status.

Psychopathologically, therefore, the anxiety symptoms of the Panic Disorder patient, as in Anxiety Neurosis, are mostly indicative of severe ego damage, that is, lack of confidence and repressed apprehensiveness about ability to handle a novel adjustive situation and hence gross overreaction to the latter with fear. However, because so many of the symptoms are somatic and highly dramatic, and also mimic life-threatening cardiovascular disease, the defense mechanisms of rationalization and displacement tend to play a much more important adjustive role than in Anxiety Neurosis. The patient plausibly uses this condition either to explain or account for his lack of vocational achievement or as an excuse for withdrawing from further participation in his vocation. At the same time, he displaces the source of the threat from his impaired self-esteem (the real cause of his anxiety) to the externally perceived danger in the panic attack.

Separation Anxiety Neurosis

This is an anxiety disorder occurring chiefly in overdependent children and adolescents (or at least having its onset then) in which the individual manifests excessive anxiety concerning actual or anticipated separation from the home or from a major attachment figure. As a result of this overdependency, the child lacks confidence in his ability to adjust alone to, or to fend for himself in, new surroundings, and overreacts with fear and anxiety to this pending situation. There is, therefore, excessive worry and emotional distress about hypothetically losing major attachment figures through misadventure, staying alone at home, or going to sleep alone. Going to and staying in school, camps, or college may precipitate major crises of fear and anxiety.

In separation anxiety cases precipitated by school entrance or attendance, most of my child patients had a history of overprotection or overdomination by their parents. In some cases, however, the parent-child relationship seemed normal enough, but the child appeared to lack volitional independence on a temperamental (genically determined) basis.

A somewhat different etiology is operative in the case of the school refuser who is typically an overvalued nonsatellizer: He is resistive to attending school because he receives there none of the special entitlements, adulation, attention, and catering that he receives at home. This condition generally responds favorably to parental firmness about school attendance.

With respect to the underlying psychopathology that accounts for the child's anxiety on anticipation of the separation (and for the fear when the separation has already occurred), it seems clear that the overdependent child, with a history of being overprotected and/or overdominated by his parents, develops significant impairment of self-esteem as a consequence of the particular relationship he has with his parents; the implication, therefore, under these circumstances is unmistakable that if left to his own devices without his parents always protecting, directing, and telling him what to do, he would not be able to fend successfully for himself and survive. This is certainly enough to impair anyone's sense of security and self-esteem, which, when threatened further, gives rise to fear and anxiety. It is on this basis, as pointed out earlier, that these children constitute one of the exceptions among satellizers who, for the reasons given, are susceptible to Anxiety Neurosis, its defenses, and complications despite their history of having undergone satellization.

The overvalued nonsatellizer who understandably refuses to attend school because he doesn't receive the unusual deference, privileges, and the adulation there that he is accustomed to receiving from his parents at home, is obviously as susceptible as any overvalued nonsatellizer to experiencing anxiety following anticipated loss of status and self-esteem.

Post-Traumatic Stress Disorder

The distinctive characteristics of this disorder are: that the patient has experienced or witnessed an extreme life-threatening traumatic event happening to himself or others, and is responding with exaggerated fear and/or feelings of helplessness and horror to same; that he re-experiences this traumatic event recurrently, intrusively, and distressfully in recollections, dreams, and nightmares; that he "relives" the event in "flashbacks" and sometimes in hallucinations; that he avoids exposure to associated aspects of the event in related places, activities, persons, thoughts, and so forth; that unsuccessful avoidance of the latter results in emotional or physiological distress; and that he doesn't expect to have a normally extended future with respect to a career, marriage, life span, and so forth.

Symptoms of more general psychiatric significance include a highly diminished interest and participation in his prior activities; feelings of estrangement, detachment, and disinvolvement from others; emotional constriction (e.g., inability to experience and express tender feelings); and signs of increased arousal: problems in falling and/or staying asleep, increased irritability and/or outbursts of rage, hypervigilance, intense startle reflex, and difficulty in concentrating.

The symptoms indicative of re-experiencing and reliving the trauma are not particularly enlightening with respect to interpreting the psychological meaning of this disorder. *Any* person, normal or suffering from a serious mental disorder, on exposure to an extreme, life-threatening, fearsome, and horrific event is bound to have recurrent distressing and intrusive recollections and dreams about same, to relive it through flashbacks, and to manifest signs of increased autonomic arousal. This is no more than the simple psychological and physiological aftereffects expected after such an experience.

However, the decreased interest and participation in customary activities, the detachment and alienation from others, the emotional constriction, and the writing off of his life in the future are all suggestive of emotional disengagement from other persons, from his current activities, and from his future life. Most of the patients whom I have examined with this disorder have impressed me as having seriously impaired self-esteem. They have reacted to an extreme life-threatening event not only with anxiety but also by saying in effect: "Life is precarious and tenuous as this traumatic event demonstrates. It doesn't pay, therefore, to get too involved in it when it could all abruptly go up in smoke. Thus, we will disengage from most of our present commitments and not make any new ones; and now that our commitments have been all but abandoned, we can no longer be threatened through them or overreact to threats against them with anxiety." In effect, therefore, this is an escape from anxiety by withdrawal from striving, from reality commitments, and hence from the possibility of frustration and failure. When unremitting, it is one step closer psychopathologically from anxiety to the depressive and Schizophrenic disorders.

Notes

1. Much of the psychopathological and ego-development background material of Neurotic Anxiety is discussed in chapter 6 in considering the similarities and differences between anxiety and depression in these two respects.
2. The following discussion in this section is largely theoretical, sometimes purely speculative, or based entirely on the author's uncontrolled (anecdotal) or personal experience in clinical psychiatry. However, where conclusions are based on the research findings of other investigators, they are presented only in summary form that identifies majority trends in the findings rather than the individual findings of particular named researchers. The rationale for using this form of bibliographic citation in this type of book is explained in the Preface.

6

Psychotic Depression and Elevation (Mania) of Self-Esteem

The tendency for anxiety and depression to occur together in the same patient has been observed by both clinicians and patients for a long time. Indeed they occur together more often than singly. Anxious depression is the most common form of depression and accounts for the popularity of various psychotropic medications consisting of irrational fixed-dose combinations of antidepressants and anxiolytics (anti-anxiety agents). However, it is not the epidemiologic concomitance of these basic symptoms as an empirical fact of psychiatric practice that should engage our attention so much as its psychopathological significance. Whether anxiety is masked depression, as some clinicians claim, or vice versa, as others contend, is not simply a matter of arbitrary subjective preference or theoretical bias. Rather, it is one of the current central issues in psychopathology with far-reaching implications for an eventual goal of psychiatry, namely, the formulation of a rational, rather than simply a descriptive, classification of mental disorders, based upon the underlying etiology and psychopathology of the various forms of mental illness.

In this chapter, I shall consider more extreme and unrealistic distortions and complications of self-esteem (both lowering and raising) than are characteristic of the anxiety disorders per se described in the previous chapter; they (the anxiety disorders) are not generally regarded as involving sufficient impairment of reality testing to be considered psychotic, as are Major Depression of self-esteem and Mania, in my opinion, in this volume. Inasmuch as anxiety states almost invariably precede the onset of Psychotic Depression of self-esteem, the latter can, therefore, be considered a complication of them (i.e., as a later and more severe stage) of psychopathology, namely, one step beyond severe or traumatic impairment of self-esteem (i.e., massive collapse). However, there is this crucially important difference between the two disorders: Although severe impairment of self-esteem is present in anxiety states, the patient's ego aspirations and goal frustration tolerance, unlike in depression, continue to remain unrealistically and tenaciously high; and he is in no sense disposed to "give up" on life.

The Anxiety Neurotic who goes on to develop Psychotic Depression, on the other hand, continues first for some time to maintain his unrealistically high ego aspirations, despite the near-collapsed state of his self-esteem, and to search for some new basis on which to restructure his ambitions. Eventually, however, the psychotically depressed patient is ready to relinquish his self-esteem claims on life in accordance with the much greater impairment (massive collapse) of his self-esteem than is true of the Anxiety Neurotic.

Before reaching this latter degree of psychopathological severity, however, the sorely beset Anxiety Neurotic merely reacts unrealistically and subjectively to the perceived precipitating threat to his self-esteem with anticipatory fear (anxiety) of future threatening situations that might possibly diminish his impaired self-esteem even further. In contrast, the psychotically depressed patient, although reacting like the Anxiety Neurotic to the precipitating psychosocial threat with greatly increased impairment of self-esteem (massive collapse), does not initially respond affectively (with depression) to the extreme diminution of his self-esteem. It is only the latter *proportionate* affective response (e.g., sadness, dejection) to this later "massive collapse" itself, and to all that this implies, that subsequently gives rise to the familiar, "indirect" affective symptoms of psychotically unrealistic depression of self-esteem.

A clinical picture that frequently presents itself shortly after this point of psychopathological transition between severe Neurotic Anxiety and incipient psychotic depression is reached, is a characteristic syndrome of acute anxiety, sadness, dejection, severe insomnia, pessimism, hopelessness, frantic aimless activity, and complete abandonment of life ambitions that is characteristic of *agitated depression,* a clinical condition that patients find extremely uncomfortable and even emotionally painful—much more so than *retarded* depressions.

Some of the more distressing indirect symptoms of Psychotic Depression are probably mediated through corresponding changes in related neurotransmitter systems (e.g., vegetative symptoms affecting sleep, appetite, sexual desire and performance). These delayed "affective" symptoms are secondary to the massive collapse of self-esteem (which occurred in response to the psychosocial situation precipitating the depressive disorder). In this context, therefore, the latter affective response to collapsed self-esteem is quite *appropriate,* and *proportionate* in quality and intensity to the instigating personality (ego) situation (i.e., the collapsed self-esteem); and this collapse, induced by psychosocial stress or threat, is then further exacerbated by the changes taking place in the neurotransmitters, as well as by the affective responses to the collapsed self-esteem.

Thus, the use of the term *affective* to describe depressive and manic disorders constitutes a misleading misconception and misnomer. The basic psychopathological response is really a psychotically unrealistic massive collapse (or groundless elevation) of self-esteem to a threatening psychosocial situation. It is only natural that the patient will then also respond emotionally to these tumultuous fluctuations in his self-esteem; but the essential or primary psychopathology obviously inheres in the devastating, unrealistic, and *disproportionate* lowering of self-esteem—not in the appropriate and proportionate "affective" response to this lowering, which response can hardly be warrantedly characterized now as an "*affective* disorder" despite the saliency of the appropriate change in mood.

Anxiety and Depression: Psychopathological Contrasts

Depressive reactions are closely related to acute and chronic states of anxiety for reasons over and above the fact that, psychopathologically speaking, severe and long-standing chronic Neurotic Anxiety, with severe impairment of self-esteem, almost invariably precedes, and, in my opinion, is a necessary precondition for, the development of depression.

Major Depression is a psychotic disorder that tends to occur either when there is an abrupt increase in actual or perceived level of stress (and accompanying threat) or when defenses against anxiety break down. At such times it is difficult indeed to maintain striving and to avoid "giving up." In the first place, the chronic Anxiety Neurotic typically has an overdeveloped self-critical faculty[1] in relation to his own abilities, performance, and prospects for success, which tends to become even more severe as anxiety level increases, thereby setting up a mutually reinforcing relationship between anxiety and depression of self-esteem. Thus, he typically tends to react later to frustration and failure with some lowering of self-esteem and disorganization of ability to perform (that is, eventually with depressed mood as well as with anxiety) that further increases his feelings of worthlessness and helplessness and generates increased potentiality for anxiety.

Contrariwise, any enhancement of self-esteem in a depressed patient (as, for example, following the use of antidepressants) tends to reduce anxiety as well as depression. The depression ordinarily accompanying this increased anxiety, however, is not prognostically ominous, because as long as the anxiety is accompanied by goal-directed and adaptive striving, and does not degenerate into panic or demoralization, it (the depression) is not *defeatist* in nature.

It need not be thought, however, that all Anxiety Neurotics who reach this stage of anxiety crisis *necessarily* pass into a condition of Psychotic Depression (collapse of self-esteem). This latter outcome is probably the case only for individuals strongly disposed genically to develop depressive reactions in psychosocial crisis situations. A fairly typical history of the onset of Psychotic Depression in an Anxiety Neurotic often includes disorganized feelings and incipient (unconsummated) behavior indicative of panic (inaction; blocking of action; unreasonable, precipitate, and uncontrolled action) followed by a more or less complete "giving up" of purposeful striving; and he sometimes verbalizes the impression that if not for this precursory panic reaction, or the inability to control same, the depressive response could have been averted.

Because of the chronic Anxiety Neurotic individual's high "goal frustration tolerance," defeat is not accepted easily even when anxiety becomes relatively acute. Thus, he continues for some time to nurture his unrealistically elevated vocational ambitions, despite the severely impaired state of his self-esteem, and to seek some new rationale on which to reconstruct them. Depression then first replaces anxiety when the Anxiety Neurotic reacts to new psychosocial stress or threat with a more intense and generalized (massive collapse) decrement in self-esteem, plus the giving-up reaction, rather than with merely severe anticipatory anxiety accompanied by an additional loss of self-esteem and no inclination whatsoever to give up. Many of my high-anxiety, severely depressed patients also attributed the onset of their condition to a preceding panic-like state characterized by complete disorganization of behavior, paralysis of will, and perseverative, futile actions in which they felt they were "going around in circles and getting nowhere" (see above).

It is on this basis that the clinical picture of agitated depression develops. A form of agitated depression also occurs commonly in menopausal women; it is precipitated in part by the threat to biosocial status and security posed by the prospect of sterility and the loss of "parental vocation" as well as by the emotional instability secondary to hormonal imbalance. In spite of the characteristic guilt-ridden and self-condemnatory trend found in this condition, ego hypertrophy (grandiose ego aspirations) betrays itself in the patient's assertion that she is the "greatest sinner in the world."

Anxiety, however, is not basically replaced by psychotic depression of self-esteem until the Anxiety Neurotic abandons his unrealistic (but tenacious) and compensatorily elevated ego aspirations. At this point of giving up, as John Milton so vividly and poetically expresses it, "Where all hope is gone is left no fear"; for now even the former chronic anxiety sufferer from grossly impaired self-esteem, with possible episodes of panic attack and agoraphobia (superimposed on a chronic Generalized Anxiety state), becomes invulnerable to further anticipatory threat to his already catastrophically damaged self-esteem.

The close phenomenological association between anxiety and depression is confirmed by the fact that the two disorders are more often seen in combination than separately, and that psychiatrists, as well as patients, experience considerable difficulty in distinguishing between them. This co-occurrence is also confirmed by MMPI (Minnesota Multiphasic Personality Inventory) findings.

The most *suggestive* and definitive empirical-clinical finding regarding the co-occurrence of anxiety disorders and Major Depression, however, is the conclusion reached in a study of relatives of individuals with Major Depression plus anxiety that the former are at greater risk for Major Depression, as well as anxiety disorders, than are the relatives of individuals with Major Depression (but) without a diagnosable anxiety disorder. It both suggests a psychopathological, genic, and personality linkage between the two disorders as well as lends support to the hypothesis advanced below that Major Depression occurs as a psychotic complication of anxiety disorders in those persons with severe chronic Neurotic Anxiety of any cause whatsoever, and who, additionally, are genically predisposed toward collapse of self-esteem as their specific form of impairment of reality testing in response to perceived catastrophic psychosocial stress—over and above that already implicated in their Neurotic Anxiety and involving further overwhelming threat to their already impaired self-esteem.

The foregoing formulation of the etiology and psychopathology of depression as a complication of Neurotic Anxiety assumes, of course, that anxiety is ordinarily the *antecedent* or *primary* condition whenever the two disorders co-exist in the same patient. It also assumes that the primary psychopathology in depression is massive and acute collapse of self-esteem rather than a primary mood disorder, which is really an affective response (depressive dysphoria) to this latter collapse of self-esteem.

Thus, the primary psychopathological basis of the association between anxiety and depression is that both conditions are basically disorders of self-esteem. The essential precondition for the development of acute Neurotic Anxiety is severe or traumatic impairment of self-esteem at some point in the life history of the patient. Given this history of gross traumatic impairment, the patient chronically overreacts thereafter with anticipatory fear (i.e., anxiety) whenever he anticipates future threats to his self-esteem that he subjectively *perceives* as possibly impairing it even further, even if these threats are not *objectively* threatening. This is the case: he feels threatened by the new adjustive situation because he lacks confidence (in view of his negative self-evaluation of his own worth and competence) in his ability to cope with the ongoing adjustive situation posed by the threat, particularly if it is novel or unfamiliar.

Depression, on the other hand, is the psychopathological state of affairs that exists when the individual reacts to extreme, subjectively perceived threats to his self-esteem (i.e., to catastrophic-like interpretations of psychosocial stress) with virtually massive *collapse* of the latter—not merely with anticipatory fear referable to prior traumatic impairment of self-esteem, as in the case of Neurotic Anxiety. In depression there is also gross destabilization of personality, reality testing and behavior, followed by secondary appropriate and proportionate mood (affective) responses to the acute and massive collapse of self-esteem.

Psychopathologically speaking, therefore, depression proceeds one important step beyond Neurotic Anxiety. Not only is the underlying impairment of self-esteem much more massive and acute (partaking of collapse), but the accompanying motivational response is also a defeatist abandonment of striving, that is, "giving up" (instead of the compensatory accentuation of achievement motivation and goal tenacity found in Neurotic Anxiety), with resulting significant decrement in, or loss of ability to, function.

Panic states, on the other hand, stand midway between anxiety and depression: The perceived threat to self-esteem is subjectively so overwhelming that self-esteem collapses massively as in depression, but only briefly, leading to severe, transitory destabilization or paralysis of behavior or to complete disorganization of adaptive functioning that is sustained for only short and self-limited periods of time (mini-depressions). Concurrently, however, the panicky individual remains acutely responsive to phobically perceived threats to his self-esteem, overreacting in all directions at once, to almost *any* stimulus, with total paralysis of action, or with precipitate or unreasonable action (because of severely diminished capacity, in his state of extreme behavioral disorganization, to discriminate between innocuous and genuinely threatening situations).

Agitated depression, in many respects, is very similar to panic reactions insofar as prevailing relationships between anxiety and depression are concerned, except that the former condition is less acute and is sustained over a relatively prolonged period of time; hence, it involves much less disorganization of behavior, the anxiety being expressed more benignly as agitation instead of panic.

Consistent with the interpretation both of depression as a more serious psychiatric condition and complication of anxiety, and of anxiety as the typically antecedent form of psychopathology (when the two disorders either coexist or occur sequentially) is the important observation that whereas almost every depressed patient exhibits anxiety, not every anxiety patient manifests depression. This is particularly, predictably, and most seriously true of severely depressed patients (i.e., those with melancholia), inasmuch as in this especially severe variety of depressive disorder one might logically suppose that the predisposing anxiety state operates more saliently as a factor promoting vulnerability to later depression than is the case in milder forms of depression.

Commonality of Ego-Development Backgrounds in Anxiety and Depression

It is hardly surprising that the so-called affective disorders (reconceptualized and renamed here as the psychotically unrealistic, depressed, and elevated [manic], self-esteem disorders) are characteristically manifested by individuals whose ego development is almost entirely that of the nonsatellizer. Since diagnosable Neurotic Anxiety almost always precedes the psychotic self-esteem disorders, and since the latter can be conceptualized most easily as complications of Neurotic Anxiety, it follows that patients with both of these disorders also exemplify a common nonsatellizing history and course of ego development.

Inasmuch as both Anxiety Neurotics and Major Depressives both stem from a common nonsatellizing parent-child relationship, it is evident that they both exemplify very similar ego-development histories and ego structures: the complete absence of any derived status; the undevalued ego omnipotence and volitional independence of infancy; no feelings of intrinsic security and adequacy; ego hypertrophy (compensatory and unrealistically and tenaciously high aspirations for earned [achievement] status) and high goal- and performance-frustration tolerance, as well as enhanced perseverance and resoluteness. These latter personality characteristics are naturally quite compatible with culturally accepted expectations and criteria regarding the attainment of adult personality status; in fact they are basically instrumental in facilitating its development and acquisition.

However, the above personality characteristics that reflect the lack of ego devaluation inherent in the child's failure to undergo satellization as a toddler also constitute at the same time the basic predispositions toward anxiety disorders and their defenses, as well as the complications of anxiety (psychotically unrealistic depression and elevation [mania] of self-esteem, Reactive Schizophrenia, and Delusional Disorder). Residual feelings of omnipotence and of exaggerated volitional independence, when present after infancy, simply reflect, of course, the relative non-occurrence and absence of ego devaluation; whereas the remaining ego characteristics predisposing the child toward these disorders are more reflective of either the direct consequences in ego structure of lack of satellization or of ego compensations for this lack. Specifically, these latter predispositions consist of those infantile ego attributes that are customarily attenuated in the course of satellization—for example, the uninhibited need for immediate hedonistic gratification, potent desires for continued maintenance of executive dependence, and moral unaccountability or irresponsibility.

In nonsatellizers, therefore, these immature ego attributes of infancy undergo maturation at the very best only selectively on an expediential basis, that is, only those particular attributes that are necessary or useful for facilitating achievement or for acquiring other forms of earned status and ego aggrandizement undergo maturation and become stable; and in the event of severe behavioral disorganization or psychosis, frank regression to the original nature of these immature ego attributes occurs since genuine unconditional (unexpediential) attenuation of them had never really taken place. There is hence no real need for these mature ego traits, when achievement and ego-status goals, which they ordinarily facilitate, have been temporarily abandoned for the duration of the mental illness (Reactive Schizophrenia, Delusional Disorder, psychotic depression or elevation of self-esteem).

As indicated in chapter 1, nonsatellization at the toddler stage occurs predominantly in children who typically are genically quite capable of manifesting normal attachment behavior in infancy and of satellizing later at about age 3, but who nevertheless fail to do so because they are overwhelmingly rejected or extrinsically valued (overvalued) by their parents. Less typically and frequently, satellization may fail to occur because the children in question are either unwilling or unable to do so because of inordinately potent (largely genically determined), temperamental traits such as excessive visceral drive and need for volitional independence and for immediate hedonistic gratification.

Satellizing (intrinsically accepted and valued) children, however, may sometimes develop Neurotic Anxiety states (and the associated defenses and complications thereof) if they have been grossly overprotected by their parents to the point of feeling very insecure in fending for themselves in school and with peers, and, thus, becoming overly dependent on parents during childhood and adolescence and even beyond. Anxiety disorders and depression are also more prevalent among adults who had satellized as children but who had lost a parent in childhood or adolescence through death or divorce.

When the severe anxiety, psychotically depressed or manic, Reactive Schizophrenic, or Delusional Disorder patient is not regressed with respect to his ego-maturity traits, or is otherwise symptom-free regarding his particular mental disorder(s), his level of ego maturation (with respect to such traits as responsibility, executive independence, frustration tolerance, perseverance, resoluteness, and deferral of immediate hedonistic gratification for the sake of advancing long-term goals) tends to be unusually high.

This is the case because these latter traits are necessary for, and enhance, achievement and the acquisition of earned status, which goals are obviously very important for these persons with such high status and prestige aspirations. The net effect of these exaggeratedly high ego-maturity traits is obviously to enhance achievement, except, of course, when achievement goals become excessively unrealistic. This is the case in very severe anxiety states, predepressive, depressive, and manic states when the psychosocial symptoms of the disorder in question are rendered more severe and are intensified by the inevitable frustration of such highly unrealistic achievement aspirations.

Ego-Maturity Weaknesses and Strengths in Ego-Hypertrophic Nonsatellizers

Whereas ego maturation in general tends to be enhanced by the developmental and psychopathological conditions leading to ego hypertrophy, two developmental weaknesses are maturationally inherent in this situation, as suggested above: (1) the characteristics of mature personality structure that do not contribute to ego aggrandizement tend to be accepted with great difficulty (this applies especially to moral responsibility); and (2) the characteristics of mature personality status that do contribute to ego aggrandizement are stable only as long as the individual remains within the framework of his hypertrophied ego structure. In the event of severe behavioral disorganization or psychosis, full-blown regression to the infantile attributes of ego-maturity occurs when their mature counterparts are completely abandoned, since they are no longer needed for the ego aggrandizement goals that have been suspended in deeply depressed or acutely Reactive Schizophrenic patients.

Conspicuous among these latter maturational disorders are deficiencies in conscience development that are found in some persons with a nonsatellizing history of ego development, namely, complete moral agenesis (aggressive Antisocial Personality Disorder), and Juvenile Delinquency secondary to unstable internalization of moral obligations. Lack of ego maturation with respect to attenuation of hedonism and executive dependence also occurs sometimes in overvalued children (who in later childhood and adolescence are subjected unexpectedly to tight discipline) as a form of aggressive retaliation against parents. Regressive manifestations of these same ego attributes are, of course, also commonly encountered as major symptoms of psychotic complications of anxiety states (e.g., in Major Depression, Mania, and Reactive Schizophrenia).

The full picture of ego hypertrophy is, of course, most floridly expressed in manic states (exaggeratedly unrealistic and uncritical expansiveness of self-esteem) and also to a lesser extent in the anxiety disorders. It is encountered frequently in somewhat less exaggerated form, in the Narcissistic and Histrionic Personality Disorders, in certain defenses against anxiety (Somatization, Conversion, and Dissociative Disorders), in Hypochondriasis, in Conduct and Antisocial Personality Disorders, in Delusional Disorder, in Reactive Schizophrenia, in the depressive disorders, in many types of alcoholism, and in Infantile Autism.

The obviously unadaptive qualities of moderate and severe manic states have generally tended to blind psychiatrists to the adjustive effects of milder and contained forms of the disorder (i.e., Hypomania), particularly in schizoid, painfully shy, overanxious, abnormally underassertive, and socially inhibited individuals who would otherwise be unable to interact socially with others, to express justifiable anger, to assert their own unconventional opinions, or to develop their off-beat creative potentialities.

Role of Self-Critical Faculty in Depression[2]

Psychopathologically speaking, as already suggested, severe and long-standing anxiety almost invariably precedes and is a necessary precondition for the development of depression. The transition from one psychopathological state to the other occurs first either when there is an abrupt increase in actual or perceived level of stress or threat or when existing defenses against anxiety break down. Second, the Anxiety Neurotic typically has a well-developed self-critical attitude in relation to his own abilities, performances, and prospects for success, which tends to become even more severe as the anxiety level increases prior to the onset of depression, thereby setting up a mutually reinforcing relationship between anxiety and depression. Impaired self-esteem, which is common to both disabling anxiety and Major Depressed states at this point of their interaction, is largely a product of an overly vigorous and unrealistically severe self-critical faculty. (In anxiety states, prior to the onset of depression, self-esteem is primarily determined not by the self-critical faculty but by the difference between aspiration and achievement levels.) If panic, rather than depression, ensues, the behavioral disorganization that results prevents the anxiety-laden individual from distinguishing between innocuous and genuine threats, thereby intensifying the anxiety.

Depression, along with anxiety (and its defenses), Mania, and Reactive Schizophrenic withdrawal, is one of the major psychological responses available to human beings when confronted by catastrophic stress and accompanying threats of massive collapse of self-esteem and of personality destabilization. The foregoing events would appear to occur under these circumstances (see above) in individuals genically predisposed to respond in this way, rather than with Reactive Schizophrenia, for example. It is hypothesized that the specific mediating psychopathological mechanism causing the massive collapse of self-esteem in depression (when either the level of stress increases greatly or previously adequate defenses break down) is a gross intensification of the self-critical attitude, which in turn is mediated by excitation of the orbital portion of the thalamo-cortical tract. (In individuals genically predisposed to Mania, of course, just the opposite train of events ensues: catastrophic stress triggers diminution of the self-critical attitude mediated in turn by inhibition of the thalamo-cortical tract.)

In support of this hypothesis are the following facts and empirically based inferences:

1. Orbital prefrontal lobotomy has a therapeutic effect on Major Depression.
2. The analgesic effect of opioids can be plausibly attributed to their euphoric action, that is, to the fact that the threatening biological implications of pain are largely discounted when these drugs induce euphoria by increasing effective levels of neurotransmitters at synaptic junctions of the above-mentioned area of the brain.
3. Endogenous opioids (endorphins and enkephalins) relieve pain in essentially the same fashion, that is, by being bound to receptor sites located on the thalamo-cortical tract.
4. Orbital prefrontal lobotomy has an even more certain effect on intractable pain than do the opioids. The analgesic effects of opioids can, therefore, be regarded as a partial pharmacological equivalent of section of the thalamocortical tract.
5. Antidepressants (as well as anxiolytics) are therapeutically effective in Agoraphobia and panic attacks. This suggests that in persons predisposed to these conditions, actual or perceived severe threat triggers sporadically occurring mini-depressions (mediated by excitation of the thalamo-cortical tract) that are superimposed on the existing anxiety state. The psychopathological mechanisms underlying such phobic conditions and panic attacks are, therefore, probably closer to those of depression than anxiety despite the fact that they are traditionally classified under anxiety states.

Thus, it would appear that opioids, both pharmacological and endogenous, induce euphoria and analgesia (through euphoria) by decreasing the effective level of catecholamines at synaptic junctions located on the thalamo-cortical tract. Increased levels of catecholamines at this site are, therefore, presumably correlated with manic elation; and, conversely, decreased levels are correlated with depression. Hence, within the normal range of concentration, one can readily conceive of endorphins and enkephalins as having biological survival value by: (1) influencing most persons, particularly youth, to be mildly to moderately more optimistic about their adaptive capacities and prospects for successful adaptation than is actually warranted by strict reality considerations; and (2) facilitating man's capacity to live placidly and to focus on resolving current problems of adaptation without being preoccupied with and dismayed by the seeming cosmic futility of such efforts in the light of the presumed finiteness of his own identity and its presumed dependence on the temporally limited biological integrity of its neural substrate. They probably also have additional survival value insofar as they mediate the placebo effect of drugs and other agents that patients believe to be therapeutic in nature.

Psychopharmacological Relationships between Anxiety and Depression[3]

With regard to the psychopharmacological treatment of anxious depression, anxiolytics primarily reduce anxiety by raising perceptual thresholds for threat, and, thus, secondarily (but less effectively than antidepressants) reduce depression by combating the *concurrent* loss in self-esteem occurring during depressive episodes as a result of further experienced threat to an already severely impaired self-esteem. Not surprisingly anxiolytics are, therefore, much *less* effective than antidepressants in the treatment of "endogenomorphic" symptoms of depression but are *more* effective in counteracting such associated anxiety symptoms as initial insomnia, tension, agitation, and decreased libido; they also elevate depressed mood but much less effectively than do antidepressants.

It is quite understandable under the circumstances that a combination of anxiolytic and antidepressant medications is more effective than either drug alone in ameliorating *both* the depressive *and* the anxiety components of anxious depression. However, there is a clear danger in using anxiolytics alone, either in anxious depression, in severe cases of Neurotic Anxiety, or for Anxiety Neurotics with a history of prior or familial depression, because their anxiety-reducing action is accompanied by a significant lowering of achievement motivation, of adaptive striving, and of goal tenacity. This latter effect is responsible for the frequent clinical observation that anxiolytics may increase psychomotor retardation and suicidal behavior in depressed patients.

From the foregoing, it would appear that the principal neurobiological and/or psychopharmacological mediating mechanism whereby antidepressants elevate depressed self-esteem is by inhibiting the neural substrate (thalamo-cortical tract and associated limbic system) ordinarily regulating the self-critical function, and thereby increasing self-esteem. Their chief therapeutic action is, thus, directed against this distinctive psychopathological process mediating depressive disorders, namely, collapse of self-esteem induced by exaggerated functioning of the self-critical faculty (as opposed to the more typical mechanism whereby self-esteem is lowered in anxiety states, that is, by increasing the gross discrepancy between aspirational and achievement levels).

Therefore, not only are antidepressant drugs the most effective pharmacological agents for combating collapse of self-esteem and its associated dysphoria (depression), but they can also be used rationally and preventively to combat both the chronic impairment of self-esteem that constitutes the chief psychopathological basis of Neurotic Anxiety, as well as the principal intrapsychic predisposing factor for the "affective" disorders themselves (and also for other psychotic complications of Neurotic Anxiety states). In this regard, it has recently been suggested, empirically, through long-standing clinical impressions and anecdotal evidence, that antidepressants are effective in the treatment of chronic anxiety states resistive to anxiolytic drugs and other therapeutic modalities. The effectiveness of antidepressant medications (tricyclics and MAO-inhibitors) in treating panic states and agoraphobia, a finding that is thoroughly consistent with the foregoing formulation of these conditions as variants of anxious depression, or as mini-depressions, is now a well-established clinical fact.

It is credible to hypothesize, therefore, from the pharmacological research data that depression is only one of four basic kinds of "psychotic" complications (that is, involving severe impairment of reality testing) of Neurotic Anxiety, and that it is mediated neurologically by the thalamo-cortical tract, which operates functionally in depressive states as an unrealistically oversevere self-critical faculty. The three other complications are Mania, "Reactive" (as opposed to "Process") Schizophrenia (Schizophreniform Disorder), and Delusional Disorders. These complications tend to arise, as pointed out above, when either perceived or actual level of stress increases or when the defenses against anxiety themselves break down. Which of these four psychotic reactions occurs under these circumstances is probably a function, at least in part, of polygenically determined differential genic susceptibility to particular mental disorders. Because of the profound impairment and distortion of reality testing in endogenomorphic depression, insofar as self-evaluation is concerned, all cases of Major Depression with Melancholia should qualify as psychosis, even in the absence of accompanying psychotic delusions.

Childhood Depression

Because of current intense interest in this issue and fluctuating views about the reality of childhood depression, some brief special attention may be addressed to it here. Until relatively recently (two decades ago), it was believed that children were not subject to depressive disorders—largely because of the widely accepted psychoanalytic view of depression as "anger turned inwards" or against oneself. It was postulated in this theoretical formulation that feelings of hate and hostility toward a significant loved person, for example, a parent or a spouse, are often too ego-alien to be even acknowledged, thus giving rise to a maneuver in which this loved-hated person is *introjected* into the patient's own self, thereby allowing his (the patient's) repressed anger against him to be expressed through displacement onto himself.

This theory has a certain amount of face plausibility inasmuch as both the presence of marked inner rage, and the concomitant absence of overt hostility and aggression toward others, are very common findings in many, but by no means all, clinically depressed individuals. However, there is no evidence whatsoever that would support the inference that this rage is the *cause* of the depression rather than merely a *nonspecific* associated symptom of the clinical condition. It is more parsimonious, therefore, to suppose that any person who perceives his major life goals and ego aspirations to be irretrievably frustrated by his depressed state tends to be consumed by impotent fury directed against himself, because he blames himself for "botching" his chances in life. Cluster analysis of neurotic depression, in fact, suggests that one distinctive subcategory of this condition is marked by extreme self-pity and *overt* hostility toward *others*.

A second major reason why the possibility of childhood depression, comparable to that found in adults, was denied so long is that psychoanalytic doctrine did not acknowledge that children's ego structure was sufficiently mature to allow for the development and expression of adult-like impairment of self-esteem. It has been abundantly shown, however, that although the structure of children's self-esteem is obviously not as sophisticated as that of adults, it is not *qualitatively* discontinuous with it.

Thus, despite introducing this largely irrelevant latter red herring into discussions of the etiology and psychopathology of depression that steered theoretical inquiry regarding the nature of this disorder into unproductive blind alleys for over six decades, Freud must still be credited with one of the most important theoretical breakthroughs in this area, namely, with discovering the crucial distinction between grief (bereavement) and depression, that is, the centrality of impaired self-esteem in the latter condition and its absence in the former. Unfortunately for the subsequent history of psychiatry, Freud's critical insight was, for the most part, ignored or, at best, overshadowed by the widely popularized psychoanalytic characterization of depression as "anger turned against oneself," which like many other misleading and oversimplified half-truth slogans in psychiatry, captured the public imagination. Partly, at least because of this misdirected emphasis on alleged underlying mood disturbance in depression, fundamentally different from its more overt manifestations (i.e., anger as compared to sadness), the early conceptualization of depression as an *affective* disorder, rather than as basically a profound disturbance (collapse) of self-esteem with secondary mood accompaniments was unfortunately consolidated in clinical psychiatry.

Depression and Mania[4]

Last, among the theoretical issues in the psychotic self-esteem disorders, there only remains to be considered the reasons for the tendency for depression and Mania to occur concurrently or alternately in the same individual. Available evidence suggests that psychogenic mechanisms can explain this co-occurrence much more convincingly and parsimoniously than can the neurotransmitter or endogenous opioid theories.

Depression occurs singly overwhelmingly more frequently than alternately or together with Mania. It is followed by one or more manic episodes in only a relatively small minority of cases, whereas manic episodes are followed invariably by depression sooner or later. However, the existence of one condition does predispose toward the occurrence of the other. As convalescence from depression sets in, some patients begin to realize how unwarranted and exaggerated their unrealistically dismal outlook on themselves and on life was in the past. Thus, in the first intoxication of release from depressive despair, the seeds of Mania are sown; for it seems no less miraculous to be delivered from a state in which the reasonable seemed impossible (depression) than to pass into a stage in which the possible, or even the impossible, seems probable, if not certain (Mania).

Conversely, when the manic stage collapses, and untenable commitments made in the glow of prior euphoria cannot be met, and high-flown aspirations cannot be actualized, the resulting "let-down" may precipitate depression on the same basis as occurred originally. A tendency toward all-or-none formulations in relation to the self-critical faculty also predisposes toward violent fluctuations in self-evaluation by interfering with the fusion of positive and negative elements that would otherwise temper each other.

The much higher degree of concordance in depressive disorders for monozygotic than dizygotic twins, and for bipolar than unipolar depression, indicates quite conclusively that these disorders are at least in part genically determined.

Although the specific type of genic regulatory mechanism involved has not yet been definitively established, it would still be fairly safe to extrapolate to the "affective" disorders the general principle that a polygenic regulatory mechanism sets limits for all commonly occurring human traits, both normal and pathological (particularly those that are normally distributed).

Polygenically determined susceptibilities to respond to catastrophic levels of stress with *either* depression *or* Mania, therefore, reflect an additive vectorial tendency, to which many genes contribute, each exerting a small positive or negative effect, that is summated separately in either direction (manic or depressive); and the strength of each summated tendency tends to be normally distributed. In other words, the summated genic effects apply separately to vulnerability to each disorder, Mania and depression, and not to an algebraically summated point on a bipolar manic-depressive continuum. Each of us has a separately determined predisposition (from near zero to extremely high) to respond both manically *and* depressively to stress; and the mechanism whereby each polar opposite predisposes the affected individual to manifest the other polar opposite is psychogenic and learned rather than genically determined.

All of the evidence from normal and pathological variability in human anatomy, physiology, and pathology runs counter to the hypothesis that spontaneous significant fluctuations in effective neurotransmitter or endorphin-enkephalin levels at crucial receptor sites in the brain, account for the tendency for the two polar affective opposites to be associated with each other in the *same* individual, presumably on some genically determined basis.

Nowhere in nature, however (or, at the very most, only in very rare, unusual, or atypical circumstances), where polygenically determined homeostatic mechanisms are mediated through the maintenance normally of narrowly fluctuating enzyme or hormone levels (and where pathological overconcentration of the enzyme or hormone leads to one functional clinical extreme and pathological underconcentration to its clinical opposite), do over- and underconcentration occur either concurrently or alternately in the *same* individual. For example, one never encounters a patient who simultaneously or alternately suffers from both hyper- and hypothyroidism or from hyper- and hypoinsulinism. This is the case because the positive and negative effects of the polygenes implicated in the maintenance of homeostatic balance in *each* disorder are not each separately summated so that sometimes only positive effects are operative while at other times only negative effects are operative. Invariably, rather, in these disorders, positive and negative effects are algebraically summated so as to *yield* overall positive or negative tendencies, the intensity of which in either direction tends to be normally distributed; and correspondingly in depression and Mania, a completely *separate* set of positive and negative genes are operative for *each* disorder.

Thus, in the "affective" disorders, as pointed out above, the polygenic regulatory system must undoubtedly be much more complex inasmuch as separate and independent genically determined predispositions seem to exist for both depression and mania. Hence, for example, positive polygenic effects for *over*concentration of norepinephrine or serotonin and/ or endorphins and enkephalins (as in a predisposition toward Mania) would not be algebraically summated with negative effects for *under*concentration of these substances (as in predisposition toward depression). Rather, positive and negative effects would be summated *separately* for *each* condition so that every individual would manifest a predisposition of given strength toward Mania as well as a separately determined predisposition of given strength toward depression, a different set of polygenes being implicated in each case.

Any possibility of linkage or association between these two predispositions, therefore, would have to be psychogenically rather than genically determined. Psychogenic correlation could be explained, as above, if and when some insight is acquired into the glaring discrepancy between the exaggerated and unrealistic self-esteem and status expectations prevailing in either polar direction, on the one hand, and the actuality of the reality situation, on the other; this induces, in turn, an understandable rebound reaction in the opposite direction. Other credible, and not mutually preclusive, explanations are: (1) that bipolar individuals tend to view themselves and the world in terms of blacks and whites; and (2) that since both depression and Mania are pathologically extreme psychological reactions occurring primarily in ego hypertrophic individuals with high levels of Neurotic Anxiety, a depressed person with this type of ego structure would be much more likely than a nondepressed person, without this kind of ego structure, to exhibit Mania, and vice versa.

Conclusion

In any case, however, if the genic regulatory system in the "affective" disorders were comparable to that occurring in hypertrophic and atrophic endocrinal tissue conditions, respectively, of the thyroid, adrenal cortex, or Islands of Langerhans, as proponents of the neurotransmitter formulation of the affective disorders contend, the co-occurrence of depression and Mania in the *same* person would be just as improbable or impossible as the co-occurrence of hypo- and hyperthyroidism, of Addison's disease and Cushing's syndrome, and of hypo- and hyperinsulinism.

The neurobiological hypothesis that depression and Mania represent polar affective states corresponding to abnormally low and abnormally high effective concentrations, respectively, of catecholamines at critical synaptic junctions is, therefore, biologically untenable. It seems more plausible, therefore, to hypothesize both that: (1) the occurrence of depression and Mania each predisposes the affected individual to an episode of its polar opposite effect, on psychogenic rather than on genic and neurophysiological grounds; and (2) that entirely separate genic predispositions exist for depression and Mania, respectively.

Primary and Secondary Depression

The interpretation of depression as a complication of Neurotic Anxiety is obviously at variance with traditional psychopathological opinion. The prevailing view differentiates a group of "primary" depressions (including the majority of depressed patients, that is, unipolar and bipolar depression) from "secondary" depression, which purportedly occurs only in the context of another psychiatric or medical illness. Each of the primary subgroups of unipolar depression also supposedly exhibits its own distinctive familial and/or genetic pattern. How is it possible, therefore, to reconcile a concept of severe (*clinical*) depression, as a complication of an underlying Neurotic Anxiety state, on the one hand, with the view that primary depressions are very common disorders, on the other, but nonetheless occur independently of such disorders as chronically impaired self-esteem with generalized anxiety?

In the first place, a diagnosis of "primary" depression does not necessarily rule out the possibility that the patient suffers from an anxiety disorder. In some cases this may seem so for a number of reasons: (1) because both patient and psychiatrist are unaware of the existence of the latter condition insofar as it implicates the former (reflective in turn of either good defenses and/or poor insight and perceptiveness); (2) because both are so impressed by, or preoccupied with, the depression that they have neither time nor inclination to search for symptoms of other mental disorders; (3) because the patient is sufficiently experienced and/or motivated to be able to conceal his anxiety from his psychiatrist and/or from himself; or (4) because the anxiety is misperceived as being only secondary to the depression, rather than vice versa.

Second, depression, like Schizophrenia, is clearly a more catastrophic psychological reaction to psychosocial stress and involves a more severe form of psychopathology than does anxiety. Relatively few cases of anxiety disorder are severe enough to be considered incapacitating, whereas incapacitating depressions (e.g., "endogenomorphic" types or depression with "melancholia") are by no means uncommon. Thus, it hardly seems credible to suppose that a *perfectly normal* person would develop a serious depression *de novo,* so to speak, that is, without first exhibiting some prior history of pathologically damaged self-esteem. Consider, for example, the depression accompanying hypothyroidism, the puerperium, pregnancy, menopause, or that following the use of anxiolytics, propanolol, cortisone, raufolfia, or other medication. Careful investigation of the premorbid personality in my experience almost invariably reveals the selective occurrence of the "secondary" depressive disorder in patients with significantly high levels of preexisting anxiety, a familial history of depression, and/or prior pathologically severe reactions to stress.

It is instructive in this connection to recall the fate of the widely accepted, so-called concept of endogenous (or nonprecipitated) depression that at one time served as one of the principal clinical arguments in support of the "spontaneous imbalance of the catecholamines" hypothesis regarding the etiology of "affective" disorders. Although "primary" depressions are theoretically conceivable in relatively anxiety-free persons with unusually prepotent genic predispositions to depressive reactions (when they encounter extraordinary degrees of stress beyond the usual range of human experience), they are rarely, if ever, found in practice. It seems likely, therefore, at least to this observer, that the concept of *primary* depression as a clinical entity will eventually suffer the same fate as that befalling the classificatory concept of so-called endogenous depression for which the absence of precipitating stress is no longer regarded as requisite, but, rather, as symptomatic of so-called melancholia.

In the future, therefore, the term *primary depression* may very well be used in a restricted sense to distinguish it from only those "secondary" forms of depression associated with impaired neural or cellular substrates of mental functioning (e.g., after use of certain drugs or hormones, organic or physiological brain damage, hypothyroidism, etc.), and concomitantly it may be definitively established that long-standing chronic anxiety, reflective of severely damaged self-esteem, may be the typical predisposing factor or antecedent condition present in almost all cases of psychogenic major depression, particularly those accompanied by melancholia. In this present clinical context, calling the depression "secondary" because it occurs in relation to another mental disorder (namely, anxiety states) would be extremely misleading, inasmuch as the antecedent or concomitant anxiety condition is an integral psychopathological precursor or predisposing causal factor, and the later-appearing depressive condition is largely a psychotic complication or decompensation reflective of collapse of the previously partly compensated chronic impairment of self-esteem (anxiety).

Clinical Disorders: Psychotic Depression
and Elevation of Self-Esteem

Psychotic Depression

As indicated above, the underlying psychopathology of this disorder is massive decompensation or collapse of self-esteem following a long-standing Anxiety Neurosis usually present since early childhood in nonsatellizing individuals. When this disorder alternates with manic or mixed affective episodes, it is referred to as Bipolar I Disorder; when it alternates with one or more hypomanic episodes, it is called Bipolar II Disorder. (A Mixed Episode consists of the occurrence of both a Psychotic Depression and a Psychotic Manic Episode on almost a daily basis for a week or more.)

I consider Major Depressive Disorder to be psychotic (even in the absence of delusions), because as a result of the gross impairment of reality testing (due to an overly severe and exacting self-critical faculty), self-evaluation of the patient's abilities, personality traits, aspirations, prospects for the future, and so forth—as reflected in his self-esteem in these respects—are *unrealistically* and disproportionately depressed, leading to objectively unwarranted and disproportionate despair and giving up. (I similarly regard Mania as a psychotic disorder for comparable reasons; but here the opposite situation prevails, i.e., objectively unwarranted, unrealistic, and disproportionate expansiveness or elevation of self-esteem as a result of inhibition of the self-critical faculty.) The *hypomanic* patient's impairment of reality testing, however, is not sufficiently extreme, unrealistic, or disproportionately expansive or elated to qualify as genuinely psychotic in his psychopathology.

Hypomanic Episodes are much less extreme than Manic Episodes; they include such symptoms as elevated or expansive mood, less need for sleep, pressure of speech, flight of ideas, extreme distractibility, and psychomotor agitation.

The clinical symptoms of psychotic depression of self-esteem last at least two weeks. They may be categorized as follows:

Very low self-esteem.[5] This includes feelings of helplessness, hopelessness, uselessness, and worthlessness; unwarranted, deep guilt feelings; abandonment of vocational aspirations and ambitions for achievement and earned status; extreme pessimism; social isolation; preoccupation with recurrent thoughts about death; and suicidal ideation, planning, gestures, and attempts.

Loss of energy or of general feelings of well-being. This is characterized by generalized anergia or decrease of energy; excessive fatigue, especially in the morning; and almost complete loss of interest, motivation, and pleasure in usual activities.

Vegetative. Symptoms include persistent insomnia or hypersomnia; increase or decrease in appetite; weight loss; and diminished sex drive.

Secondary impairment of psychological functioning. This refers to impairment of thinking, concentration, and memory; slowing (retardation) of speech, movement, and thought; and indecisiveness.

Affective. This is characterized by extreme sadness and dejection (rarely, only irritability).

The placement of some of these symptoms in their designated categories is obviously quite arbitrary since they could be placed with equal justification in other categories just as well. The vegetative category contains psychophysiological functions that are delicately balanced and hence are easily disrupted by large fluctuations in feelings of physical and emotional well-being and self-esteem or by gross emotional upset.

Instead of regressing like the Reactive Schizophrenic to a less mature goal structure and seeking ego aggrandizement in a subjective reality of his own making, another alternative is open to a severely stressed and threatened Anxiety Neurotic: He may accept the defeat of his ego aspirations, wallow in the misery of his impaired self-esteem, and renounce all further striving. Soon he is overcome by emotional depression and physical and mental retardation. Suffering and hopelessness are acute, and the individual is so completely overwhelmed by his unworthiness that he sees little point in continuing to live. The sense of future time in relation to the ego is lost, and there is a strong desire for death. This often leads to refusal to eat, and frequently to suicidal attempts. There is no purposeful withdrawal from reality as such; but preoccupation with his own worthlessness, profound physical and mental retardation, extreme depression of mood, and abandonment of striving make participation in social reality completely untenable. When this stage is reached, anxiety no longer occurs since self-esteem could not possibly sink any lower, and since both ego aspirations and the future cease to have any meaning. Where there is no hope, as John Milton suggests, one cannot fear defeat and its loss of self-esteem because it is the destruction of hope that primarily makes for defeat and for fear (anxiety) of it.

In some instances, inordinate and unexpected anger, hostility, and aggression are observed that are quite incongruous with the patient's overall dejected and subdued emotional state. These feelings are typically not directed against anyone in particular, but rather are an expression of rage, self-disgust, and reprisal against all those who participated in frustrating and thwarting his ambitions over the course of his lifetime.

The full (psychotic) Depressive Episode appears to be qualitatively continuous in terms of kinds and depth of feeling tones with transitory depressive fluctuations in mood and self-esteem, as well as heightened level of anxiety. In the latter condition (as in the prodromal stage of a Psychotic Depressive Episode), however, the symptoms are much milder, fewer in number, and do not last very long; these quantitative differences are sufficiently conspicuous to appear to be qualitative in nature. In untreated cases, a Depressive Episode may last as long as six months or even longer, terminating in a Manic Episode (precipitated sometimes by antidepressant medication treatment), in a Dysthymic Disorder (chronic, relatively low-grade, nonpsychotic depression, lasting two years or more), or full remission of all symptoms.

In dementia of the elderly, the onset of the cognitive deficiencies invariably precedes the onset of the depressed self-esteem and affect; they are also much more conspicuous than the latter and are less responsive to pharmacological treatment. Affectively, the grief of bereavement resembles depression and may even seem intense and persistent enough in duration to qualify as a major (psychotic) Depressive Episode. Subsequent investigation, however, invariably indicates that the sadness and tearfulness are emotional reactions to the loss of a loved one rather than to massive collapse of self-esteem. Most mourners also manifest a great deal of unresolved guilt toward the deceased loved one inasmuch as it is too late for the mourner to beg his forgiveness or for him to grant it; to reduce his guilt, therefore, the mourner can only expiate his sins against him in his imagination and observe self-imposed penances.

Psychotic Mania

In contrast to the emotional pain and distress experienced by the Psychotic Depressive, the Psychotic Manic enjoys and is very well pleased by his elevated self-esteem condition, by his feelings of increased well-being, and by his emotional reaction of elation to these feelings, which are comparable to a cocaine "high." His inflated self-esteem is also manifested by a nondelusional kind of grandiosity which assumes an undeserved self-importance and/or omniscience; sometimes instead of a general expansiveness he exhibits an overall irritability. In contrast to the depressive who is disinvolved and disengaged from his normal interests, activities, and aspirations, the manic patient is excessively involved in the latter. This is illustrated by his purposeful psychomotor activity and by his overinvolvement in pleasurable activities that could have painful consequences. The verbal equivalents of his frenetic psychomotor pace are pressure of speech, "racing" thoughts, flight of ideas, circumstantiality, and high distractibility.

In order to have sufficient time to plan and carry out all of his ambitious enterprises and activities, the manic individual has less need for sleep and actually spends considerably less time sleeping than persons not manifesting this disorder. Since his low need for sleep and abbreviated sleeping time are congruent with his high work and activity plans and schedules, he welcomes rather than resents or feels distressed by his lack of sleep, and does not manifest sleepiness, fatigue, inefficiency, confusion, or irritability, the common symptoms of sleep deprivation in nonmanic persons or individuals not in a state of cocaine intoxication.

Unlike depressive reactions, which are basically manifestations of very serious trauma and damage to the self-esteem aspect of ego and personality, and have little or no compensatory or defensive value, Mania can quite plausibly be considered an effective defense (adjustive but not adaptive) against not only threats to self-esteem but also against the massive collapse of self-esteem made in response to this threat and against the affective response (sadness and dejection) to collapsed self-esteem. The manic patient's self-esteem is not only greatly elevated and enhanced, but he is also prepared to act on it in thought, speech, plans, intentions, level of activity, and even in self-imposed limitation of sleep.

Dysthymic Disorder

This is a chronic, relatively low-intensity, long-lasting, and more tolerable form of depressive disorder which lasts two or more years. Depressive symptoms are present for a majority of the days in this latter time period, as well as for the greater part of each day. Although dysthymic symptoms are numerous and severe enough to result in some emotional distress and impairment of vocational, interpersonal, and intrafamilial functioning, the degree of distress and impaired functioning is much less than in Psychotic Depression of Self-Esteem (Major Depression). Much of the experienced symptomatic difference between the two disorders reflects, in fact, the much lesser impairment of self-esteem in Dysthymia. Many Dysthymic patients get quite "used" or resigned to the disorder and are able to function reasonably well with it. In any case it has few of the crisis features of Major Depression; hospitalization is rarely necessary. Despite the relative lack of severity of the symptoms as a whole, and the only mild impairment of self-esteem, disproportionate pessimism, and hopelessness about the future tend to prevail. The onset of Dysthymic Disorder is insidious and tends to occur relatively early in life—typically earlier than Major Depression. Some cases of depression (especially when untreated) originate as Major Depression, but are eventually terminated chronically as Dysthymic Disorder instead of with full remission of all symptoms. More often, however, Major Depression is superimposed on an existing Dysthymia. The co-occurrence of the two conditions is often referred to as "Double Depression."

Cyclothymic Disorder

Cyclothymic Disorder is a chronic, cyclical condition related in part both to Bipolar II Disorder and to Dysthymic Disorder. Like Bipolar II it involves frequent hypomanic episodes over a two-year period alternating with depressive symptoms that (unlike Bipolar II) are not severe enough to be considered part of a Major Depression. Like Dysthymic Disorder, it is a chronic condition spanning at least a two-year period and involving depressive symptoms that are comparable in severity to those of Dysthymic Disorder and sufficient to give rise to moderate emotional distress.

The hypomania of Cyclothymic Disorder is relatively mild but still is usually severe enough to cause moderate occupational or social impairment. In some cases, however, there is either a real or an apparent improvement in functioning due to disinhibition of the self-critical faculty, the inhibition of which was responsible for the hypomania in the first place.

Notes

1. Actually, in persons without mental disorder, as well as in Anxiety Neurotics, current level of self-esteem is ordinarily determined as a ratio between accomplishment and level of aspiration. In depression, however, after "giving up" occurs, self-esteem is determined mostly by the self-critical faculty alone, mediated neurologically (via neurotransmitter level changes) by the thalamo-cortical tract because this mechanism allows for wider fluctuations.
2. See note 2 in chapter 5.
3. Ibid.
4. Ibid.
5. It is interesting to note that even in the depths of depression there is some attempt to preserve ego grandiosity through displacement of affect. The patient admits worthlessness, but sometimes for some irrelevantly innocuous reason. Depressions also are sometimes complicated by obsessive perplexity reactions which serve the same defensive functions as ordinary obsessions.

7

Other Psychotic Complications of Anxiety

Reactive Schizophrenia[1]

In contrast to *Process* Schizophrenia, the onset of *Reactive* Schizophrenia (Schizophreniform Disorder in DSM-IV) is relatively sudden and abrupt (semi-paroxysmal), and the duration of the illness is shorter, that is, at least one month but less than six months. Generally speaking, occupational and social functioning are not necessarily impaired during some phase of the disorder (but might be), as is invariably the case in Process Schizophrenia; and the course of the disorder is also typically more benign. Last, its ultimate outcome, in terms of the patient's ability to function on discharge, as well as he was able to during the premorbid period, without exhibiting the characteristic post-Schizophrenic emotional and behavioral stigmata of Process Schizophrenia, is superior by far.

The symptoms of Reactive Schizophrenia are very similar to those of Process Schizophrenia: delusions, hallucinations, ideas of reference, disorganized speech and thinking, alogia, disorganized, bizarre, or catatonic (rigidly negativistic) behavior, flat and inappropriate affect, irrationality, avolition (decreased voluntary responsiveness), looseness of associations, tangential speech, and silliness. Delusions and hallucinations are often bizarre. Hallucinations are typically auditory but may rarely implicate the other sensory modalities. (This occurs rarely enough to be suggestive of malingering.)

The symptoms that are present and most prominent in a given case of Reactive Schizophrenia are largely a function of the subtype in which a given patient belongs:

> *paranoid*—both bizarre delusions and auditory hallucinations, frequently with associated ideas of reference, are prominent, but not disorganized speech, catatonic behavior, or flatness or inappropriateness of affect;

catatonic—exaggerated and apparently purposeless motor activity; negativism, rigidity, and mutism; bizarre and stereotyped posturing, manners, and grimacing; and catalepsy or stupor;

disorganized—flat and inappropriate affect, as well as disorganized speech or behavior, are prominent;

residual—absence of the prominent symptoms of the paranoid, catatonic, and disorganized subtypes, and the presence of such so-called negative symptoms of flattened and inappropriate affect, irrationality, alogia, and avolition.

In Reactive Schizophrenia (in contrast to Process Schizophrenia), a relatively extreme and acute form of withdrawal adjustment occurs in ego-hypertrophic individuals (typically nonsatellizers, as opposed to the typical satellizers in Process Schizophrenia) in response to catastrophic environmental stress. In contrast to the depressive disorders also, Reactive Schizophrenia is more likely to occur in introverted individuals (withdrawal and disengagement naturally occur more readily in introverts); but the introversion is seldom as marked as in Process Schizophrenia, and is by no means an indispensable condition of its occurrence, inasmuch as pronounced extroversion occurs sometimes in the reactive form of the disorder.

The more crucial premorbid predisposing factor in the Schizophrenic disorders is failure in ego maturation (i.e., of desatellization in the *process* type, and of ego devaluation satellization in the *reactive* type). In the prodromal phase, the ego structure of the Reactive Schizophrenic, as a nonsatellizer, consists of exaggerated ideas of volitional omnipotence and of inordinate volitional independence; the absence of derived status, of intrinsic security and adequacy, and of an inner core of intrinsic self-esteem; low functional self-esteem; unrealistically high and tenacious aspirations for achievement and earned status prodromally; and selective, expediential development of those ego-maturity traits that foster achievement; and high Neurotic Anxiety level.

In Reactive Schizophrenia there is typically a history of ten or more years of more or less neurotic adaptation to adult reality and of multiple defenses against anxiety before abrupt withdrawal from emotional investment in the real world and (in the event of chronicity) disinvolvement from mature adult goals take place. Reactive Schizophrenia is typically precipitated in the course of Anxiety Neurosis by a new catastrophic threat to self-esteem, or by a breakdown of previously adequate defenses, to which the patient reacts by abrupt withdrawal and disengagement from adult goals, from reality, from interpersonal relationships, and from adult standards of maturity. All of this, of course, presupposes severe impairment of reality testing. Grossly regressive symptoms (e.g., fecal smearing) also occur as in *Process* Schizophrenia.

In the classical or *Process* form of Schizophrenia, the psychosis is merely the culmination or end result of the natural evolution of the pre-Schizophrenic personality: It is the almost invariable and insidious outcome of the continued existence of this type of personality make-up—or, at any rate, if a mental disorder occurs in such a personality, no other type of psychotic reaction seems as probable.

On the other hand, in an individual not endowed with the pre-Schizophrenic personality, another type of Schizophrenic reaction may occur which is an abortive attempt at adjustment upon confrontation with overwhelming environmental demands. Such an individual has previously adopted normal or other abnormal, but non-Schizophrenic, techniques of adjustment and actually and potentially has a better adjustive capacity than the classical *process* type. This second variety of reaction occurs later in life, begins more acutely, is more exogenous in origin, and runs a more benign course. There is often a strong affective component present, as in the catatonic variety, or various compensatory paranoid trends. This reaction is not a cumulative or well-nigh inevitable result of a predisposing personality disorder, but a transitory Schizophrenic-like complication or decompensation in a chronic Anxiety Neurotic who is abruptly overwhelmed by one or more of the common vicissitudes of life.

The relatively rare occurrence of Schizophrenia in children supports the hypothesis that the process type is the outcome of maturational failure relative to the preadolescent and adolescent periods. Reactive Schizophrenia, on the other hand, tends to be a terminal type of maladjustment in the overanxious nonsatellizer, not generally appearing before the third or fourth decades of life. It would be a fair inference, however, to expect juvenile Schizophrenics to conform more to the process type because of the heavy loading of constitutional and predisposing factors that obviously must operate in such cases. If our hypothesis is correct, the reactive type would tend to follow overt rejection of the child by the parent, whereas the process type would tend to be preceded relatively more often by overprotection and underdomination.

Schizoaffective Disorder

The unusual feature of this disorder is that it appears to consist of two co-equal components indicative of complication or decompensation in Anxiety Neurosis—a Reactive Schizophrenic aspect and a depressive and/or manic reaction to a new threat instigating massive collapse of the patient's self-esteem. Both aspects of the Schizoaffective response appear to be different but parallel reactions to his collapsed self-esteem: (1) a reactive psychotic withdrawal and disinvolvement from adult interpersonal reality and striving for status and achievement; and (2) a marked deflation or inflation of self-esteem (these two latter reactions to a perceived catastrophic threat, reflective of inhibition or maximization of the self-critical faculty, lead to impaired reality testing and unrealistic perception).

Thus, both the Schizophrenic and the depressive or manic reactions in Schizoaffective Disorder are integral parts of a total reaction to this catastrophic threat, rather than additional components (depressive or Schizophrenic) added on to, or superimposed on, the disorder as, for example, an affective reaction to the existing collapse of self-esteem in Psychotic Depression or Schizophrenia. The mood is reactive and proportionate to the prevailing depression or elevation of self-esteem.

Delusional Disorder

This disorder is marked by the presence of a more or less plausible, credible, understandable (within its cultural context), and persistent delusion (lasting at least one month) that is not bizarre. Thus, unlike Schizophrenia, delusions in this disorder are more reality oriented or the products of less impaired reality testing than is the case in Schizophrenia. Auditory hallucinations, as well as such negative symptoms as avolition, alogia, and flattened and inappropriate affect, are less common than in Schizophrenia. On the other hand, ideas of reference are much more prominent. Generally speaking, occupational and social functioning are relatively unimpaired unless the content of the delusional system is implicated in these areas of functioning. Delusions may be persecutory, erotomanic, somatic, grandiose, or sexually jealous in content.

On the whole, despite the indications of better reality testing than in Schizophrenia (the nonbizarreness of the delusions, the absent or less prominent hallucinations, the less disengagement and withdrawal from mature adult goals and relationships, and the absent or fewer negative symptoms), there is still probably sufficient impairment of reality testing to regard the disorder as a psychosis, although less so, of course, than Schizophrenia. In substantiation of this judgment the delusions of this disorder generally respond to antipsychotic medication.

As far as the underlying mental mechanisms of the delusions are concerned, some elements of projection are almost always involved where an individual believes that he is the victim of aggression, assault, conspiracy, and so forth: he simply projects his own injurious actions and intentions onto someone else, for example, a personal enemy, and believes that he himself is the target of the malevolence in question. By this maneuver—by attributing the culpability to another—he also effectively disowns these unacceptable intentions; and with the help of some rationalization, he can then use the persecution, hostility, and conspiracy to explain why he hasn't been more successful in life.

Unfortunately, however, it is in the diagnosis of Delusional Disorder that the dearth of ordinary common sense has been most conspicuous among some psychiatrists and other mental health professionals. The evaluation of Schizophrenic delusion does not usually present this problem to the same extent because their bizarre and outlandish nature obviously stamps them as psychopathological. But in Delusional Disorder, not only are the delusions generally not bizarre, but in many cases they are also based on eminently possible events or are quite plausibly inferable from them in terms of everyday experience. Persecution, discrimination, exploitation, oppression, and denial of others' rights, including secret and malevolent plotting and conspiracy, have always been ubiquitous occurrences in interpersonal, intergroup, and community life.

Thus, for example, if an elderly man, recently admitted to a psychiatric hospital, asserts in the course of his mental status examination that his daughter and son-in-law have virtually been holding him prisoner, beating him if he complains, and defrauding him of his life savings, the mental-health professional must obviously explore *two* possible explanations from a commonsensical standpoint: either the patient is simply stating the actual facts in the case (with or without some overstatement) or else he is delusional. The first possibility, however, must self-evidently be thoroughly investigated and ruled out before the second one can be warrantedly accepted for diagnostic purposes.

But far too many psychiatrists, in my experience, bowing either to popular misconceptions stemming from the overpsychologization of belief in our culture, or to irrational clinical blind spots of their own, rush to make a diagnosis of Delusional Disorder without first ruling out the factual possibility of false imprisonment, fraud, and elder abuse. Further, in addition to the cultural bias operating here, psychiatrists are undoubtedly influenced in making such a diagnosis in this case by the fear of incurring negative criticism from colleagues, either for missing such an "easy" diagnosis in a patient with such glaring, textbook symptoms or for being hopelessly naive and indecisive in suspending diagnostic judgment pending investigation of the latter's "far-fetched psychotic tale."

The cultural bias to which the psychiatrists are pandering (in this case which they helped to create and foster in the first place) is derived from the widespread lay misconception that anyone who complains vigorously and persistently of injustice, persecution, conspiracy, discrimination, or victimization of any kind, especially at the hands of relatives, ostensible friends, supervisors, employers, or public officials must be regarded and treated as "paranoid" (i.e., suffering, by definition, from persecutory delusions). The public apparently prefers to believe this fiction than to acknowledge that persecution is, and always has been, an unfortunate but very real occurrence in human relations. This is a good example of the previously stated observation that most people (with obvious exceptions) are generally reluctant to admit the existence of deliberate evil-doing in the world, even preferring to use the euphemism "mental illness."

Note

1. Terms such as *Reactive* and *Process* Schizophrenia were devised in the past to represent perceived differences in personality development, psychopathology, etiology, and clinical course for different identifiable types of Schizophrenia, and as a means of going beyond the conventional descriptive approach to the disorder. In 1949, for example, the author published one such paper. These terms, however, are seldom used today despite their psychopathological, clinical, and heuristic value.

8

Personality and Mental Disorders Due to Maturational Failure in Desatellization

The mental and personality disorders considered in this section primarily reflect a deficit, deficiency, or failure in the final stage of ego maturation, namely, in the process of desatellization, which ordinarily takes place mostly in adolescence. This stage essentially marks a transition between the personality or ego structure of childhood and adolescence, on the one hand, and of young adulthood, on the other. The personality maturation that takes place at this time is, of course, neither the first nor the only instance of ego maturation that takes place during the satellizing period of ego development. Progress in the attainment of such ego-maturity goals as executive independence, responsibility, frustration tolerance, impulse control, and so forth, is continuous throughout the prior stages of ego development; what is basically new, however, in the desatellization process is that the rate of maturation it encompasses is higher, the degree of change achieved is much greater, and the accompanying ego-status changes (part of the maturation process in the larger sense of the term) are more striking. For example, elevated aspirations for volitional independence and earned status are disproportionately more abrupt in their rise, as well as more thoroughgoing in those adolescents who do not exhibit maturational failure.

Complicating considerably the interpretation and diagnosis of this maturational condition involving defect or failure in desatellization at adolescence, described above, is the existence of a phenotypically very similar condition of maturational failure that, genotypically, is completely different in terms of developmental background and etiology. The first condition considered above naturally presupposes a difficulty or inability to go beyond a strong satellizing orientation, both in establishing basic interpersonal relationships and in seeking a derived rather than an

229

earned type of status; it could be overcome only by adopting a volitionally more independent orientation predicated more on equality and reciprocity in relationships or on a more intense quest for earned status.

Of course, when the respective past personality histories of the two individuals in question are known, then their two contrasting ego-development backgrounds with respect to the phenotypically similar conditions of maturational failure in adolescence, remove any possibility of confusing their differential interpretation and diagnosis.

By definition, a failure in desatellization presupposes a prior history of a better-than-average degree of satellization, the effects of which fail to be adequately attenuated in the course of adolescent personality development; whereas, on the other hand, the other phenotypically similar, but genotypically opposite, case of adolescent maturational failure is obviously that of a nonsatellizer who is sacrificing his elevated aspirations for earned status in order to obtain reactive, counteraggressive revenge against a hated authority figure (usually a parent) by deliberately sabotaging all efforts to undergo the transition to adult personality status in adolescence. Ego maturation for such an individual obviously does not consist principally of desatellization, since satellization never occurred in the first place; nor, by the same token, does failure in ego maturation mostly involve a lack of desatellization inasmuch as this individual self-evidently couldn't fail to desatellize if he had not undergone satellization in the first place.

Nevertheless, the person manifesting the classical symptoms of Inadequate and Immature Personality Disorder actually is in most instances a satellizer par excellence who finds the challenge of desatellization extremely difficult to meet and overcome. As indicated earlier, this difficulty usually reflects either an overaccentuation of an extreme of one dimension of the parent-child relationship (i.e., parental overprotection or over- or underdomination), or an excessive disparity between parent and child with respect to such temperamental (largely genically determined) traits as volitional independence, assertiveness, dominance, and so forth.

Both types of inadequate and immature personality disorder—the basic type indicative of failure in desatellization and the reactive, counteraggressive type that resembles it only phenotypically—will be discussed in this chapter along with: (1) the most common type of narcotic addiction; and (2) the mental disorder (i.e., Process Schizophrenia), both reflective in part of this first type of maturational failure. Other manifestations of reactive, counteraggressive personality disorder (i.e., not the hostile and vindictive sabotage of adult personality development) but, rather, Conduct Disorder, juvenile delinquency, Antisocial Personality Disorder, and Narcissistic Personality Disorder) will be considered in chapter 9.

Inadequate and Immature Personality Disorder

The defects in ego organization that result from maturational failure have already been briefly described. It will be recalled that ego devaluation, as well as attenuation (preliminary maturation) of infantile ego attributes, take place normally in satellizers and oversatellizers. However, the next step in maturation that usually occurs in preadolescence and adolescence, that is, desatellization and the acquisition of adult personality status (volitional independence, striving for long-range fulfillment of adult ego goals, increased executive independence, frustration tolerance, societal moral responsibility, etc.) fail to eventuate. Hence, lack of maturation rather than regression is the hallmark of this disorder.

Because of the presence of intrinsic security and adequacy, however, Neurotic Anxiety does not occur and relatively meager reality accomplishments can be tolerated with equanimity. Aspirational tenacity (goal frustration tolerance) is low, whereas self-esteem and performance frustration tolerance is high. The type of behavior disorder that finally prevails in this type of aberrant ego development is largely influenced by the factor of introversion-extroversion. In either case, characteristic modes of gratifying the hedonistic goal structure are found. And since satisfaction is neither sought nor can be gained through normal adult goals, there is some compensatory retrogression to even more childish levels of goal striving, especially when the individual is removed from the supervision of parents for whose sake only minimal attenuation of hedonistic impulses occurred in the first place.

The predominantly extroverted inadequate personality satisfies his hedonistic needs in reality by finding ways of gratifying his pleasure-seeking and childish goals. Since it is obviously impossible for an adult to adapt to an adult world of reality while retaining the goal structure of a child, successful adjustment at a mature level fails to take place.

Because of lack of emotional identification with normal goals, the extroverted inadequate personality is unable to sustain his motivation in striving for them or to derive any satisfaction from their realization. His attitude toward life is passive and dependent. He demonstrates no desire to persevere in the face of environmental difficulties or to accept responsibilities that he finds painful.

But despite his underlying sense of intrinsic adequacy, the failure to acquire extrinsic status would still be quite frustrating and traumatic were it not for a protective inhibition of the self-critical faculty. Otherwise, it would explode the fiction of serene adequacy so vital to his sense of puerile security. Thus, we find the strange paradox that in the personality disorder in which the most inadequate adaptation to life is made, there are no subjective feelings of inadequacy. Thanks to an impaired self-critical faculty, the inadequate personality is able to deny the very existence of his difficulties and problems as well as his obvious inadequacy. By making unwarranted assumptions about his capacity for meeting new situations, he obviates the necessity for painful planning or preparation. By denying his failures and exaggerating the efficacy of his adjustment, he is thereby required to put forth less effort toward a positive solution of his problems. He becomes preoccupied with the search for an easy, effortless, unearned form of pleasure. All of these factors contribute to his resulting instability and nomadism that is characteristic of this group as a whole, as well as his overriding predisposition to narcotic addiction.

Etiology

Overprotected child. The principal variable predisposing an extroverted young adult individual to Inadequate and Immature Personality Disorder (maturational failure in adolescence relative to desatellization) is the history of his parents' child-rearing attitudes that would indicate whether he was an overprotected, overdominated, or underdominated child. All three of these latter individuals are satellizers.

The overprotecting parent has compulsive needs for providing a completely sheltered environment for his offspring. Thus, he makes an effort to provide for the latter an environment that is free of any type of hurt, disappointment, frustration, or painful contact with the harsher realities of life. This goal is achieved most effectively by isolating him from all experiences which could possibly result in such consequences, and by refusing to allow him to plan to do things for himself for fear that injury or failure might result.

It is clear, therefore, that the overprotected child, turned adolescent, cannot under these conditions acquire volitional and executive independence and self-direction; aspire to long-term earned status; persevere in his tasks; learn impulse control, frustration tolerance, and responsibility— in short, all of the mature traits necessary for adult personality status and functioning. He is focused instead on attaining immediate hedonistic gratification and on perpetuating both his executive dependence and the derived status of his childhood.

Overdominated child. In terms of both source and expression, parental overdomination is largely the opposite of underdomination—even though the general consequences of both attitudes are quite similar with respect to their impact on ego maturation. However, there is much greater possibility of heterogeneity in the child's response to overdomination than to underdomination.

This heterogeneity proceeds from variability in: (1) the brusqueness, hostility, kindliness, or affection with which the overdomination is administered by the parent; and (2) the self-assertiveness of the child. The first variable governs the acceptability of the overdomination to the child. The second variable determines the type of resistance that will be offered if the overdomination is unacceptable, that is, active rebellion or passive sabotage. With respect to the origin of the overdomination in the parent-child relationship, one possibility is the concomitance of unusual dominance (on genically determined temperamental grounds) on the part of the parent and of unusual submissiveness (on similar grounds) on the part of the child. More often, however, the explanation lies more in the parents' own upbringing or in his current occupational or marital circumstances.

Where the domineering parent's discipline is benevolent, consistent, and acceptable to the child, rebellion or sabotage tend to be rare responses. Continued acceptance of the parent's authority under these circumstances, thus, results in only *partial* failure in maturation. The child is given all of the necessary experience by his parents for acquiring volitional and executive experience for later use in aspiring to, and implementing, adult goals competently, that is, all except the experience needed both in making his own decisions and in independently initiating the operations following from them under his own self-direction, without authoritarian control or supervision.

Underdominated child. In most cases, the underdominated child is a product of a marked temperamental disparity in self-assertiveness between parent and child. Sometimes, however, it reflects the parent's desire to either emulate or repudiate his own upbringing. Typically, the prevailing combination of self-assertiveness is that of a temperamentally unassertive and submissive parent and a temperamentally aggressive, dominant, and assertive child. Like the overprotective parent, the underdominating parent is highly reluctant to frustrate the child, but for a different reason (largely because of his submissiveness, not because it would increase his own anxiety by projection). In both cases there is unusual tolerance for the child's hedonistic motivations, his demands for immediate gratification, and his lack of frustration tolerance and of impulse control. The underdominated child has a superabundance of the self-assertive aspects of volitional independence, but lacks the personality traits that would make possible the implementation of this independence.

What is perhaps most distinctive of the overly permissively reared child's relation to his later maturational failure is his dearth of direct experience with the limiting and restrictive features of reality (because his parents have set no limits). As a result, he is, therefore, unable to take these factors into account in choosing roles, in setting goals, and in making demands on others that do not exceed the latter's limits of tolerance. His behavior, thus, is typically out-of-bounds and inappropriate since he has never learned the limits of acceptable conduct. In his relations with children and other adults, he is aggressive, petulant, and capricious. His bullying, domineering, and importunate behavior learned in relation to his parents is carried over into relationships with peers and other adults. He has a large fund of derived status to which he clings, and his parents are unduly lax and tolerant in not pressing him to acquire any earned status.

Needless to say, the reactive, counteraggressive, and vindictive nonsatellizer who develops the phenotypically similar inadequate, immature personality disorder has very similar symptoms of this disorder but his developmental background, the reasons for his development of the disorder, and its psychopathological meaning and significance are all markedly (genotypically) different. The latter individual is also just as predisposed as the inadequate, immature personality to becoming addicted to narcotic drugs (see below).

Narcotic addiction. The large major narcotic addiction treatment centers in the United States all reported unanimously in the 1950's to 1970's that the most frequent diagnostic type of narcotic addiction in their patient populations was the Inadequate and Immature Personality Disorder (although some facilities used different but equivalent diagnostic labels for this entity). On psychiatric examination, these addicts were found to lack long-term, adult, and mature aspirations and goals (academic, vocational, marriage and a family). In addition, they lacked the mature adult character traits necessary for implementing and actualizing these goals: a sense of responsibility, volitional and executive independence, frustration tolerance, impulse control, ability to defer immediate hedonistic gratification, social recognition, self-reliance, self-direction, reliability, persistence, and resoluteness. The narcotic addict, in short, presented in almost pure culture most of the major clinical symptoms of Inadequate and Immature Personality Disorder in addition to those of narcotic addiction per se. (There are, of course, other diagnostic categories of narcotic addicts, i.e., those who take small controlled doses to relieve anxiety or depression; persons with Antisocial Personality Disorder; and normal nonaddicted youths in depressed urban areas who abuse the drug because it is expected of them in their slum-urban peer groups. It was estimated that almost two-thirds of the inmates in these narcotic-addiction treatment institutions were individuals who had been diagnosed as manifesting Inadequate and Immature Personality Disorder.)

From the ranks of the inadequate and immature personalities are recruited vagrants, hobos, drug addicts, petty criminals of all varieties, poolroom and racetrack hangers-on, carnival operators, confidence men, and others. Of all these characters, the narcotic drug addict makes the most satisfactory adjustment (from his own point of view). Drug addiction results in positive, immediate, pleasurable (euphoric) sensations that satisfy the quest for effortless, hedonistic satisfaction. It dulls the self-critical faculty to the point where the addict becomes easily contented with his inadequate, hedonistic adjustment to life, and is more easily able to evade and overlook responsibilities; and where in the complete absence of any actual accomplishment, he feels supremely satisfied with himself and his future. By virtue of its analgesic properties and general dulling effect on consciousness, the drug also provides a partial escape from the disturbances and distasteful elements of reality. Thus, if he is actually required to work and assume responsibility, the hard, distasteful edge of the task is softened, much in the way a self-indulged child will fulfill his chores as long as he has a lollipop in his mouth.

The inadequate personality who does not discover opioid addiction leads a very unstable, nomadic type of existence characterized by a precarious and marginal vocational adjustment and by frequent, unnecessary changes of employment. He is also predisposed toward alcoholism, addiction to other drugs, and all thrill-seeking forms of vice. He is able to adjust marginally in an optimal environment, that is, one structured in terms of his irresponsibility, passivity, and hedonistic needs, but in no other.

The euphoric effects of narcotics are highly adjustive (but never adaptive) because they give rise to intense feelings of self-contentment and well-being in the complete absence of any objective justification for same in reality—in fact, even in the presence of good reasons for otherwise feeling the opposite, for example, lack of academic or vocational achievement, no job, no spouse, or no prospects. The component elements of this euphoria include: (1) inhibition of the thalamo-cortical tract, with elevation of self-esteem (the principal element of the drug-induced euphoria); (2) a "rush"—orgasm-like abdominal feelings of pleasure after intravenous injection of narcotics; (3) inhibition of the urgency of the primary drives (e.g., hunger and sex) (their deprivation no longer seems so threatening); and (4) abolition of all pain and discomfort.

Process Schizophrenia

This is the classical chronic Schizophrenia, the type that filled our mental institutions in the decades prior to and shortly after World War II. In contrast to Reactive Schizophrenia considered above, it is less acute and more insidious in onset, occurs in a younger population, and tends to run a more chronic and less benign course. Before the antipsychotic drugs were available, about half of the first-admission Schizophrenics improved sufficiently enough to be discharged after one month; the remainder were assigned almost indefinitely to back wards. For the reactive type these figures were somewhat better than for the process type. After Chlorpromazine came into widespread use, the statistics improved substantially for both types. Unfortunately, however, a sizable proportion of discharged patients had to be readmitted, creating a therapeutic situation known as the "revolving door" problem.

Not only is there greater impairment of occupational and/or social functioning in the premorbid phase of the disorder than in the reactive type, but there is also considerable characteristic post-Schizophrenic cognitive or behavioral stigmata. What is perhaps most distinctively and differentially pathognomonic of the two types of the disorder is that the process type appears to be the slow, insidious, and inevitable culmination of a long, slow process of deteriorative personality change toward inadequacy, whereas the reactive type is a more or less acute reaction to a psychosocial threat that has catastrophic implications for the individual. Characteristically, the Process Schizophrenic, in my experience, does reasonably well in elementary school, at home, and with his peers, that is, when his predominant interpersonal orientation is still satellizing and he has little or no aspirations for achievement, earned status, volitional independence, emancipation from parents, and so forth. Premorbid symptoms first appear when he encounters the above problems.

Process Schizophrenia represents a marked and functionally complete withdrawal type of adjustment in which the ego is removed beyond the reach of an unsatisfactory objective reality, and imbedded in a subjective, autistic reality of its own making. It occurs in the motivationally inadequate individual who fails to undergo adult ego maturation in goal structure. A strong constitutional predisposition toward introversion facilitates the development of the withdrawal reaction. He is too "tender-skinned," egocentric, and inclined toward indirect emotional participation in reality through the medium of symbols and intellectualization to venture the alternative of seeking hedonistic gratification in reality against the opposition of parents and cultural agents (the inadequate and immature personality disorder). Introversion also becomes a compensatory adjustive mechanism since it permits gratification of immature ego demands in fantasy.

Handicapped by this personality make-up—having no stake in the adult world of reality motivations and little opportunity for gratification of infantile desires (as long as he is required to adjust according to adult standards)—the individual gradually withdraws whatever emotional energy he has invested in adult goals in reality. He does this not because of an overwhelming sense of failure following the frustration of normally motivated desires (for he has no such sense of failure), but because he "concludes" that reality is an unsuitable medium for the gratification of his immature ego demands, and forsakes it for the obvious superiority of the world of fantasy with whose enchantments he has been progressively flirting. Some precipitating event eventually occurs, often trifling and insignificant enough in itself, which convinces him that adult motivations and reality living represent losing propositions; and that he would fare better by dropping all pretense of adult reality adjustment, and frankly expressing his true desires in fantasy.

In catatonics, the severance and disinvolvement of self from reality and mature standards of goal structure are most complete and abrupt. This transition to the patient's subjective reality and to a lower level of goal maturity may be accomplished within the space of several days or even several hours, and is most apt to occur in proud, vigorous, and volatile individuals capable of intense, uninhibited rage responses.

The paranoid reaction tends to negate frustration by distortion of the environment (rationalization and projection). This condition must be differentiated from the relatively rare disorder, *paranoia,* in which adult goals are not abandoned and loss of contact with reality is neither desired nor attained; but the patient's perception of that portion of his psychological field, which is most significant for him, is so distorted by a self-consistent delusional system that actual participation in a shared social reality impinging upon this field becomes impossible. Outside of this rather extensive field, however, the attitudes, values, and perceptions of patients with paranoia are entirely reasonable and realistic.

The symptoms of Process Schizophrenia are very similar to those of Reactive Schizophrenia described above. In any given individual case, the predominance of the particular symptoms is largely a function of the subtype of the disorder that he manifests. The following list of symptoms is arranged by functional category or psychological interpretation of their meaning or significance. A given symptom may also have two or more functions:

1. Withdrawal Adjustment: social and interpersonal withdrawal; emotional and cognitive detachment, disengagement, and disinvolvement from adult reality goals, aspirations, relationships, and activities; negativism, rigidity, mutism, stupor, abulia or avolition.
2. Ideation, behavior, and emotional expression that appear bizarre because patient and observer are operating from different planes of reality (especially flattening, inappropriateness, and silliness of affect; posturing); and the former's reality-testing and self-critical faculty are also impaired. In the case of hallucinations, delusions, and ideas of reference, the mechanisms of projection, disowning, and rationalization are additionally involved.
3. Disorganization of Speech and Thinking: reflects disorientation due to impairment of reality testing and self-critical faculty. This also applies to tangential thinking and loosening of associations.
4. Regression to Infantile Behavior Patterns: reflects true retrogression or descent to a lower level of adjustment; release of existing immature tendencies when the censorship repression of an intact reality-testing mechanism is removed; and failure to undergo normal personality maturation.

In the development of the disorder, maturational (desatellization) failure is the predominant psychopathological developmental process. After the disorder has progressed for several years, however, regressive deterioration (personality, intellectual, and behavioral) become more salient as the patient loses complete touch with functioning in the real world.

With the advent of antipsychotic medication in 1955, the prognosis of Process Schizophrenia has greatly improved, but the "revolving door" problem, due to nonresponsiveness of some patients to the antipsychotic medication and to failure of other patients to continue taking the medication after discharge from the hospital, persists. The use of monthly injections of depot preparations has greatly ameliorated the latter situation.

Infantile Autism

Despite the superficial resemblance between Process Schizophrenia (juvenile or childhood) and Infantile Autism (onset before age three, by definition) and the prior tendency of child psychiatrists to group these latter disorders together, they are really quite different. In Autism there is marked impairment of reciprocal social interaction (verbal and nonverbal) and of ability to relate to adults and peers; lack of ability to share interests and to communicate verbally or nonverbally; restrictive, repetitive, and stereotyped patterns of interests and activities; and lack of imaginative and symbolic play.

In Process Schizophrenia, on the other hand, emotional, social, and cognitive development are more or less normal until the desatellization crisis of adolescence. Then emotional and social withdrawal set in and there is detachment from activities, interests, motivations, relationships, and ego aspirations. Ego development in the juvenile Schizophrenic reaches a certain high point, namely, the end of the satellization period, and then maturation (desatellization) fails to proceed any further toward adult personality status. In untreated cases, regression occurs. Development in Autism never really proceeds satisfactorily. From the very beginning there is gross incapacity in emotional, social, language, play, and interpersonal areas. In view of the fact that there is very little reciprocal social interaction occurring, there is really no need for communication skills to develop. Either rapid improvement or further deterioration may take place at adolescence.

9

Aggressive, Antisocial, and Narcissistic Personality Disorders in Nonsatellizers

Chapter 8 was devoted to the psychopathological consequences of maturational failure in desatellization among satellizers. For purposes of contrast, the personality disorder epitomizing this latter maturational failure—Inadequate and Immature Personality Disorder—was compared to a phenotypically similar reactive form of the disorder in nonsatellizers, in which the developing individual vindictively sabotages the goals of adult personality maturation. A common situation in which this cessation of maturation occurs is when a parent paradoxically imposes more, rather than less, restrictive discipline during adolescence because he fears, and wishes to forestall, sexual activity on the part of his adolescent daughter. Clinically, the symptoms and outcome of this latter reactive disorder are not at all dissimilar to those of Inadequate and Immature Personality Disorder.

The present chapter also deals with aberrant personality maturation in which the ego-status and ego-maturity goals of personality maturation are distorted and/or displaced by a combination of temperamentally aggressive and hedonistic tendencies and by the absence of conscience mechanisms. Compared to Reactive Maturational Failure, the developmental defect in these latter disorders is manifested by aggressive, antisocial, and often conscienceless and delinquent or criminal conduct instead of by failure to attain adult personality status. Another striking difference is the fact that in reactive maturational failure the impetus for the vindictive sabotage leading to the failure originates in the attitudes and actions of the parent; whereas in antisocial personality disorder (typically occurring in nonsatellizers) it originates in the extreme aberrant, temperamental, and developmental (genically determined) proclivities of the potential antisocial personality.

Antisocial Personality Disorder

Antisocial Personality Disorder is defined as "a pervasive pattern of disregard for, and violation of, the rights of others that begins in childhood or early adolescence and continues into adulthood" (American Psychiatric Association [1994: 645]). The widely used diagnostic term at one time for this disorder was *psychopathy*; and such persons are still popularly known as *psychopaths* or *psychopathic personalities*.

In evaluating the ego development of some individuals who conform to this definition, it seems reasonable to anticipate that some persons will be strongly predisposed on developmental and temperamental grounds to develop antisocial personality disorder. Developmentally, as nonsatellizers, their infantile ego traits, such as ideas of volitional omnipotence and independence, as well as executive dependence, were never really devalued, leading to a residual state of ego hypertrophy. Temperamentally, it is also quite possible for them to be very independent, volitionally as well as inordinately aggressive, assertive, and even opinionated, ruthless, and arrogant, with strong needs for immediate hedonistic gratification, with intense and uncontrolled rage reactions, and with poor impulse control. Despite their compensatorily high and tenacious, but unrealistic, aspirations for achievement and earned status, due to a lack of derived status and of intrinsic security, adequacy, and self-esteem (which also requires good character reputation and a nondelinquent, noncriminal record in order to be properly implemented), these latter negative temperamental traits may, therefore, be sufficiently potent to permit the development and expression of antisocial, delinquent, or criminal tendencies.

Another set of developmental variables that operate during the desatellization crisis must additionally be considered at this point. It will also be recalled that nonsatellizers during preadolescence and adolescence tend to take a selective and expediential orientation toward the internalization of culturally approved ego-status and ego-maturity traits—internalizing all ego-status and some ego-maturity traits such as volitional independence and unrealistically high and tenacious aspirations for achievement for the two reasons noted above. Expansive ego aspirations then do tend to elevate self-esteem—at least in the beginning.

Additionally, such ego-maturity traits as executive independence, responsibility, frustration tolerance, perseverance, and resoluteness, which are all essential for implementing ego aspirations, are also internalized without too much difficulty because on a purely expediential basis they tend to actualize aspirations for achievement and high status.

However, willingness to (1) acquire more executive independence, (2) defer immediate gratification of hedonistic desires for the sake of advancing long-term goals, and (3) inhibit aggressive, illicit sexual, and antisocial impulses, although undoubtedly expedient from the standpoint of achievement motivation and ambition, are quite other matters in practice. They may well exceed the antisocial personality's limited self-control and capacity for resisting temptation, notwithstanding the palpable and expedient advantages of not so doing.

Moral Development

Moreover, there are also certain societal ego-maturity traits of a moral nature, such as honesty, veracity, fairness, reciprocity, equity, integrity, and so forth that are culturally admired in the abstract but that not only do not promote the implementation of ego aspirations, but may actually retard same. It stands to reason, therefore, that the potential antisocial personality will neither internalize these traits as moral values nor internalize a sense of moral obligation to conform his conduct to them. Hence, behavioral volition of these values will not elicit such conscience reactions as acknowledgment of culpability and expressions of remorse, shame, or guilt. This combination of the worst temperamental aggressive traits listed above and the conscienceless lack of inhibition of immoral behavior (plus the lack of attendant remorse, shame, and guilt feelings) more or less defines the psychopathological essence of Antisocial Personality disorder.

It is apparent, therefore, that although the requirements for, and expression of, ego hypertrophy attributes in potential antisocial personalities would generally facilitate the development of a more mature adult personality, two "fatal flaws" nevertheless tend to negate the maturing effects of the ego hypertrophy and tend selectively to accentuate their antisocial propensities:

1. The characteristics of adult personality status that do not contribute to ego aggrandizement are not easily accepted or internalized. This applies especially to moral values, deferred gratification of hedonistic needs, and impulse control.
2. These same characteristics are additionally stable only as long as the individual remains within the framework of his hypertrophied goal structure.

In the event of psychosis or severe behavioral disorganization, full-blown regression to their infantile precursors will occur, since genuine, unconditional attenuation had failed to take place—merely acceptance for the sake of expediency.

Although it is obviously difficult for an uninhibited antisocial personality who acts out his aggressive, violent, and ruthless impulses to strive at the same time for the fulfillment of his legitimate hypertrophied ego needs (for status, position, power, wealth) and ambitions, it is not impossible if the individual is unusually competent, in which case he could either lead a "double life" or become a master criminal. The latter possibilities would be consistent with his well-known penchant for deceit and manipulation.

By definition, the antisocial personality represents a continuation and exacerbation, by at least the age of eighteen, of cruel, impulsive, vicious, irresponsible, ruthless, vindictive, and unfeeling tendencies, devoid of any remorse or guilt, that have been expressed, at least in the three prior years (usually since early childhood), by behavior consonant with a diagnosis of Conduct Disorder. Antisocial Personality Disorder, as indicated above, is not the general or typical outcome in delinquents diagnosed as manifesting Conduct Disorder but, rather, a by no means rare and "worst possible case" of what the latter could conceivably become, given his idiosyncratic temperamental, developmental, and situational circumstances.

Such cases as they progress (almost imperceptibly) from Conduct Disorder to Antisocial Personality Disorder are characterized often by an early history of parental rejection or abuse. However, the needs for counteraggression and vengeance are so great that considerations of expediency are generally ignored and open rebellion against all parental norms and values occurs. These latter needs for vindictiveness and retaliation combine a reactive element of counteraggression against parental rejection and/or abuse with temperamentally aggressive, assertive, and impulsive tendencies.

Conduct Disorder

In contradistinction to its sometimes sequel, Antisocial Personality Disorder, DSM-IV defines Conduct Disorder as a "repetitive and persistent pattern of behavior in which the basic rights of others or major age-appropriate societal norms or rules are violated" (American Psychiatric

Association [1994: 84]). Such conduct is often qualitatively indistinguishable from that involved in Antisocial Personality Disorder with which it merges. Four main categories of behavior may be involved in conduct disorder: (1) aggressive conduct causing or threatening physical harm to other persons or animals; (2) nonaggressive conduct causing property damage; (3) deceitfulness or theft; and (4) serious violations of rules. The incidence of Conduct Disorder and juvenile delinquency in slum-urban areas is greatly increased, of course, by the general status deprivation in the culture to which all adolescents, irrespective of social-class membership, are subjected; by high unemployment, poverty, high crime rate, and illicit drug trafficking and abuse; and by substandard housing, racial and ethnic prejudice, lack of recreational opportunities, and so forth. Typically, as a result of the disruption of behavior or personality, work efficacy and social and academic functioning are disturbed.

A substantial majority of children and adolescents who are diagnosed as exhibiting Conduct Disorder (including delinquency) in childhood and adolescence undergo more or less complete remission by the time they reach young adulthood; only a minority apparently enter the ranks of chronic adult criminals or antisocial personalities. As is true in the case of drug abuse, it is also the case, of course, that all children and adolescents living in depressed urban areas are not implicated in Conduct Disorder or juvenile delinquency (although few escape such involvement at one time or another); yet the definition of conduct disorder requires *repetitive,* not single or only occasional, involvement. Finally, indicating definitively that depressed socioeconomic conditions alone do not cause juvenile delinquency, and that idiosyncratic temperamental and developmental factors must always be taken into account, is the fact that middle- and upper-class children and adolescents not infrequently become delinquent.

Conceptualizations of delinquency. The history of social attitudes toward delinquency, including the various competing philosophies current today and over the past five decades, reflects the dilemma society finds itself in when it is forced to make moral judgments regarding guilt, culpability, and punishment without any adequate criteria of moral accountability. For most people, delinquency is still a matter of unethical behavior based on inherited moral weakness, an indication that the individual has voluntarily succumbed to the temptation of illegitimately benefiting himself or giving vent to aggressive impulses at the expense of his fellow citizens. However, more sophisticated points of view, namely the legal, psychological, and socio-logical, prevail at the level of presumed expert opinion.

The law is primarily concerned with protecting the interests and safety of individuals, groups, and society. With this end in view, the most prac-tical assumption to make is that in the absence of evidence to the con-trary, unlawful acts are willfully committed and render the offending individual liable to punishment. The strict legal test for criminal respon-sibility requires only that the accused person know right from wrong and be able to appreciate the nature and quality of his act. However, in defer-ence to the recognized contribution of emotional factors to the commis-sion of crime by mentally disordered individuals, certifiable "insanity" or mental derangement itself is often accepted by the judiciary as an ex-emption from clinical responsibility, and "uncontrollable impulse" as at least a mitigating factor.

Proponents of the psychological and sociological schools of thought, however, charge that the criterion of "willful and premeditated intent" is entirely irrelevant to the question of moral accountability since it is based on the premise of "free will." Our quarrel with the legal definition of re-sponsibility, on the other hand, rests on other grounds. In the first place the law is much too concerned with the material and formal rights of in-dividuals and concerned too little with intrinsic immorality. The vast ma-jority of acts of cruelty, injustice, and treachery are unfortunately lawful and unpunishable.

Second, the application of the test of willfulness and intent in most in-stances is not made in a context of psychological analysis of the personal-ity structure and development of the individual. Instead the actual motivation is frequently obscured by concentration on legalistic niceties and on the legal rules of evidence; and final judgment may depend more on technical points in the statutory law and on details of precedent in common law—both of which are essentially irrelevant in most cases since they are not taken into account by the offender—than on considerations of equity and justice. Criteria such as "uncontrollable impulse" also are vague and often applied in a mechanical fashion without careful consideration being given to their relative weight in the causation of a particular act of delinquency.

According to the undiluted sociological point of view, delinquency is an individual behavioral manifestation of social disorganization and pa-thology. Individuals whose opportunities for normal personality devel-opment and constructive endeavor are frustrated by virtue of poverty, unemployment, slum conditions, and so forth, therefore, tend to react with antisocial behavior. Hence, the argument runs, it is society and not the individual who really is the culprit. The latter is deviant only as long as he is exposed to an unjust or disorganized society. As a single factor theory of delinquency, however, this formulation breaks down in failing to explain why children from optimal social environments become wayward, and why the majority of children in a given urban slum area terminate their criminal careers as young adults despite fairly regular participation in delinquent activities during childhood and adolescence.

The psychological (also psychiatric and psychoanalytic) approach is similar to the sociological in deemphasizing the role of individual volitional control, but differs from the latter in locating the main etiological factor in the dynamics of early personality development rather than in social pathology. Psychoanalysts contend that criminal behavior is a symptom of mental disturbance. They view the delinquent as an individual equipped with a poorly developed ego and superego but driven by powerful instinctual forces. The delinquent, for example, is seen as fixated in the early narcissistic, sexually polymorphous stage of psychosexual development. Although social conditions are recognized as contributory factors, greater stress is placed upon various aspects of the early family situation which impinge upon personality development. Nonanalytic psychiatrists are more concerned with the influence of the parent-child relationship on the latter's socialization process rather than with its effect on his sexual maturation. Both, however, would agree that delinquency is primarily a problem of disordered personality development arising from unfortunate relationships between the child and significant persons in his psychological field rather than a manifestation of disturbance in grosser patterns of social organization.

In our conclusion regarding the social and legal management of delinquency to be offered below, two basic assumptions will be made:

1.   Delinquency like any other behavioral outcome is a result of *multiple causality*. Relevant variables that must be considered in every case include heredity, personality development, other psychological factors (e.g., intelligence, suggestibility), personality disorder, transitional pressures in development, emotional instability, situational factors, family and social environment, and so forth. Usually, however, one of these factors is prepotent in a given case, allowing it for purposes of convenience to be placed in one of the categories of the classification.

2. While allowing that psychological or social causes of delinquency can be identified, the writer is nevertheless in agreement with the moral and legal approaches to the problem in believing that identification of the effective cause in an individual case does not necessarily absolve the offender from moral accountability. Objectively valid criteria of culpability are discoverable.

There has been too great a tendency in modern psychological thinking about criminality toward divorcing all behavior of its ethical content. From the standpoint of individual behavior, there is a moral aspect to most purposeful human activity, the psychological reality of which is too compelling to be ignored. And while this aspect is so closely interwoven with the aspect of psychological disturbance that the two can hardly be separated, the relative significance of each in a given case of delinquency is usually clear enough to allow some judgment as to the individual's moral and legal accountability.

The type of delinquency characteristic of disorganized urban areas tends to be a transitory phenomenon for most individuals which is not carried over into adult life. This fact also points to the absence of complete homogeneity in exposure to moral values within a single social class; for despite the geographical segregation of the social classes and continual reinforcement of lower-class value systems, the moral code of the dominant middle class is eventually adopted by the majority of erstwhile slum dwellers.

Even in the preadolescent and adolescent periods, some of the youths in these areas are more heavily influenced by middle-class values than they are by the prevailing norms in their own social-class group. While this may be a consequence of exclusion from their own peer culture, it may also be a cause of same. We have already referred to the fact that predatory gang behavior tends to become fixed when status deprivation is perceived by the adolescent as the outcome of social discrimination attributable to such permanent characteristics as racial origin, instead of as a self-limited affliction shared by all individuals, more or less, in a given age group.

Sporadic delinquency is also common enough in adolescence even without the contributory influence of adverse social conditions. Prolonged status deprivation leads to an anti-adult and anti-authority orientation in the peer group which sometimes explodes violently in the form of aggressive, antisocial activity. Adolescent emotional instability also takes this aggressive form more readily if it is compounded by group interaction, since group resistance is much more effective than individual rebellion and provides moral sanction and anonymity to the participants. The mere pressure for conformity to group norms in adolescence is often sufficient to provoke occasional acts of delinquency in youths who otherwise have high moral standards; and, where there tends to be no large-scale segregation by race or social class, as in small towns and villages, organized delinquent gangs are not generally found.

Another factor facilitating the development of delinquent trends in adolescents is the moral confusion and ethical laxity they perceive in the culture at large. Since at this time the sense of moral obligation tends to diverge from parental loyalties, and since models of emulation for a rational and reciprocal ethical code are eagerly sought on a societal basis, the existing moral vacuum tends, unfortunately, to be filled by the readiest and most visible set of standards available.

Delinquency, which is rooted in aberrations of conscience development because of deviant parent-child relationships (e.g., severe neglect, abusive rejection), has a far more serious prognosis as an expression of Antisocial Personality Disorder. In these instances the needs of counteraggression and vengeance are so great that considerations of expediency are cast aside, and complete and overt rebellion against parental standards may take place. Not only does a sense of personal moral obligation fail to develop, but also any internalization of ethical values whatsoever. The same hostile, rebellious attitude is later carried over in relation to social norms, which the individual identifies with the hateful figures of his parents. Thus, there is no possibility of developing a sense of justice or obligation on rational grounds. Even the interests of self-aggrandizement are subordinated to the need for wanton destructiveness and aggressive retaliation against all moral and legal authority.

As could easily be anticipated, the overall incidence of Conduct Disorder and delinquency is very much higher in males than in females. The latter, however, are much more likely, when they do exhibit these disorders, to manifest such offenses as lying, truancy, sexual promiscuity, running away from home, substance abuse, and prostitution. The girls who vindictively sabotage adult personality maturation (and go on to develop Inadequate and Immature Personality Disorder), because they were paradoxically subjected to a more restrictive discipline at adolescence, could take the same reactive stance against their parents (if their conscience is unstable and if they are temperamentally very independent and aggressive) and just as easily develop an aggressive conduct disorder. Since adolescent boys typically have fewer conflicts with parents than girls do over self-determination, decision making, and restricted movement issues, rebellion over these matters is less likely to be a cause of parent-child strife, conduct disorder, or juvenile delinquency.

In conclusion, my theoretical position on the essential nature of the delinquency problem, that is, on the primary category of variable(s) to which it inherently belongs phenomenologically, as well as etiologically and developmentally, is that basically delinquency is a moral problem or a problem in moral behavior. To be sure, the internalization of moral values and of moral obligations, the honoring or violation of these moral values and of the obligation to conform conduct to them, the inhibition of impulses contrary to internalized moral values, the feelings of guilt and remorse when moral obligations are dishonored, and the role of guilt as a deterrent to immorality are all complex and related psychological phenomena and processes which make possible the functioning of conscience.

Nevertheless, the overall principal thrust of all of these psychological or psychopathological mechanisms underlying the actual operation of the component aspects of conscience is a moral one—because their entire purpose is to make or further a moral determination of conduct, that is, good conscience or bad conscience: to make a moral or immoral judgment or decision; to initiate, express, or inhibit a moral or immoral action; or to develop an effective and stable conscience or the opposite of same. These are all inherently moral rather than psychological issues even though, when tracing their development, we may do so largely in terms of corresponding psychological processes that are used for other emotional, motivational, and self-related concepts. This formulation, of course, also allows for the consideration of all relevant variables impinging on delinquency: socioeconomic, racial and ethnic, mass-media, family, cultural, school, and peer groups; psychopathological, situational, and substance abuse.

Narcissistic Personality Disorder

This is a personality disorder characterized principally by notions of controlled grandiosity with respect to self-perceived abilities, aptitudes, talents, achievements, self-importance, and so forth. The individual with this disorder tends to crave and seek the admiration and praise of others, to believe that he is a special and unique person and, thus, entitled to special treatment, deference, and compliance with his expectations. Because he is supremely egotistical and egocentric, his focus of interest, concern, and ego involvement resting squarely and exclusively on himself, he neither knows nor cares about the feelings, needs, or psychological reactions transpiring in others, and thus lacks ordinary empathy for them. Because of his very high estimate of his own status, position, and achievements, he believes that his colleagues must necessarily be envious of him (and sometimes also vice versa), and is often arrogant and overbearing in his attitude toward them. Having little genuine concern for them, he also perceives them mostly as persons to be used or exploited for his own benefit.

How and why did the narcissistic personality get to be the way he is? First, as an adult who had been a nonsatellizer since childhood, he has little or no derived status or intrinsic security, adequacy, or self-esteem. To compensate for the latter situation, he internalizes unrealistically high and tenacious ego aspirations for achievement and earned status and a corresponding set of inflated and effective ego-maturity traits to implement his high ego-status aspirations. Unlike the satellizer he lacks completely an inner core of self-esteem to carry him through life's vicissitudes in his striving for achievement. Ordinarily, therefore, he would be prone to anxiety reactions and would also be subject to the discouragement of a vigorous self-critical faculty via arousal of the thalamo-cortical tract as the intervening neural substrate in this phenomenon.

Thus, given the basic personality structure of ego hypertrophy, chronic feelings of insecurity, inadequacy, and impaired self-esteem, of intense incessant striving for earned status and achievement (with lack of self-confidence and strong doubts about the intrinsic merit of his achievements), which is precisely the opposite of his overt personality structure, the narcissistic personality must have evidently evolved this highly adjustive, organized, and canalized set of compensatory defenses against his anxiety and impaired self-esteem which he found both effective and compatible with his basic temperament and his nonsatellizing ego-aggrandizing orientation to life.

Another important facet of basic personality structure that figures prominently in the emerging Narcissistic Personality Disorder is the individual's aggressiveness, assertiveness, domineering and overbearing proclivities, and tendency to "take over" wherever possible.

The primary need for compensatory defense in the narcissistic personality is against the frustration, failure, and loss of self-esteem (and associated anxiety) that arise because of his unrealistically high and tenacious aspirations for achievement. All of these adverse consequences are not only counteracted by his perceptually self-inflated and exaggerated aptitudes, capacities, and accomplishments, but the latter also become sources of positive or elevated self-esteem that are completely credible in his own eyes. Like the psychopathological mechanism in hypomania, this transformation in the perceived competence and excellence of his own capacities and work products is effected by an inhibition of his self-critical faculty. However, this is not easily confused with hypomania because his mood is very sober and matter-of-fact; there are no signs of elation or exultation. Further, this mechanism is very stable and reliable, lasting perhaps for years and giving invariable, guaranteed inflated self-perceptions.

By taking only his own opinion and judgments into consideration in reaching his conclusions regarding the relative superiority of his own abilities and achievements over those of others (and also being more than a little biased in his own favor in making such judgments), he takes no chances whatsoever of being disappointed in the outcome of this self-judgmental comparison with his peers.

Egocentrically, he also tends gratuitously to assume that his peers have the same exalted opinion of himself that he does (and perhaps he even intimidates them somewhat into expressing such an opinion); in any case it lends external and objective support for his own judgments. All in all, this narcissistic coping mechanism is a very efficacious form of compensatory defense, which, being relatively closed, organized, and isolated from potentially disturbing influences and people, provides a very stable form of defense that is not likely to break down under direct threat or stress.

Finally, it is necessary to explain how and in what ways Narcissistic Personality Disorder is compatible with and expresses the very conspicuous, aggressive, assertive, intimidating, overbearing, and arrogant personality traits and behaviors typically found in this disorder, and, thus, justifies additionally its placement in the category (chapter) of antisocial or egocentric personality disorders that occur chiefly in nonsatellizers. There is no doubt but that if one not only possesses narcissistic proclivities, but also all of the associated temperamentally exaggerated, aggressive, and overdominant personality traits listed above in this connection as typical of Narcissistic Personality Disorder (and if at the same time one is *not* unduly impulsive, violent, emotionally uncontrolled, ruthless, full of hate, etc.), one will *not* express these traits (as individuals with

Antisocial Personality Disorder do), that is, as aggressiveness, assertiveness, and so forth, but, rather, as excessive self-love, self-indulgence, self-ishness, self-conceit, self-importance, egocentricity, egoism, undue need for admiration, and inflated self-perceptions of one's abilities and achievements. Also, because there is such little relative concern for others in this preoccupation with self, empathy for them is reduced to an insufficient and conspicuous minimum. For similar reasons the narcissistic personality tends to be overbearing and arrogant in his relations with others and to "use" or exploit them for his own benefit.

References

American Psychiatric Association. *Diagnostic and Statistical Manual of Mental Disorders,* Fourth Edition (Washington, D.C.: American Psychiatric Association, 1994).

10

Defenses Against Anxiety

Classification of Defenses

The psychopathological basis of most defense mechanisms lies in the imperious need for anxiety reduction. Defense efforts are elicited even before anxiety appears, that is, as self-esteem first begins to be threatened; and when the threat becomes intense enough to evoke the affect of anxiety, the original need for defense becomes even more imperative. As a means of bringing together some of the scattered material in this chapter relating to defenses against anxiety, a brief cataloguing of the various types of defenses will be attempted below.

Four types of defenses are distinguished: (1) direct forms of ego enhancement of an aggressive, compensatory, and independent character; (2) conciliatory, submissive, and dependent forms of defense; (3) various indirect and devious means of ego enhancement, which attain their goal without primary reliance on either aggressive or submissive tactics; and (4) mechanisms that provide escape from anxiety situations.

Direct means of ego enhancement include: (a) strong prestige drives for money, success, power, superior status, and so forth; (b) the affectation of boastful, blustering, supercilious, and belligerent attitudes, or the simulation of tremendous calm, poise, nonchalance, and indifference to social conventions; (c) aggressive attacks on the opinions, behavior, or reputations of other persons in the hope of showing to advantage in relation to the deflation of their stature; (d) the unleashing of destructive tendencies as a means of demonstrating one's power in influencing the course of events; and (e) finding substitutive gratification in the achievements of other individuals who are regarded as ego extensions of self, for example, the overvaluing parent.

Conciliatory forms of defense are illustrated by the following types of behavior: (a) sympathetic, charitable, and tolerant attitudes toward others as a means of soliciting comparable lenient treatment from them; (b) stressing one's anxiety and helplessness as a bid for sympathy and immunity from aggression; (c) repression of hostile impulses in order to insure one's own safety; (d) failure to perceive the hostility of others lest one feel obliged to retaliate and, hence, risk one's own security; (e) justifying the hostility of others for the same reason; (f) a need to be liked by *everyone* in order to feel secure, entering into friendly relationships indiscriminately with all comers; (g) exaggerated conformity to social demands, excessive compliancy to authority; (h) complete surrender of individuality in group activity; (i) abandonment of individual initiative and the prerogatives of independent action; (j) endeavoring to form satellizing-like relationships with others; and (k) suppression of self-assertive and hostile tendencies by reaction-formation, and enacting overtly a mild, humble, self-effacing, friendly, and diffident role. In this way one's negative but true personality traits and behavioral tendencies in interacting with others are not only completely suppressed and hidden from public view, but they are also thoroughly displaced overtly by their opposites, thereby deviously misleading the associates of the individual.

Denial, as a defense mechanism, involves a simpler and more direct and often brazen and self-assertive contradiction of the veridicality of past incidents, events, observations, motives, beliefs, and so forth, that are palpably true according to the testimony of documentary evidence, witnesses, and knowledgeable persons. Other involved persons often tend to be overimpressed by the persistence and consistency of the denial and, therefore, accord it greater credibility than it deserves. The defensive value of denial largely inheres in its making possible avoidance of an admission of culpability and, thus, of the guilt feelings and anxiety that might follow.

Indirect and devious defenses against anxiety are legion in number: (a) rationalization of failure and escape from competitive striving through psychosomatic symptoms of anxiety, hypochondriasis, fatigue states, and hysterical conditions; (b) displacement of the source of the threat to a more specific, concrete, identifiable, and manageable danger (phobia); (c) monopolization of consciousness by a displaced and innocuous source of threat (obsession); (d) displacement of the object or target of the threat to another person, for example, the anxious parent who overprotects his child; (e) minimization of frustration and loss of self-esteem through ego disinvolvement, depersonalization, and impairment of the self-critical faculty (e.g., Mania); (f) delusional distortion of the environment (ideas of grandeur and persecution); (g) disowning and justifying unacceptable impulses (projection); (h) achieving compensatory ego gratification through regression in goal maturity; (i) compensatory ego satisfaction through compulsive eating, activity, or sexuality; (j) finding security through compulsive rituals; (k) compulsive rigidity, inflexibility, and perfectionism in performing tasks in order to eliminate excessive fear of uncertainty, tentativeness, and improvisation; (l) undue advance preparation in meeting new situations; and (m) reliance on familiar and stereotyped methods of problem solving.

Escape mechanisms include: (a) avoidance of new, potential anxiety situations; (b) repression or denial of anxiety; (c) adopting an impersonal, third-person reference to problems productive of anxiety; (d) withdrawal from social situations that generate anxiety, for example, asceticism, intellectualization, absorption in fantasy; (e) self-insulation from emotional involvement in interpersonal relations to avoid the possibility of rejection; (f) finding a part-time escape from reality, for example, alcoholism; (g) constriction of the field of activity to limit the magnitude of the area from which threats can arise; (h) self-frustration to avoid anxiety situations or the necessity for accepting a realistic half-loaf solution to grandiose ego aspirations.

Defensive Reactions against Anxiety: Diagnostic Entities

The varied and numerous types of adjustive mechanisms through which these defensive reactions are mediated have already been described above. Here I shall only attempt to relate some of these mechanisms to the formal clinical entities employed in clinical psychiatry. Their evolution is facilitated by the increased state of behavioral reactivity induced by the heightened state of anxiety. Psychosomatic symptoms, for example, may have a dual function: They may explain failure to attain eminence in areas where tremendous effort has obviously been expended to achieve success, or they may be utilized to justify to self and others withdrawal from threatening situations (rather than face the risk of possible failure).

The simplest defenses against anxiety utilize the mechanisms of rationalization and displacement in elaborating upon the physiological accompaniments of anxiety states. The *hypochondriac* reduces anxiety by becoming preoccupied with these physiological complaints and believing that they are indicative of organic disease. This conscious attention to normally autonomous physiological functions further impairs their efficiency. Belief in organic illness rationalizes both failure and avoidance of striving, and displaces both the source and object of the threat with more palatable and less traumatic surrogates. Actual organic symptoms of illness can also be developed *de novo,* apart from the usual manifestations of anxiety (e.g., hysterical anaesthesias, blindness, paralysis, tremors, seizures, tics) through the convergence of intense need to escape from catastrophic threats, extreme suggestibility, and fortuitous environmental or physiological accident. For example, a hypersuggestible combat soldier with intense combat fear can develop hysterical blindness by misinterpreting the momentary loss of sight induced by the glare of an exploding shell.

In *phobias,* displacement of the source of the threat from impaired self-esteem to specific avoidable objects and situations occurs. The selection of surrogate objects is not arbitrary but depends upon some symbolical connection with the actual threat. In *obsessive* disorders, the source of the threat is not displaced or made more tangible and specific, but consciousness is monopolized by a relatively innocuous and symbolically related idea that relieves anxiety by creating an all-consuming distraction. *Compulsions* add the element of magic and ritualistic defense and provide a rigid formula for meeting new situations, thus banishing anxiety in relation to the unreasonable need for absolute certainty. Compulsive activity is also a simple unadjustive consequence of acute behavioral disorganization.

Obsessive-Compulsive Personality Disorder

Obsessive-compulsive defenses against anxiety constitute one of the most common of all such defenses. However, the majority of individuals using them have no inkling whatsoever regarding their meaning, psychological significance, or role in their psychopathology. Their inappropriateness, intrusiveness, and interference with normal ongoing thought processes, as well as the unpleasant intimation the patient senses that he is being "controlled," that is, compelled to do things he doesn't want to do, against his will (in the case of compulsions), sometimes induces patients to seek treatment; but when they do, it is almost invariably for the obsession or compulsion per se rather than for the underlying anxiety state for which these symptoms serve as defenses.

The content of a given obsession in this disorder focuses excessively and unreasonably on the orderliness, perfectionism, trivial details, and arbitrary control of a given situation, sacrificing adaptive flexibility and improvisation for their sake. The patient is overconscientious, rigid, and miserly; he throws nothing out and saves everything. Although the net effect of these maneuvers is intrusive and unwanted and, thus, distressing, the obsession and compulsion possibly avert one of the psychotic complications of anxiety, provided, of course, that they remain intact (i.e., don't break down) and that some new and novel catastrophic threat doesn't arise for which the patient lacks sufficient self-confidence to handle successfully.

Compulsions are somewhat more complex than obsessions in their modus operandi. They seem designed to provide long-term security by adding to obsessions the apparently invincible elements of magic and ritualism. Dependence on stereotyped ritualism also eliminates the need for improvising new adjustments. Not infrequently compulsions enact obsessive images, thoughts, and impulses, thereby enhancing their defensive properties.

The onset of this disorder typically tends to be insidious and the course more or less chronic and variable. Paradoxically, the nature of the obsessive-compulsive symptoms per se is often such as to generate more of the same anxiety they were intended to reduce in the first place. Although most patients eventually recognize that their obsessions or compulsions are excessive and/or unreasonable, relatively few develop spontaneous insight into their psychological significance and explanation as defenses against anxiety.

Specific Phobias

In specific phobias, there is moderately severe and enduring fear (or anxiety) of clearly demarcated, perceptible, circumscribed, and unambiguous objects or situations. The actual defense mechanism is simple and straightforward, more so perhaps than in any other defense against anxiety, involving displacement of the source of the threat from intangible and poorly identifiable impaired self-esteem in the patient to specific and tangible objects and situations in the environment. Self-evidently, the more discrete, identifiable, and tangible an object or situation is, the more easily and effectively it can be avoided. The situation or surrogate objects in the environment for displacement of the source of threat within the patient (i.e., impairment of his self-esteem and self-confidence) is by no means arbitrary, but is symbolically related. Actual confrontation with the phobic object invariably induces a severe fear or anxiety reaction, perhaps even a panic attack.

The simplicity of this displacement mechanism in specific phobias may account for their therapeutic susceptibility to such simple behavioral techniques as desensitization and positive reinforcement. As was also true in the case of obsessions and compulsions, most patients appreciate that the fear of the phobic object or situation is excessive and unreasonable. Onset is typically gradual and usually occurs in childhood; but it can be later, particularly if it is induced by a traumatic incident. If it persists into adulthood, it tends to be lifelong.

Social Phobia

This is a pronounced and enduring fear of social situations, and particularly of those social situations involving a solo performance as a result of which serious embarrassment could occur. Actual confrontation, however, with the latter situation evokes an immediate anxiety reaction that could possibly be an anxiety or panic attack. For this reason, individuals who suffer from social phobias learn from experience how to recognize such situations and their potential negative effects on themselves, and, thus, learn how to avoid or shun them if they can; sometimes, of course, they are unavoidable. As in the case of specific phobias and obsessions and compulsions, the degree of fear or anxiety is so gross, disproportionate, and inappropriate that the patient typically recognizes them as excessive or unreasonable. However, this awareness does not prevent the social phobia from significantly impairing occupational, academic, or social functioning or causing serious emotional distress. The embarrassment these individuals anxiously anticipate with respect to publicly performing certain acts, usually results in reaction to anticipated physiological and motor signs of "nervousness," as well as from doleful predictions of a complete performance debacle.

The shyness and timorousness inherent in anyone who responds with such exaggerated fear and embarrassment to social occasions and social performance exposure and requirements suggests an individual whose personality is highly rejection-sensitive, hypersensitive to, and intolerant of, criticism, and who has very low self-esteem. The onset of this condition, therefore, tends to be gradual and cumulative during adolescence and the course is chronic and lifelong, with wide fluctuations.

Contrary to the patient's understanding of his disorder, however (and often of his therapist's understanding as well), identification of the "traumatic childhood or adolescent incident" in cases of social and specific phobias explains *only* why in each case the particular object or social situation (as opposed to many other possibilities) became the overt depository of the original and displaced source of fear or anxiety (i.e., the impaired self-esteem of the patient) and, hence, the manifest, canalized phobic stimulus. Some insight into the phobic condition is undoubtedly acquired in this manner, but the major insight—that is, the actual reasons for the impairment of self-esteem, its consequences, and its relationship to the phobia—still remains to be acquired.

Somatization Disorder

The following three mental disorders to be discussed—somatization, hypochondriasis, and conversion—all have in common a form of overt physical symptom(s) as the manifest presenting symptomatology of this category of disorder. Additionally, it is generally accepted that these physical symptoms have a psychological cause or basis (i.e., that they are psychosomatic). In somatization disorder, for example, there are multiple, recurring somatic complaints that either seem serious enough to warrant clinical treatment or that result in significant occupational, academic, or social impairment.

Symptoms of this somatization condition, for example, pain, tend to be highly diffuse (i.e., to originate from multiple sites) and usually also include gastrointestinal, reproductive (sexual), and neurological complaints, which patients tend to describe in highly exaggerated and effusive terms. Frequent physical examinations, laboratory tests, special diagnostic procedures, and even exploratory surgery abound in these cases, but all to no avail. Invariably none of the subjective complaints are substantiated by objective findings from these diagnostic techniques. Furthermore, the pattern of reported complaints, even if they are substantiated by objective tests, do not generally correspond to any known medical disorder or combination of disorders.

Psychosomatic symptoms such as those found in somatization disorder probably serve at least two significant adjustive functions; they are used by the patient to (1) explain both his absolute and relative vocational failure—either why he failed dismally by any standard or why his extraordinary efforts to achieve eminence resulted in no more than average success; and (2) explain why he is withdrawing from the threatening vocational competition in which the possibilities of both failure and incessant anxiety reactions are so high for persons with impaired self-esteem but only average ability.

Why does that segment of the population exhibiting clinically significant Anxiety Neurosis choose psychosomatic symptoms as a preferred and canalized rationalizing defense against its anxiety? One possible explanation may be that they have a genetic predisposition to overreact to stress or threat with physical or physiological symptoms. They may also be genetically predisposed to take undue notice of such symptoms and to be greatly predisposed by them to react similarly to stress. On the other hand, this same differential tendency may be the result of acquired experience rather than a product of differential genetic influence. That is, individuals exhibiting Somatization Disorder frequently attempt to rationalize failure by pointing to the handicaps under which they operate because of many organic and functional (really psychosomatic or somatization) symptoms. This disorder, for example, can originate in a child if his loving parent adopts a somatization defense against anxiety. Beginning when the child is old enough to understand the signs and meaning of physical illness, the latter soon grasps the relationship between stress and physical illness, and will then regard such illness as the "natural" way of reacting to stress or threat. In the end, he too will become thoroughly impressed by, and sensitized to, this reactive mode and will stand a good chance of developing a full-fledged case of Somatization Disorder himself.

The onset of this disorder is gradual and insidious. Once established in adolescence or early adulthood, it tends to be highly canalized and, thus, very resistive to total extinction, although fluctuations in degree of severity are the rule.

Hypochondriasis

The Hypochondriac is a person who is preoccupied with fears of having, or believing that he actually has, a serious medical disease. His fears and belief are based on a misinterpretation of one or more physical signs or symptoms. Pathognomonic of this disorder, however, is the fact that his belief and fear of having such a serious (often fatal) disease exist and persist indefinitely despite complete medical reassurance to the contrary.

Hypochondriasis reduces anxiety by using the mechanisms of displacement and of rationalization to elaborate unjustifiably on the ordinary physiological accompaniments of anxiety. The Hypochondriac focuses persistently on these physiological symptoms and believes implicitly that they reflect serious organic disease in his case. The latter conviction is then utilized to explain away both his relative failure in life and his retreat from further striving. It also displaces impaired self-esteem as the source of the threat. Hypochondriacal symptoms are neither malingering nor factitious. Belief in organic illness rationalizes both failure and avoidance of striving, and displaces both the source and object of the threat with more palatable and less traumatic surrogates. (The same mechanisms are also operative in "fatigue" and "exhaustion" states, except that the individual focuses on the fatiguing consequences of anxiety instead of on other somatic complaints.)

As one might readily anticipate, this type of catastrophically threatening belief, and its associated fear, cause significant emotional distress (including anxiety) as well as impaired academic, vocational, family, and social functioning. In so doing they counterbalance the original anxiety reduction (or defense against anxiety) achieved by misinterpreting the physiological symptoms of anxiety as indicative of serious organic disease. As an adjustive device, therefore, hypochondriasis is apparently no more effective than it is adaptive.

The onset of hypochondriasis is generally gradual and insidious, beginning most often in young adulthood. The disorder tends to run a chronic course, as one might easily anticipate from its strong canalization; but fluctuations in severity are common. Although hypochondriacal symptoms seldom have any objective basis in fact, they are definitely not deliberately feigned. However, a certain amount of habitual verbal "embroidery" in describing symptoms is common and expected.

Conversion Disorder

Thus far in our consideration of subjective somatic symptoms or complaints that have no objective basis in fact (somatization disorder, hypochondriasis), the focus of clinical concern has been on long-standing, preexisting medical symptoms that arose from misinterpretation of the usual physiological accompaniments of anxiety. In conversion disorder, on the other hand, the focus of clinical attention is on recent organic-like symptoms that are newly developed from the very beginning, so to speak, apart from the usual manifestations of preexisting anxiety. These symptoms also tend to have a neurological focus (e.g., loss of a voluntary motor or sensory function), which explains their general nature. The physiological basis of the conversion symptoms is suggested by both (1) the intense psychological or moral conflict that precedes the onset of the symptoms, and (2) the patient's spatial distribution of the neurological deficit (e.g., cutaneous anesthesia) on the basis of a layman's "common-sense" notions rather than on the actual anatomical innervations involved.

The avoidance of the feared combat duty in the example mentioned above is often referred to as the "secondary gain," motivating the conversion deficit symptom. The "primary gain," on the other hand, according to psychoanalytic doctrine, reflects (1) symbolic resolution of a repressed conflict and strengthening of the repression by the conversion symptom, and (2) reduction of anxiety. These psychoanalytic propositions do have a certain common-sense appeal that could be substantially increased, in my opinion, by substituting terms such as "motive" and "defense against anxiety," which have a more unambiguous and parsimonious meaning than "primary" or "secondary" gain and "symbolic resolution of an unconscious conflict."

The onset of conversion disorder is usually between late childhood and early adulthood. Because it often depends on extreme, unusual, or dramatic experience coinciding with a moral dilemma or perceived catastrophic threat to self-esteem, the onset is typically acute. For the same reason the disorder is not chronic or continuous, but, rather, episodic.

Hypomania

Reference was made above to the partial adjustive value and role of Hypomania as a possible defense against anxiety (and depression). On the one hand, the decreased intensity and extremeness of the symptoms compared to Mania make it more appropriate and less risky and potentially destructive as a defense against anxiety than Mania itself, which is both seriously unadaptive and unadjustive. On the other hand, the nature of Hypomanic symptoms (mild grandiosity, euphoria, pressure of speech, feeling of well-being, circumstantiality, expansiveness, decreased need for sleep, increased energy), with some exceptions (e.g., irritability, unreality of the euphoria, etc.), is such that it counteracts almost specifically the impaired self-esteem and self-confidence of anxiety states. However, even the reduced extremeness of Hypomania from Mania, and the specific opposition it offers to some of the negative qualities of anxiety, are insufficiently adaptive and adjustive in itself to make it a suitable defense mechanism against anxiety. This is the case despite the fact that bipolar II (Hypomanic) patients seem to enjoy it very much and are very reluctant to submit to treatment that would terminate or prevent this condition.

Unlike displacement, rationalization, projection, and delusional distortion of reality, all of which involve some limited impairment of the self-critical faculty, Hypomanic reactions imply an even milder degree of such impairment as an adjustive mechanism (or defense against anxiety). Unlike the situation in delusions, it is not specifically related to a single belief or to a unitary group of beliefs; instead there is a general groundless elevation of self-esteem and a corresponding general euphoric alteration of mood, greatly increased self-confidence, and optimism, an expansive belief in one's abilities and prospects, diminished social inhibition, and reduced adherence to a sense of social propriety.

By any standard, however, Hypomania is still insufficiently reduced from Mania to be truly adjustive. The reality testing is not as seriously impaired as in Mania but is still not adequately reality oriented enough to be adaptive; and the particular qualities of Hypomania that specifically counteract the negative features of anxiety also have the same disadvantage of unreality. Other symptoms of Hypomania, such as overinvolvement in pleasurable activities with high-risk potential, can obviously lead to unfortunate, harmful, or dangerous consequences.

Dissociative Amnesia

This disorder consists essentially of an individual's loss of access to a portion of his memory that is personal, significant, unusually emotionally traumatic in origin, and reversible under such drastic therapeutic measures as hypnosis. Dissociative amnesia as a process or defense mechanism constitutes a splitting off and isolation from the main body of consciousness of a related body of memories of past experiences so that the individual cannot voluntarily recall them. The fact that the inability to recall this material is total rules out any explanation based on normal cognitive forgetting.

Lack of availability or retrievability of the inaccessible memories does not, of course, mean that it cannot and does not influence perception, thinking, attitudes, and motives while inaccessible. Functionally, dissociative amnesia is very similar to the nature, mechanism, purpose, and consequences of "repression," except that the latter process ordinarily tends to be more reversible, more discrete, and to involve more circumscribed segments of related memories.

The onset of dissociative amnesia, like the emotional trauma that self-protectively initiates it, is characteristically acute and abrupt. Diagnostically it is manifested as an otherwise inexplicable and sizable retrospective hiatus in memory. Removal from the traumatic circumstances of origin may sometimes result (without hypnosis) in spontaneous recovery of the ability to recall the memories in question. Given the grossness of the memory deficit in question, it is not at all surprising, of course, that it leads to serious academic, vocational, or social impairment. In some cases the disorder becomes chronic. Relative to the dissociated experiential material per se, the resulting amnesia may be divided into subtypes characterized as localized, generalized, selective, continuous, or systematized. As to the reasons for the amnesia itself, it is quite evident that it serves to protect the individual from memories of extremely traumatic and emotionally hurtful experiences impairing self-esteem or severe guilt-arousing experiences.

The onset of dissociative amnesia is frequently in childhood because of the vulnerability of children to physical, sexual, and emotional abuse. However, because such memories are often too hurtful and traumatic to remain accessible to recall, they are sometimes rendered inaccessible by the mechanism of dissociation. Nevertheless, as a result of the recent popularization both of childhood sexual abuse and of the claimed associated dissociative amnesia (and fugue), numerous controversial cases have recently come to clinical attention in which women in their 30's claim to recover under therapy, vivid repressed memories of being sexually abused, molested, and raped as children by an adult male relative (father, brother, uncle, etc.).

Although some of these memories are undoubtedly substantially valid, the vast majority are tainted (as is all distantly retrospective memory, especially in children) by the considerable loss of veridicality characterizing any retrospective memory over an extended period of time. Repressed memories do not remain "frozen" while they are dissociated and inaccessible, but interact with, and are altered by, memories of new experience, of reading material, of conversation, of movies, TV, dreams, and even case histories of sexual abuse in psychiatric journals. Thus, the patient's memories that are dredged up by the therapist may be a far cry from what actually happened in fact thirty years earlier.

Dissociative Fugue

Dissociative fugue is very similar in adjustive mechanism and purpose to dissociative amnesia, but is more complex psychopathologically. Instead of a retrospective gap in remote past memory, the amnesia (total or partial) is for the *recent* past, bordering on the present. It may also include some confusion about the individual's personal identity and the possible adoption of a new identity; these latter features are what usually bring the patient to clinical attention during the course of the fugue.

Another invariable pathognomonic feature of a fugue (although it doesn't necessarily seem to be intrinsically related to the underlying psychopathology) is that the patient takes an abrupt unplanned trip away from home or from the customary locus of his daily activities. This latter aspect may possibly have some psychological significance since the patient not only dissociates his recent past memory and personal identity data from the mainstream of his consciousness, but also attempts by travel to distance himself spatially from the customary activities that define his current personal and occupational identity.

Like dissociative amnesia, the onset of a fugue usually follows emotionally traumatic events that are too painful to be acknowledged and incorporated as accessible aspects of memory. Unlike dissociative amnesia, however, it is recent past that is part of current identity (not remote past), which is dissociated and becomes inaccessible. Simultaneously the individual seeks to distance himself spatially from his customary activities, appears confused about his present identity, and may possibly assume a new identity.

This attempt to shed present identity and the memories of the recent past that are an integral part of such identity—presumably because they are extremely painful or arouse deep guilt feelings—constitutes a rather extreme defense against anxiety, even if the individual does not typically attract much clinical attention. From the standpoint of ego psychology, identity constitutes the inner core of the ego; thus, nothing is more serious or ominous in psychopathology than a breakdown in the intactness of individual identity, which is the ultimate recipient of all the stress, threat, parental pressure, and so forth, to which the ego is subjected, as well as the ultimate actor in such developmental processes as ego maturation, satellization and desatellization, the acquisition of volitional and executive independence and of aspirations for achievement and earned status, and the operations involved in conscience formation.

Dissociative Identity Disorder

Thus far, in considering the dissociative mental disorders, we have proceeded from the least to the most serious (both in terms of degree of dissociation and of implications for psychopathology and behavior): (1) Dissociative Amnesia (inaccessibility of remote past memory); (2) loss or change of identity (Dissociative Fugue); and (3) multiple, independent personalities, each controlling behavior (Dissociative Identity Disorder) when ascendant or dominant relative to the other personalities. The former name of this disorder (Multiple Personality Disorder) describes its chief characteristics very well: two or more distinctive personality states, each independent of the others, and taking control intermittently of overall behavior.

In at least two respects, however, the former name of the disorder seems psychologically more precise than the present one. First, the term *personality* refers to all of the traits, mental sets, attitudes, motives, intentions, sensitizations, and so forth of the whole person and how he is disposed to act in any given situation or in response to any given stimulus. Thus, "the personality controlling behavior" is a much more inclusive concept than "identity," which refers only to an individual's sense or awareness of himself as both an enduring person and as a separate, unique, distinctive, and independent personality. The concept of identity does not include any of the predispositions of a given personality (genetic or experiential) to behave in a designated way.

Second, from the above distinction between personality and identity it is clear that only a personality, and not an identity, can "take control" of behavior. Of course, in persons who don't have Dissociative Identity Disorder, their one normal personality still has a corresponding identity; and individuals with identity disorder, who dissociate their personalities into several parts, have several personalities, each with its own identity and its own proper name.

In many cases, the multiple personalities spun off from the patient's original personality tend to complement each other with respect to role, function, and temperament. One obvious use to which an auxiliary personality may be put in this disorder is to act as a circumscribed memory recipient for emotionally traumatic experience or information that the individual as a whole does not want to know about or be able to recall; functionally, of course, although the mechanism is quite different, this is equivalent to dissociative amnesia, a condition that is also found in this disorder.

Like Dissociative Amnesia, only more so, there is a frequent history of childhood physical or sexual abuse in individuals with this disorder. Psychopathologically, and in general terms, this association makes a good deal of sense; but for several reasons stated above memories about *particular* persons and acts may be entirely lacking in validity and veridicality. To the reasons delineated above for this discrepancy between memory and experience might be added the well-known instability and imprecision of childhood memories, and the ease with which they can be distorted, as well as the susceptibility of persons with this disorder to authoritative suggestion (as from a therapist). Dissociative Identity Disorder is diagnosed much more frequently in adult females than in adult males.

Further exploration in some cases of a patient's feelings toward the older male relative whom she accuses of sexually abusing, molesting, or raping her as a child (but whose memories of same were supposedly obliterated or rendered irretrievable by repression or dissociation, and then supposedly recovered later through psychotherapy) suggests that these allegations are largely motivated by hostility, hatred, and desire for vengeance stemming from real or fancied wrongs or grievances in the remote past. Hence, definitive demonstration that these "memories" are completely invalid and without any basis in fact would probably have little or no effect on changing her expressed belief about their reality. This is the case because she anticipated these memories, and then hugged them to her bosom when they appeared during psychotherapy, perceiving them as a possible means of destroying the personal and professional reputations of the alleged incestuous sex offender, and of also justifying her hatred, hostility, and vindictiveness.

Depersonalization Disorder

This is a generalized, highly subjective, and intellectualized disorder, not attributable to dissociation, impaired reality testing, or overactive self-critical faculty, in which the individual is somehow disinvolved, detached, and alienated from himself, with the result that he does not feel as if it is really he who is acting, doing, and behaving. A companion general attitude toward experience, that is, derealization—a feeling and orientation toward the external world that external reality is unreal and is not what it seems to be—is found as a symptom in many diverse mental disorders together with Depersonalization Disorder: Post-Traumatic Stress Disorder, depression, Schizophrenia, Panic Disorder, and so forth. Both disorders also occur by themselves and not in conjunction either with each other or with other mental disorders.

Psychopathologically, depersonalization appears to be an extreme defense against anxiety in which the self is protected against a hostile, frustrating, threatening, deprecating, and demeaning interpersonal and social environment by disinvolving and withdrawing it from relationships with persons, activities, and so forth, in the real world. Thus, the individual with this disorder appears as a deanimated robot to himself when he introspects or observes himself functioning in a world that no longer seems real because he no longer has a personal stake in it.

Depersonalization symptoms occur both as an acute defensive and self-protective mechanism of desperation against anxiety in the early stages of such psychotic complications of anxiety as Reactive Schizophrenia, depression, manic episodes, and so forth, and also in the chronic stages of these same disorders when patients seem not only reconciled to their disorders, but also use mechanisms such as depersonalization to perpetuate them. A clinical distinction is made above between depersonalization as an acute adjustive or defensive mechanism and as a breakdown product of advanced ego damage.

General Considerations Regarding Defenses Against Anxiety

The numerous and varied types of defense mechanisms against anxiety have been classified and briefly described above. Most of this chapter, however, has been devoted to an attempt to relate these mechanisms, and relevant developmental considerations, to some of the formal diagnostic entities employed in clinical psychiatry. The elaboration of these mechanisms tends to be facilitated by the altered state of behavioral reactivity induced by anxiety; and their general functions tend, if possible, to bolster self-esteem, increase feelings of security, and rationalize avoidance of threatening situations.

Neurotic Anxiety has been described as an acquired reaction sensitivity in an individual with impaired self-esteem to over-react with fear to any stimulus that threatens to impair self-esteem further. It is a psychopathological outcome of faulty ego devaluation combined with a history of catastrophic trauma to self-esteem; fundamentally, therefore, it is a disease process, a reflection of ego damage rather than a compensatory mechanism.

Nevertheless it must be conceded that anxiety does have some adjustive value per se:

1. Before it assumes disorganizing proportions, it mobilizes the individual's adaptive efforts and increases his motivational tenacity. By alerting him in advance, it allows him to prepare responses to threatening stimuli that otherwise might precipitate panic if confronting him unawares. Although this interferes with the capacity for improvisation, it does prevent behavioral disorganization in response to threatening situations which the individual cannot or chooses not to solve by avoidance behavior.
2. It serves as a warning signal to withdraw from certain situations that threaten to bring him defeat and lowered self-esteem. If this entails the loss of gratifications associated with possible success, it also forestalls the painful humiliation that failure would evoke. This protective value of anxiety, however, cannot be utilized in the form of outright avoidance, since fear of failure is not an acceptable justification for withdrawal in our culture. Hence, avoidance must be rationalized by some other device such as illness, gross ineptitude, the virtue of asceticism or self-denial for the sake of others, and in extreme cases by the plea of incapacity due to behavioral disorganization, for example, panic, agitation.
3. Anxiety is sometimes employed as a bid for help, sympathy, deference, or executive dependence. But since this adjustive use of anxiety is socially hazardous and implies a degree of helplessness that is highly threatening to self-esteem, it is not generally utilized except under conditions of panic.

Although many of the defenses against anxiety help considerably to reduce its tensions and distastefulness, simple conscious anxiety is still a more desirable state of affairs from the standpoint of eventually evolving a constructive adjustment. The defensive reactions tend to become fixed, to acquire a canalized adjustive value, and to limit the variability of behavior, which is one of the main hopes of effecting a more wholesome type of adaptation. We must also amend our earlier interpretation of the defenses against, and the complications of anxiety, to include their role of rationalizing (making more acceptable) the adjustive value of anxiety per se as a technique of avoiding situations where loss of self-esteem is feared.

We have held throughout that the main reason for anxiety, that is, over-reaction with fear to an ostensibly inadequate threat (judged in terms of its objective hazardousness to persons not suffering from Neurotic Anxiety), is an inner feeling of inadequacy reflective of impaired self-esteem. When panic sets in, however, this reason is compounded by the resulting loss of discriminative ability, which further prevents the individual from distinguishing between adequate and inadequate threats. The importance of constructing an adequate and effective defense against anxiety, therefore, inheres in the dire consequences of failure in this endeavor.

When the burden of anxiety exceeds the individual's level of tolerance because of a breakdown in his defenses or because of new and catastrophic environmental threats to his self-esteem, severe psychotic complications of anxiety may ensue. These reactions represent such marked disorganization of behavior that normal interpersonal relationships or participation in a shared social reality become impossible. The disorganization is in part a reflection of the deterioration of behavior and personality occurring in extreme or panic levels of altered behavioral reactivity, a form of damage that has no adjustive value per se. In part, they represent an attempt at adjustment beyond the established framework of ego organization from which the patient derives his usual sense of personal identity, and beyond the social reality that he shares with significant persons in his psychological field. In this sense, and in the sense that they remove him from the field of impossible adjustive situations exceeding his adaptive capacity, they may be considered to have some defensive value.

How are such adjustive crises produced? The Anxiety Neurotic ordinarily learns how to avoid potentially traumatic situations that he feels might end disastrously in terms of his self-esteem, for example, rejection by a person with whom he wishes to establish a close emotional relationship. Through various rationalizing techniques he manages to justify avoidance of forming such relationships even though this involves self-frustration and loss of possible gratifications, which he deeply desires.

Let us carry the adjustive stress one step further. Suppose that our anxiety patient is confronted with accepting a vocational adjustment below his level of aspiration, a situation that is highly traumatic in terms of his hypertrophic goal structure. Neither fear nor protestations of "being too good for such a job" are valid enough reasons to persuade oneself or others that a practical, modestly oriented adjustment is unsatisfactory when no other employment is available. When hard-pressed by the inexorable logic of accepting this situation, anxiety may give way to panic, which in turn disorganizes behavior, makes any type of adjustment impossible, and induces blocking, paralysis, and exaggerated self-criticism. The patient can then claim complete incapacity as a result of "nervous breakdown," justify his dependence on others, and enjoy a reprieve from accepting a half-loaf solution that does violence to his needs for prestige, power, and exalted ego status.

While immersed in this agitated state of panic, marked by gross impairment of self-esteem, self-deprecation, and dependence on others, a constructive solution is still possible as long as the patient continues to strive on an adult reality plane. If he can perceive the new adjustment as only a short-term setback that does not irreparably frustrate his needs for ego aggrandizement, he may be persuaded to accept it as a temporary expedient. If, on the other hand, he feels that his ambitions are completely blocked and that reconciliation to a life of acknowledged mediocrity of status is inevitable, he may choose instead a psychotic adjustment removed from normal adult strivings and from participation in social reality.

Brief Miscellaneous Defenses

Aggression and hostility are among the simplest and commonest outcomes of frustration, and are sometimes used defensively to allay anxiety. But as pointed out earlier, they are themselves highly productive of anxiety because of the anticipation of retaliation, and because they threaten to disrupt the placatory defensive techniques that are more effective in our society.

Self-esteem and security can be enhanced by *delusional* distortion of reality in which: (a) guilt, responsibility, unacceptable motivations, and so forth, are disowned and projected onto others; (b) rejecting and unappreciative individuals are unjustifiably deprecated; and (c) the status and accomplishments of self are uncritically inflated or perceived to be the objects of systematic victimization. A related technique is to proclaim the wickedness of all earthly aspirations, to renounce same, and interpret the renunciation as proof of unusual virtue (asceticism), or to believe in one's divinely inspired mission to redeem mankind (religious delusions).

Martyrs assume the role of neglected, self-sacrificing individuals who voluntarily neglect their own interests and aspirations to enhance the welfare or career of others. This not only explains their own lack of eminence but also bestows upon them a saint's mantle of selflessness and devotion. The latter claim is not unfounded in fact, since martyrs either allow themselves to be exploited by others or else manipulate situations in such a way that they are obliged to suffer martyrdom. They frequently start their careers as rejected eldest children in large families who are deprived of childhood joys and are burdened with the responsibility of caring for younger siblings. The role of martyrdom may be assumed initially as a reaction-formation against resulting feelings of hostility and resentment or as a form of expiation for the guilt feelings referable to same. In addition to the latter rationalizing and ego-enhancing values of the device, some martyrs also achieve secondary ego gratification by identifying themselves with the accomplishments of those for whom they sacrifice their own lives and aspirations.

Malingering

Malingering is not a defense against anxiety. It was arbitrarily positioned as the last diagnostic entity to be discussed in this book, partly because it is not really a substantive psychiatric diagnosis as such (but has to be placed somewhere), and partly because it can compound and confuse the diagnosis of any and all other clinical entities. Psychiatric clinicians generally are not sufficiently aware of the possibility of malingering in evaluating patients for diagnostic purposes, and as a result make many serious diagnostic errors that could be easily avoided if malingering were always kept in mind as a viable possibility, especially where the findings in the case are equivocal or where a marked discrepancy exists between the objective evidence in the case and the subjective claims reported by the patient.

Malingering is a very common phenomenon, particularly in facilities providing incarceration as detention. Just to be removed from these conditions constitutes incentive enough for malingering. Other external incentives that motivate malingering include evading work or military duty, obtaining financial compensation, evading criminal prosecution, and obtaining narcotics under false pretenses. It should be suspected in those cases where the patient is uncooperative during the diagnostic evaluation and in following the treatment regimen, where he is referred for evaluation by his own attorney, and where he has a diagnosis of Antisocial Personality Disorder.

As a general rule, the particular psychiatric symptom that is chosen for false representation or exaggeration as malingering is completely subjective and dependent on the patient's subjective report, for example, auditory hallucinations. If he asserts that voices have told him to kill himself and other people, it is difficult to contradict him, and he knows it, because only he "hears" the voices. The same is true of suicidal ideation, another favorite ploy of malingerers.

Notwithstanding what has been said above about the deceitfulness of malingerers and the various crass materialistic incentives they have for malingering, it is necessary at this point to qualify some of these negative implications. The rigid dichotomy between malingering, on the one hand, and exhibiting and reporting only genuine symptoms, on the other, is highly idealized and simply doesn't exist in practice. Almost all patients, to a variable degree, falsify their symptoms—invent ones they don't have; deny others they do have; exaggerate, minimize, or rationalize. They may "borrow" the symptoms of other patients if they believe such are interesting or necessary to establish the diagnosis, or may do the same thing just to please the psychiatrist and confirm his diagnosis. On the other hand, the motive for embroidering his symptoms may be to impress or astound the psychiatrist. In any case it is apparent that many relatively innocent motives for intentionally falsifying psychiatric symptoms exist that are not materialistic or deceitful and that malingering is not the black-and-white problem it appears to be at first glance.

11

Conclusions

Brief Overview: Ego Development and Psychopathology

The major implication of naturalistic (empirical) ego development for an etiological-psychopathological classification system of the mental disorders in psychiatry can be inferred logically from the following plausible proposition (supported by clinical findings): That the most tenable and felicitous course of ego development, from the standpoint of mature, stable, and productive personality functioning (and the later avoidance of disabling personality distortions and mental disorders) is the modal type prevailing panculturally, namely, satellization during childhood followed by desatellization during adolescence and early adulthood.

Failure to satellize typically results in compensatorily and unrealistically high and tenacious needs for achievement, severe impairment of self-esteem, Neurotic Anxiety and its various distortive defenses, and possibly increased susceptibility to Conduct and Antisocial Personality Disorders as well as to such psychotic complications of anxiety as depressive disorders, Reactive Schizophrenia, and Delusional Disorder. Failure to desatellize, on the other hand, often leads to a Motivationally Immature and Inadequate Personality structure that is predisposed accordingly to chronic academic and vocational underachievement, the amotivational syndrome, substance abuse, and Process Schizophrenia.

Psychopathologically speaking, Neurotic Anxiety of whatever origin constitutes the chief generic form of neurosis and may be defined as an anticipatory fear response in which the patient, who typically has a history of severely impaired self-esteem, overreacts to novel adjustive situations that threaten to cause further impairment of his already severely impaired self-esteem.

Rejected children manifest anxiety soon after the rejection aspect of the parent-child relationship becomes perceptible to the child, because of the

277

obviously severe narcissistic injury inherent in rejection per se; whereas overvalued children, who fail to undergo normal ego devaluation (because the extrinsically valuing parents deliberately seek to maintain and foster the fiction of infantile ego omnipotence as portentous of future greatness and, hence, useful for their own vicarious ego enhancement), usually do not satellize or become devalued and, accordingly, do not often exhibit severely impaired self-esteem and Neurotic Anxiety until late adolescence.

Overprotected and overdependent children, on the other hand, generally satellize and are typically midway between the latter two conditions with respect to age of onset of Neurotic Anxiety, manifesting generalized anxiety during middle childhood or after loss of the more significant parent due to death or divorce. However, they also differ from the latter rejected and overvalued children described above in their lack of hypertrophic ego aspirations; whereas rejected and overvalued children are typically predisposed to further impairment of self-esteem simply because of their compensatorily, unrealistically, and tenaciously high achievement needs, and also because, unlike satellizers, they have after childhood no residual inner core of self-esteem protecting them from life's vicissitudes.

Neurotic Anxiety and its underlying impaired self-esteem, as stated above, constitute the common predisposing factors toward psychotic complications, all involving marked impairment of reality testing. These occur only when either the defenses against anxiety break down completely or the individual overreacts to actual, or merely perceived, stress threatening catastrophic collapse of his self-esteem, becoming thereby destabilized and dysfunctional. Then, depending on his particular genic predispositions toward psychotic reactions, his psychotic complication of anxiety takes the form of Major Depression, Mania, Reactive Schizophrenia (Schizophreniform Disorder), Brief Reactive or Atypical Psychosis, or Delusional Disorder.

Neurotic Anxiety itself may either be acute and/or chronic with acute exacerbations, and either generalized, circumscribed (Panic Disorder), or phobic (displacement of perceived source of threat to tangible or avoidable objects or situations). Agoraphobia, with or without panic attacks, for example, is an acute and/or chronic condition intermediate between anxiety and depression (i.e., a "mini-depression"), whereas demoralization and agitated depression are, respectively, more or less severe and more or less acute forms of anxious depression that are actually more prevalent than either pure anxiety or pure depression.

Motivationally Inadequate Personality Disorder (unfortunately and unjustifiably deleted from DSM III and IV) of whatever origin, but typically occurring in oversatellizers, fails to undergo both the ego-status and ego-maturity aspects of desatellization, that is, does not develop both appropriately mature adult ego aspirations and needs for volitional independence and the appropriately mature adult personality traits (e.g., responsibility, self-reliance, goal and performance frustration tolerance, executive independence, realistic self-appraisal, perseverance, and resoluteness) necessary to implement these aspirations.

A combination of motivational inadequacy and marked introversion tends to predispose the individual to emotional disengagement from adult reality and people, social withdrawal, retreat into fantasy, and relatively rapid personality and cognitive deterioration (Process Schizophrenia). More extroverted inadequate personalities, on the other hand, are predisposed toward all forms of hedonistic self-gratification in reality, for example, drug-induced euphoria if such is available, and to underachievement and instability in school and vocational life, to unstable marriage, and to all of their complications.

Implications of Ego Development for Psychotherapy

At first glance, the reader may gain the impression that my approach to psychiatric treatment is inherently and deliberately eclectic. This is definitely not the case although, on the surface, it appears to be so because so many different therapeutic modalities (e.g., individual, group, and family psychotherapy; pharmacotherapy; electro-convulsive therapy; "behavioral" therapy; crisis intervention), as well as seemingly antagonistic therapeutic principles from a great diversity of theorists, are advocated in this volume for general or specific purposes. It should be borne in mind, however, that particular therapeutic modalities may be effective for reasons much different from those advanced by the theorists who originated them, and may, in fact, be intrinsically unrelated to the latter's theoretical positions. Further, it must be appreciated that just because a given mental disorder (e.g., Schizophrenia) is benefited therapeutically by a physical or pharmacological agent, its cause cannot necessarily be assumed to be neurobiological in nature.

In the present state of the art we cannot afford to dismiss *any* effective therapeutic modality even if there is gross ignorance or disagreement regarding how or why it works. The only defensible constraint that can be imposed on a theorist in this regard, therefore, is that he justify the various therapeutic principles and modalities he approves of in terms of their consonance or consistency with his theoretical position.

The Overvaluation of Psychotherapy

We have witnessed for some time a vast but not inexplicable overvaluation of the field of psychotherapy. Exaggerated and unwarranted claims are being made for this relatively new addition to medicine's therapeutic armamentarium. In some quarters it has taken on the status of panacea, promising to all within its reach a fuller and richer life, greater personality integration and self-realization, and freedom from tension, anxiety, and disabling psychological symptoms of all varieties. This trend, of course, has its cultural supports. In the first place, there is the tremendous prestige of science in general and of medicine in particular to draw upon. It was relatively easy, therefore, for psychotherapy to establish itself as a branch of medicine and to borrow medicine's mantle of scientific prestige and authority. In the process two weaknesses in the analogy have escaped general detection. It was forgotten first that clinical medicine is built upon a firm foundation of anatomy, physiology, biochemistry, pathology, pharmacology, and so forth, whereas psychotherapy enjoys precious little of an empirical scientific substructure. It is only relatively recently that any attention at all has been given to the problems of evidence of efficacy in psychotherapy.

The second weakness in the analogy of psychotherapy with medicine is that theoretical structure of clinical medicine is cogent, self-consistent, and in harmony with the concepts of its parent sciences. In psychotherapy, on the other hand, there are innumerable warring factions with completely antagonistic theories and little consensus with respect to fundamental issues; yet each group claims expertness and reputability, while often formulating its system with consummate disregard for established principles of general psychology.

A second cultural support favoring the overvaluation of psychotherapy has been the sudden public awakening to the importance, prevalence, and economic cost of mental illness. The high incidence of psychiatric casualties in World War II increased official willingness to remedy the shortage of psychotherapists; and postwar economic prosperity created for the first time an actual surplus of demand over supply in terms of ability to pay for needed services. The federal government underwrote training programs in clinical psychology, numerous new clinical positions opened up, and many general psychologists climbed on the more promising and more remunerative clinical bandwagon. Concurrently private practice in psychiatry greatly expanded.

A third cultural support is traceable to the current tendency to over-psychologize all aspects of modern living. We have already noted this trend in relation to moral problems from which a strong attempt is being made to remove all ethical content and to restate issues simply in behavioral terms. A similar situation has arisen in relation to social, political, and economic problems, which some psychologists attempt to explain on a psychological plane alone. Within such a conceptual framework, psychotherapy naturally looms as a logical cure for all of the world's ills.

A fourth cultural support stems from a long-seething overreaction to a core of ideological trends prominent in the first half of the present century which emphasized principles inherently limiting man's capacity for behavioral change. Illustrative of such ideas are Freud's concepts of the id and of a phylogenetically predetermined sequence of psychosexual development; Jung's "racial unconscious"; the concept of "repetition compulsion"; the emphasis upon the prepotent influence of infant experience upon adult personality structure; the notion of a universal Oedipus conflict; Hall's theory of individual psychological growth as a recapitulation of cultural development, and so forth. The almost inevitable overreaction to this kind of ideology was the assertion of a rather naive *tabula rasa* doctrine: Human nature was, allegedly, held to be infinitely plastic and malleable; problems of psychological development had no universal common denominator, but reflected in every instance only the operation of unique cultural conditions; genetic and constitutional factors were only of minor importance since man is primarily a creature of his social environment and could be molded into any form his culture wishes him to take.

This new *tabula rasa* trend was not without its influence on psychotherapy. It led to unbounded confidence in the patient's capacity to reconstruct his personality on a more wholesome basis, regardless of his previous history, as long as the stimulus and motivation for same were endogenously derived. This point of view naturally led to a deemphasis of developmental diagnosis and to a concentration upon the current adjustive situation. Perhaps both the optimism and the exclusive preoc-

cupation with current problems stemmed from the predominant experience of nondirective therapists with clients having only minor adjustive
difficulties, largely of a situational nature.

However, this unlimited optimism with respect to an adult's ability to
remake his personality is not only unsupported by any empirical evidence,
but seems highly unlikely in the light of theoretical considerations with
respect to the reversibility of basic personality patterns. A not-to-be ignored consideration also in determining the limits of possible change is
the relative benevolence of an individual's environment and the degree
of control he can exercise over it. In the case of children, for example,
this latter factor is especially important.

It is clear, therefore, that the scientific status and role of psychotherapy
must be seen in clearer perspective before much progress can be made.
Principles of psychotherapy must be related to principles of psychology.
Hypotheses regarding the processes of psychotherapy must be empirically validated and related to outcomes. Clinicians must cease demanding exemption from the canons of scientific evidence and must be willing
to regard diagnoses as hypotheses to be proven rather than as unchallengeable facts; clinical hunches and impressions, on the other hand, should
motivate the search for general psychodynamic principles and for definitive psychological diagnoses rather than be offered in and of themselves
as the equivalent of empirically established data. And, lastly, psychotherapists should avoid arousing extravagant and unwarranted hopes for cure,
hopes, which when frustrated, only augment adjustive stress. Criteria must
be established indicating when psychotherapy can be useful, what the
objectives are, what limitations exist, and the maximum change that can
be expected in terms of developmental history, personality structure, age,
diagnostic entity, and the environmental situation of the patient.

Finally, considering that retardation, failure, and distortions in ego development are among the most common and serious forms of psychopathology, and that each of these disorders is both many years in the making,
as well as the product of long-term relationships with parents, teachers,
peers, and so forth, it seems somewhat naive and simplistic to expect reversal with insight-oriented psychotherapy of these maturational defects
after just a few months of weekly psychotherapy and the questionable
retrospective acquisition of "insight."

The logistics of the maturational retardation and failure situations would
suggest, rather, that reversal of maturational retardation is more likely to

occur if the patient were placed for an extended period of time in a variety of therapeutic environments, which would be structured maximally to overcome his particular adjustive difficulties and to facilitate his idiosyncratically delayed maturation. This would be similar in principle to the milieu therapy that typically takes place in in-patient settings, except that the length of the therapy would be incomparably greater and would take place in a variety of community settings. The same therapeutic model, of course, could be used just as well for other nonmaturational disorders, for example, anxiety, Schizophrenia, and depression, all of which take many years to develop. Conceptually, it is equivalent to a long-term "environmental manipulation" approach to therapy.

The Overvaluation of Unconscious Motivation and Insight

Contributing to the current overvaluation of psychotherapy, but on a conceptual plane rather than as a cultural support, is the psychoanalytic overemphasis upon unconscious motivation as the central etiological mechanism in the production of neurotic symptoms. If behavior disorders could be interpreted as symbolic expressions of, or defenses against, repressed unconscious motives, then it seemed reasonable to expect complete cure as soon as the patient could be made to appreciate the motivation underlying his symptoms (insight). When this failed to happen in all but a few dramatic cases, analysts explained that unconscious "resistance" was operative, that intellectual understanding was insufficient, and that emotional acceptance and practical application of insight to current life situations ("working through") were also necessary. Emotional acceptance, they argued, was facilitated by catharsis of the affect involved in the repressed complex; and since the source of such complexes supposedly resided in childhood psychosexual development, catharsis could be best effected therapeutically by a "transference" relationship in which the therapist plays the role of parent figure to re-elicit the expression of repressed childhood motives and attitudes. These additional techniques, according to this way of thinking, do not invalidate the crucial role of insight but, rather, implement and enhance it.

Nondirective therapists also stress the role of perceptual reorganization through insight, but decry therapist participation except for purposes of reflection and clarification of the client's feelings. Interpretation and "transference" are taboo, and attention is focused on current conflicts apart from their developmental origins. It is claimed that emotional acceptance of insight is facilitated by the creation of a permissive atmosphere, which minimizes resistance to change by emphasis upon self-discovery of underlying attitudes and motivations, and by emotional relatedness on the part of the therapist to the client. Reinforcement of insight is also possible through diagrammatic representation, the use of relevant, instructive films, and opportunity for observation and therapy in reality and role-playing situations.

Acceptance of the therapeutic value of insight, however, does not necessarily imply acceptance of the theory that *all* neurotic symptoms reflect the operation of repression and unconscious motivation. Many neurotic symptoms can occur with complete possession of insight; and lack of conscious accessibility is not necessarily a precondition for lack of insight, since oftentimes the relation of symptoms to conscious motives is not appreciated. The reason for this, as has already been noted, is that repression is not the primary cause of anxiety, ego immaturity, and other forms of ego damage, but a defense against anxiety which facilitates the development of neurotic defenses and interferes with the evolution of more constructive solutions. Hence, it is unrealistic to expect that the acquisition of insight can by itself repair lack of self-esteem or create feelings of security and adequacy. More constructive relief from anxiety might conceivably be achieved by optimal manipulation of the environment, reorganization of goal structure, altering the quality of interpersonal relationships, increasing tolerance for unalterable disabilities, and creating a new set of environmental expectations.

Also, as suggested earlier, an ever-present danger in the patient's acquisition of insight is that he obtains plausible explanations for his mental disorder, which he might then very well use for retaining rather than discarding it—if he happened to be resistant to being "cured" of his symptoms or mental disorder.

Despite the sacrosanct status of "transference" in psychoanalytic therapy, it is necessary to point out that not only is an adult patient virtually incapable of relating as a three-year-old to the therapist, in the same sense as to one of his parent figures at that time—too many significant emotional, personality, and cognitive changes have occurred in the interim to modify personality structure—but even if he could, it would still be inadvisable for him to do so. Psychotherapy can be realistic and useful only if patients relate to therapists in terms of their current personality status and organization; this is clearly the case because if they do decide to make significant changes in their personality structure, they will obviously do so as adults, not as simulated three-year-olds.

A final qualification or caveat is in order regarding the widespread teleological belief in the culture regarding the "adjustive" or "compensatory" nature of *all* symptoms, a belief that was uncritically borrowed from medical pathology. *Some* symptoms undoubtedly do have compensatory functions and properties, for example, most defense mechanisms. Escape mechanisms, for their part, facilitate the withdrawal of self beyond the reach of environmental threats, for example, social withdrawal and isolation, negativism, and so forth. Psychopathological indications of *noncompensatory ego damage,* on the other hand, include loss of self-esteem, anxiety, agitation, depression, and depersonalization. Thus, since it stands to reason that most psychiatric symptoms reflect damage (e.g., distortion, disruption, disorganization) to ego and personality rather than "adjustive" or "compensatory" efforts to improve the patient's adjustment or adaptation to his environment, it is just as futile to believe that all psychiatric symptoms are compensatory (and to base all treatment strategies on this belief), as to believe that all behavior is motivated.

The Place of Diagnosis in Therapy

While it is true (as claimed by nondirective therapists) that present personality structure represents a *precipitate* of all the relevant developmental influences entering into its formation, mere attention to the current adjustive problem, without definitive diagnosis in terms of developmental history, is not likely to lead to permanent therapeutic benefits. Meaningful insight into the present adjustive situation cannot be gained by patient or therapist by examining only the end product of development. Neither sequence nor process of growth is deducible from eventual outcome although the latter necessarily reflects their operation.

The practical clinical significance of this consideration enters into one of the first decisions that the therapist is obliged to make in every case he undertakes: Are the adjustive difficulties of the patient an outcome of current transitional or situational pressures, or are they reflective of serious abnormalities in ego devaluation or maturation? Until this question can be answered, no intelligent decision with respect to prognosis, length, depth, urgency, and type of therapy indicated can be made.

Nevertheless it need not be imagined that all therapy must be post-poned until a definitive diagnosis is possible. In acute cases, supportive or psychopharmacological therapy, environmental manipulation, and re-lief from immediate pressures and frustration are indicated to forestall the possibility of imminent psychotic breakdown. Where such breakdown has already occurred, shock therapy or pharmacotherapy may be neces-sary to make the patient more accessible to interpersonal influences. In less acute cases, concurrently with developmental diagnosis, progress in solving current problems of adjustment must be made if the later acquisi-tion of insight is to have any practical significance; otherwise not only does exploration of the past become an academic pursuit, but also anxi-ety increases and deterioration of the environmental situation occurs (es-pecially in the spheres of vocational adaptation, social relationships, and personal independence), making actual implementation of insight all but impossible.

The common psychoanalytic practice of ignoring situational factors until complete insight is acquired is partly a reflection of the Hippocratian concept of the finiteness and single source of drive and affect to which most analysts subscribe. According to this reasoning, as long as affect and drive are bound up in repressed neurotic complexes, the acquisition of more wholesome adjustive mechanisms is impossible since the latter could not be energized by necessary emotional and motivational compo-nents; only after insight is attained can this "frozen" affect be liberated for psychotherapy. However, if we adopt the more plausible assumption that "functionally autonomous" motives can arise as the result of new life experience, then new techniques of adjustment can be successfully sustained even though emotional energy is tied up in unsolved conflicts. It is also a common experience that motivation develops retroactively as a result of the interest aroused and the gratification obtained from suc-cessful performance of an activity that might have been grudgingly un-dertaken in the first place.

The Place of Direction in Therapy

The same fetish of permissiveness that took over the field of parent-child relationships has also gradually captured the field of psychotherapy. Almost by definition in some quarters, the more permissive a therapist is, the less he structures the therapeutic situation; the fewer his expecta-tions, the less he tends to "judge" the patient; the wider his limits of tolerance and the less authority he wields, the more superior his professional attitudes and methods are accounted to be.

The nondirective therapist takes the position that change cannot be imposed upon the individual from without but must originate endogenously. He takes issue with the traditional medical approach in which the physician diagnoses the disorder, explains to the patient the genesis and meaning of his symptoms, and prescribes the necessary treatment. Instead the patient does all of these things by himself; and the therapist by clarifying and reflecting the former's own productions merely helps him to make better use of his own inherent resources for acquiring insight and instigating change.

This insistence upon the fact that in the final analysis it is only the individual himself who can actually effect a reorganization of his own personality structure is logical enough providing that it is qualified by certain realistic limitations. In the first place, ego maturation takes place under the impact of mature social expectations and within a realistic framework of interpersonal relations, which does not ignore relevant moral problems. Second, because lasting personality change can occur only when there is genuine internal acceptance of the need for same does not mean that it can or must *always* be endogenously stimulated. Because self-generated insight is generally superior to equivalent insight communicated by the therapist does not imply that the latter is worthless or has no beneficial effects. Further, many patients are generally incapable of ever formulating insights, and all patients have blind spots about certain issues.

Lastly, patients obviously cannot assume the major responsibility for self-direction when they are disorganized, panic-stricken, or hopelessly caught between the vicious cycle of anxiety and the fixed, perseverative, and maladaptive responses that it tends to engender. The degree of responsibility and self-direction that a patient can assume cannot be fixed dogmatically at the start of therapy and maintained throughout, but must be flexibly modified to meet the requirements of both his original condition and subsequent improvement therein. In many critical situations, supportive therapy, environmental manipulation, reliance on medications and physical therapy, and interpretation by the therapist are also indicated.

The Need for Realistic and Moral Expectations

Throughout this volume we have stressed that ego maturation does not occur spontaneously but largely in response to new interpersonal and social expectations. This principle is supported by evidence from the social psychology of attitude formation and attitude change. Goals, ego attributes, and attitudes toward self also change in response to cultural demands and supports, since individuals are dependent upon their social milieu for status, approval, love, acceptance, security, and a sense of belonging.

To the patient, the therapist represents the expectations of the social reality to which he has not yet succeeded in adjusting adequately. Much of the stimulus for change in motivation, attitude, and adjustive behavior during the period of treatment will come from the expectations of the therapist in his role of social reality surrogate. However, if the latter takes the position that it is the patient's prerogative to structure the framework of expectancy and set the limits in the relationship, the patient not only feels under no pressure to abandon his unrealistic, autistic, or immature frame of reference, but also feels justifiably encouraged to seek adjustment within such a framework with the tacit approval, support, and sanction of the therapist. The latter, for example, must continue to insist on the patient's acceptance of the need for vocational adjustment on a realistic level, rather than remain noncommittal when confronted with grandiose and impractical ambitions that blithely ignore insuperable obstacles of ability and job opportunity.

Part of this framework of realistic and mature expectations in which the therapeutic setting is embedded consists of a code of moral values. Most significant human behavior has an ethical aspect that cannot be ignored without sacrificing much of its essence insofar as interpersonal relationships are concerned. If the therapist articulates no moral expectations and fails to express ethical judgments, the patient is justified in assuming that the former either approves of his immoral behavior, or else considers that any type of ethical solution he (the patient) is satisfied with is also satisfactory to the therapist. In the latter case, therapy takes place in an amoral setting, and the patient is supported in his belief that he is above the moral law, which applies to ordinary mortals. Silence on the part of the therapist condones immorality and whitewashes guilt feelings.

Both therapist and patient must face the problem of guilt and moral accountability squarely. If guilt feelings are unfounded, they should be discounted; if they are warranted they should be acknowledged and dealt with constructively. Proper timing, good rapport, and tact on the part of the therapist are necessary, as well as a constructive approach rather than an attitude of final condemnation. However, if in spite of skillful handling the patient discontinues therapy because of the therapist's expression of moral judgment, it is doubtful whether he could have benefited from it in the first place. The pragmatic approach to ethical problems employed by many nondirective therapists, that is, moral behavior is desirable simply because it pragmatically and systematically makes for more wholesome, stable, and predictable interpersonal relationships, actually has little moral content and lends support to current philosophies of expediency.

Above all, the therapist should never become a party to using euphemisms or condoning immoral or criminal behavior as merely a variety of mental illness. As long as an individual is psychologically capable of inhibiting impulses leading to such behavior at the time that he committed it, he is morally and legally accountable for it and subject to whatever social sanctions that are culturally prescribed for it.

It is equally unrealistic to deny the inherent authority residing in the role of therapist and to set up the dictum that therapeutic benefit is limited in instances where the therapist is in a position of authority in relation to the patient. In the first place, the very fact that one individual appeals for help on the basis of another's expert knowledge and experience inevitably injects an authoritarian aspect into the relationship. Second, if the therapist plays his necessary role of representing cultural expectations and defining limits in the therapeutic relationship, he automatically becomes invested with authority. Whether he wishes to create a limited "transference" situation or not, the patient inevitably reacts to him as an authority figure (but as one adult to another), since the relationship recapitulates so many features of the parent-child relationship. Lastly, the therapist's effectiveness depends upon his being perceived by the patient as an individual of strength, someone to be respected rather than pushed around like an ineffectual, underdominating parent. Without authority he can set no realistic limits; and in the absence of such limits, therapy can only compound existing ego damage.

It does seem reasonable to expect that there will be less resistance to genuine emotional acceptance of insight if such insight is the product of self-discovery rather than of interpretation by the therapist. However, self-discovery is by no means an indispensable condition for the acceptance of insight. Satellizers, for example, are more willing to accept the therapist's interpretations than nonsatellizers. Interpretation is also necessary in acute phases of anxiety when panic destroys all ability to think clearly, and in cases where the acquisition of insight is persistently blocked by stubborn "blind spots."

In a large number of cases also, in which the patient is either hostile, withdrawn, suspicious, or diffident, it is necessary for the therapist to take the initiative in the relationship rather than passively allow the former to explore the situation by himself. As the more mature and independent person in the relationship, he has to be willing to make the advances if any need to be made.

Anyone who has had experience in treating hostile children and adolescents also recognizes that "warmth, love, understanding, and acceptance" (maximal permissiveness) is no magic formula that will automatically diminish the latter's aggressive proclivities. Such is only partly the case in instances of counteraggression induced by environmental deprivation, and not where hostility is a deeply ingrained orientation toward life or a fixed form of defense against anxiety.

By structuring the therapeutic situation in this fashion, the therapist does not necessarily make the patient unduly dependent upon him. Real danger of dependence only arises if direction and support are maintained too long or longer than warranted by the patient's adjustive capacity, especially if during this time no progress has been made toward economic independence. The therapist's presence and support then becomes necessary conditions upon which the patient's security depends. The therapist also becomes reluctant to terminate the situation since he prefers to earn his living in a familiar setting. The risk of dependency is much greater in the case of satellizers, since nonsatellizers do not tend to form deep emotional attachments to their therapists, merely accepting their direction on the basis of its objective validity. Since there is no subservience of self in the latter's acceptance of assistance, volitional independence is not essentially surrendered.

Special Indications for Directive Therapy

Indications for special forms of directive therapy exist in: (1) acute (prepsychotic) cases of maladjustment; (2) cases rendered inaccessible to interpersonal intervention because of psychotic inaccessibility; (3) the treatment of children and adolescents; and (4) cases of chronic anxiety and other forms of chronic maladjustment.

The first therapeutic consideration in agitated and panic states of anxiety, when patients are confused, helpless, desperate, and on the verge of either Major Depression or Reactive Schizophrenia, is symptomatic relief of anxiety and frustration. In terms of psychotherapy, this may involve the extension of immediate emotional support and the use of reassurance, suggestion, prestige authority, and cautiously advanced interpretation. The patient's environment must be simplified by the elimination of unnecessary pressures and harassments of all kinds; and the therapist must be prepared to intervene actively in the former's personal affairs, and if necessary help make swift decisions for him. Pharmacological therapy may be necessary to keep acute anxiety, depression, or psychosis under control and prevent the patient from seeking relief in psychotic mechanisms. Explanation of how the surrender of adult strivings in a reality setting may lead to psychosis sometimes has a protective effect. The use of nondirective techniques in such a situation, however, can only end in disaster.

In psychotic states where the patient is either preoccupied with his own subjective reality or too overwhelmed by his defeat to remain in contact with objective reality, it is first desirable to make him more accessible by means of antipsychotic or antidepressive drug therapy before psychotherapy has much chance of success. This difficulty in communication, however, can be greatly reduced in Schizophrenia if the therapist is willing to think and feel in terms of the patient's reality in the early stages of treatment. However, this maneuver obviously requires a degree of individual attention which would be impossible without increasing the number of psychiatrists in mental hospitals by several thousand percent. For practical reasons, therefore, pharmacological methods of treatment are presently indispensable.

The use of physical methods of therapy represents in no sense an abandonment of a psychological theory of mental disorder. If we are ready to concede that an altered state of behavioral reactivity can be induced by fatigue, hormonal imbalance, brain injury, syphilitic encephalitis, uremia, and so forth, it is no less logical to grant that favorable modification of mental disorder can be brought about by manipulation of the anatomical or physiological substrate of behavior and of consciousness. The more plausible theories of the action of shock therapy (i.e., selective disorganization of the more recently acquired neurotic behavior patterns, removal of undesirable cortical control, and deliberate impairment of the self-critical faculty) are quite compatible with psychological approaches to behavior disorder. The use of psychotropic drugs to correct neurotransmitter imbalance is similarly compatible with a psychogenic orientation to mental disorders.

Psychiatric Treatment of Children and Adolescents

This naturally requires considerable reliance on environmental manipulation for two reasons: (1) independent acquisition of insight is difficult for children because of limitations in their verbal ability; and (2) both children and adolescents are largely under the immediate control of powerful adults (parents or parent surrogates) who in most cases are largely responsible for the adjustive difficulties involved, and without whose cooperation, improvement in the interpersonal environment and implementation of insight would be impossible.

Since the personality of the parents constitutes the most important factor affecting the child's ego development, it can be safely predicted that psychotherapy with the latter can bring little lasting improvement until favorable modification of parental practices and attitudes is obtained through parenting and/or family therapy. As a matter of fact, this is what is actually found in child guidance centers. Where the parent-child relationship is essentially wholesome, simple mediation or interpretation of parent and child to each other is often helpful. Acceptance of these therapeutic principles, however, does not in the least rule out an attempt to secure the child's active participation in the process of change. Through recognition, objectification, and acceptance of his feelings (by means of role playing and play therapy in a shared reality), the child patient is often enabled to acquire and implement insights and achieve greater security, integration, and maturity of personality structure.

Directed guidance is also necessary in chronic maladjustments such as anxiety disorders if progress is to be made in solving current problems of adjustment, and if fixed and rigid defensive mechanisms that prevent efficient learning and working are to be overcome. The Anxiety Neurotic who has acquired maladaptive ways of learning, perceiving, and setting goals is not free independently to select and utilize beneficial insights (that might arise in the course of therapy) because of potent reaction sensitivities that predispose his behavior along rigidly canalized lines of a defensive nature. Guidance in restructuring his environment and response repertory is needed, for example, selective ego disinvolvement from untenable situations, lowering of aspirational level, formation of selective satellizing-like relationships, emphasis upon economic security with creative avocational opportunities, avoidance of excessive advance preparation in new learning situations, increasing tolerance for conscious anxiety, minimizing the tendency to achieve security and forestall defeat through abnormal circumscription of the environment, and so forth.

Concluding Remarks

The chief practical implication that a psychology of ego development holds for the treatment of mental disorders is reiteration of the well-established principle that prevention is far more effective than therapy. If before and during the crisis of ego devaluation, a child is accepted and valued for himself, he will satellize and acquire an intrinsic sense of security and adequacy that will prove highly resistant to environmental vicissitudes and will protect him from Neurotic Anxiety. Then if before and during the crisis of ego maturation he is spared from overprotection, underdomination (permissiveness), and overdomination, and given opportunity to undergo desatellization, it is unlikely that he will fail to acquire the mature ego attributes of adult personality structure.

Failing the protection of these preventive measures, it should be realized that the earlier therapy is instituted, the greater the possibility that damage and distortion are correctable. However, in the light of the paucity of empirical evidence regarding both the rationale for and the outcome of psychotherapy, it behooves psychiatrists and clinical psychologists to adopt greater caution and humility in appraising the scientific status, the applicability, and the probable success of their therapeutic techniques.

It must also be appreciated that some psychopathological changes and effects (e.g., severe or catastrophic impairment of self esteem following a child's rejection by his parents and the resulting generalized or Neurotic Anxiety) are wholly or partially irreversible, and that complete cure is conceivable only if radical therapeutic measures (e.g., promotion of satellization to parent surrogates or of satellizing-like relationships to parental or nurturant figures) are instituted in early childhood. In my psychiatric experience, however, it has not been possible to effect complete cure of Neurotic Anxiety beyond the age of seven, and the best that could be hoped for therapeutically thereafter was varying degrees of amelioration.

Index

Achievement motivation, 106n; and affiliative drive, 45, 46; and cognitive drive, 45; components of, 45–46; and ego-enhancement drive, 45; gender differences in, 47; and parent attitudes, 47–48

Adequacy, feelings of; and intrinsic adequacy, 173–174

Addiction, narcotic, 234–236; adjustive properties of, 236; in desatellization failure, 234–236; other types of, 235

Adolescent personality, 62–64; and assimilation of values, 95; compared to childhood, 64; and crisis of desatellization, 62; compared to infancy, 62–64; and earned status, 64; and ego maturity traits; 64–65; and executive independence, 64; and hedonistic motivation, 64; and moral responsibility, 64; and sex drive, 62; and volitional emancipation, 84

Adult-youth alienation, 84–90; consequences of, 86; in primitive cultures, 85; role of peer group in, 86–87; in Western culture, 85–86

Agitation, 176

Agoraphobia, 190, 278

Anxiety, 163, 168; as defense, 271–273; free-floating, 171–172; and motivation, 181–182; and self-critical faculty, 182–185

Anxiety, constructive, 181

Anxiety, defenses against, 255–257; compensatory, 163; conciliatory, 164–164; delusional, 186; denial, 165; direct, 163; ego-enhancing, 163; escape, 163, 165; through "martyrdom," 183

Anxiety neurosis, 161n; as agitation, 176; causes, 163–166, 189; course of, 189;

complications of, 175–176; cure of, 189–190; as defense, 174–176; defensive reactions to, 174, 175; and depression, 174–176; as ego damage, 174–176; exacerbated by stress, 189; as escape, 173; escape reaction to, 171–175; in nonsatellizers, 189; in overprotected child, 178; in overvalued child, 166, 176–178, 277–278; prognosis for cure of, 186; prognosis for palliation of, 186–190; and reactive schizophrenia, 176; in rejected child, 52n, 165–166, 277–278; in satellizers, 189, 278; source of threat in, 175; symptoms of, 187

Anxiety, situational, 179

Anxiety, transitional, 179; cultural factors in, 179–181

Antidepressant medication, 208

Antisocial personality disorder, 241, 242–244; as conscienceless, 241; definition of, 242; ego maturity in, 243, 250; ego status goals in, 243; in nonsatellizers, 242; predisposing factors in, 242; temperamental traits in, 242

Anxiolytic drugs, 207–208; anxiety-reducing mechanism in, 207; depression-reducing mechanism in, 207; as causes of depression, 208

Autism, infantile, 149, 239; course, 149, 239; compared to schizophrenia, 239; symptoms, 239

Biosocial status, 10; as individual achievement, 10

Body image, 20

Cognition, 7–10; difference from perception, 9–10; examples of, 9; and perceptual maturity, 9–10